URBAN INDIGENEITIES

URBAN INDIGENEITIES

Being Indigenous in the Twenty-First Century

Edited by DANA BRABLEC and ANDREW CANESSA

THE UNIVERSITY OF ARIZONA PRESS
TUCSON

The University of Arizona Press
www.uapress.arizona.edu

We respectfully acknowledge the University of Arizona is on the land and territories of Indigenous peoples. Today, Arizona is home to twenty-two federally recognized tribes, with Tucson being home to the O'odham and the Yaqui. Committed to diversity and inclusion, the University strives to build sustainable relationships with sovereign Native Nations and Indigenous communities through education offerings, partnerships, and community service.

ISBN-13: 978-0-8165-4882-8 (hardcover)
ISBN-13: 978-0-8165-4883-5 (ebook)

Cover design by Leigh McDonald
Cover art: Elena Valera / Bahuan Jisbë, *Handicraft Sellers*, 2013
Typeset by Sara Thaxton in 10/14 Warnock Pro with Acumin Variable Concept and Alternate Gothic No1 D

Library of Congress Cataloging-in-Publication Data
Names: Brablec, Dana, 1987– editor. | Canessa, Andrew, 1965– editor.
Title: Urban indigeneities : being indigenous in the twenty-first century / edited by Dana Brablec and Andrew Canessa.
Description: Tucson : University of Arizona Press, 2023. | Includes bibliographical references and index.
Identifiers: LCCN 2022051950 (print) | LCCN 2022051951 (ebook) | ISBN 9780816548828 (hardcover) | ISBN 9780816548835 (ebook)
Subjects: LCSH: Urban indigenous peoples.
Classification: LCC HT151 .U6715 2023 (print) | LCC HT151 (ebook) | DDC 305.8—dc23/eng/20221208
LC record available at https://lccn.loc.gov/2022051950
LC ebook record available at https://lccn.loc.gov/2022051951

Printed in the United States of America
♾ This paper meets the requirements of ANSI/NISO Z39.48-1992 (Permanence of Paper).

CONTENTS

URBAN INDIGENEITIES

Introduction

Indigenous Peoples in the Cities of the World

DANA BRABLEC AND ANDREW CANESSA

Finding the Indigenous in the Urban and the Urban in the Indigenous

We are all familiar with the image of the Indigenous person in forests or mountains living close to and in harmony with the natural environment, enjoying a traditional lifestyle distant from the realities of a modern world. The reality is that an increasing proportion of Indigenous peoples today live in urban areas (UN Habitat 2010). They are builders and cleaners, teachers and lawyers, market women and masons, living in towns and cities surrounded by the people and pollution that characterize life for most of us in the twenty-first century.

Despite this basic reality of contemporary Indigenous life, the vast majority of studies on Indigenous peoples still concentrate on the rural Indigenous. There are a number of reasons for this. Even though Indigenous peoples have lived in cities for centuries and even created some of the largest cities of their era (e.g., Cuzco in Peru, and Tenochtitlan in Mexico), from the time of Rousseau, Hobbes, and Locke, Europeans and their descendants have seen Indigenous peoples as living in a "state of nature" and so were not only blind to an Indigenous history in cities, but even when they did appear in urban spaces, they were considered to be no longer Indigenous *by definition*. This close association of indigeneity with the wild spaces continues right through to the twenty-first century, where the "authentic" Indigenous subject is deemed to live in the forests and mountains far from urban life and, if not in a state of nature, certainly in harmony with it. To situate so resolutely the Indigenous beyond the urban is not only to ignore history but also to deprive Indigenous peoples of their cultural agency and their ability to create identities in any space they choose. The social sciences in general have been largely complicit in this, although there are some notable exceptions (Howard and Proulx 2011; Furlan 2017; Horn 2019). This book, written by Indigenous and non-Indigenous authors, is the first to look at urban Indigenous peoples globally and to present the urban Indigenous experience not as the exception, but as the norm it is.

According to the International Labour Organization (ILO), there are approximately 477 million Indigenous people belonging to 5,000 different groups in 90 different countries. While increasing Indigenous urbanization is a global phenomenon, there is some significant variation between regions. About 70.5 percent of the urban Indigenous population lives in Asia and the Pacific, followed by 16.3 percent in Africa, 11.5 percent in Latin America and the Caribbean, 1.6 percent in North America, and 0.1 percent in Europe and Central Asia. In some Arctic regions, urbanization rates for Indigenous peoples reaches 85 percent (Laruelle 2019; Rozanova-Smith, Ksenofontov, and Petrov, chap. 8, this volume). These tendencies are also present in other regions that have witnessed an increase in Indigenous urbanization rates, such as in the cases of Tanzania with the Maasai, India with the so-called Scheduled Tribes, and New Zealand with the Māori, just to name a few examples (Permanent Forum on Indigenous Issues 2007). Urban Indigenous peoples are also one of the fastest-growing populations in North and South America, as well as in much of the rest of the world (Hall and Fenelon 2016). As Ikemura Amaral (chap. 3, this volume) notes, this Indigenous peoples migration may occur not simply within the nation state but also across national borders (see also Cruz Manjarrez 2013; Foxen 2007; Simpson 2014). It is not only Indigenous people who cross international borders but also the very concept of indigeneity itself. Andrew Canessa (2018) has explored how contemporary indigeneity as a concept circulates globally through international institutions (see also Pelican 2009; Hodgson 2011).

The increase in migration of this population to cities in search of education or employment opportunities has a number of consequences that can undermine a sense of collective belonging and Indigenous identity in two ways. The first, and perhaps most obvious, is that Indigenous peoples in urban areas are living next to people who are not Indigenous. Urban Indigenous people usually constitute a small minority in the city and, in many cases, an almost invisible minority. Brablec (chap. 4, this volume) and Uzawa (chap. 5, this volume) both give examples in Santiago, Chile, and Tokyo, Japan, respectively, where this is the case. Being Indigenous in such environments often requires a seeking out of Indigenous spaces and people and, in cases such as that of the Ainu in Tokyo (Uzawa), may occasion a new appreciation of Indigenous identity focused on something as simple as a particular restaurant.

Being a very small minority in a very large urban area unavoidably entails more frequent and closer contact with the dominant society and inevitably becomes more hybrid. In that context, maintaining Indigenous identities requires awareness and mobilization—in other words, a conscious political act. Indigenous peoples are also less visible in cities, not only vulnerable to the pressure to conform but also made invisible by dominant societies unwilling to recognize them. There is, however, nothing determinant about urban migration for Indigenous peoples. It may, indeed, result in erasure or it may very well provide the opportunities for the recovery of presence and memory.

Another feature of rural-urban migration is that it can occur at an extremely rapid rate. Rozanova-Smith, Ksenofontov, and Petrov (chap. 8, this volume) explore the consequences of such migration in the Russian Arctic region, focusing on young people in two cities since the migration predominantly involves younger members of Indigenous communities. Young people are more likely to be educated in the national language, so migration is easier, but it is also the case that climate change and environmental degradation in Indigenous regions means that there are simply fewer opportunities for younger people in Indigenous territories. These intergenerational differences and issues are explored in some detail by Rozanova-Smith, Ksenofontov, and Petrov, but they are also important features of the works of del Valle Casals and Borea (chaps. 7 and 1, respectively, this volume).

Indigenous peoples' prospects have changed dramatically since the early decades of the twentieth century, owing to the continuing rural-to-urban migration that has resulted, in the majority of cases, from a systematic usurpation of Indigenous territories by the states that encompass them. For example, since the 1980s, the consolidation of liberal market economies has involved structural transformations in Latin American countries that resulted in the remaining Indigenous territories being targeted as fertile lands for development projects such as dams, forestry, mining industries, and highways. With the fast development of Latin American cities, new work opportunities were created for medium- and low-skilled jobs. Cities were transformed as attractive magnets for Indigenous peoples, fostering rural-to-urban waves of migration to escape from rural misery or simply in search of better opportunities. Sometimes, Indigenous people feel that there are no significant development possibilities for them in rural communities or on reservations. Recognizing that cities are filled with opportunity, Indigenous peoples will continue to inhabit urban areas, and their populations will continue to grow. This has been the case in Canada since the 1970s, the decade since which Indigenous peoples are more likely to live in cities than in rural areas (Hall and Fenelon 2016). In some other cases, these geographical movements have been accentuated by situations of political violence and climate change. It is, of course, important to point out that Indigenous peoples' migration is not always voluntary. Even where it may appear voluntary, there may be a systematic and subtle coercion. As Canessa's (2012) work in highland Bolivia shows, schooling in Indigenous communities may be so biased toward urban values that young people feel they have little choice but to leave their Indigenous village. This compulsion can take many forms, not all of them economic or narrowly political.

Whatever the push and pull factors, migration for Indigenous people always entails a reimagining of what it means to be Indigenous. This may be because they face an oppressive racism that compels them to hide or deny their indigeneity, or it may be that their Indigenous identity is intimately tied to rituals and relationships with human and nonhuman beings that are weakly present—if at all—in urban settings. From the perspective of those urban dwellers, however, this is not necessarily the case at all. They may develop new energetic forms of Indigenous consciousness in the urban milieu and find sites in the city where new cultural forms are adapted or created from scratch, which articulates a very urban Indigenous identity. This can take myriad forms, from women's wrestling bouts (Haynes 2013) to Aymara hip-hop (Swineheart 2012) to architecture (Runnels 2019). None of these may be rooted in rural lifeways, but on what basis could one possibly argue they are not Indigenous if they are meaningful representations and expressions of Indigenous people?

Identity and Authenticity

Despite the challenges Indigenous peoples face in urban areas, they have responded to their new urban situation by developing new forms of survival, new networks and forms of mobility, and new political and cultural strategies of resistance. As maintained by Howard and Proulx (2011), issues of identity reclamation and retention, both individually and collectively, are central for urban Indigenous peoples worldwide. We consider identity building as a form of resistance to oppressive and assimilatory colonizing forces. An objective of this volume is to interrogate the theoretical formulations that correlate mobility with acculturation and assimilation on the one hand, and stasis and authenticity on the other. By questioning ideas of identity purity and homogeneity, while acknowledging the Indigenous use of authenticity as a tool to defend endangered cultures, our collaborators establish that there can be no pure and authentic identity for Indigenous people, either for those who stayed or for those who traveled. In fact, many identity markers, such as territorial origin, kinship, and blood quantum, are common in both rural and urban contexts. Other themes that arise in the chapters are related to identity perceptions and classifications. That is to say, while Indigenous people are carriers of connections to their homelands, of ties of tradition and kinship (Furlan 2017), they are creating their own communities in cities, complicating what it means to be Indigenous. A similar trend is exemplified by Brablec's (2021) work, which reveals how urban Indigenous individuals and groups inhabit, negotiate, and challenge authenticity-based definitions of Indigenous identity in cities. By traversing urban spaces and practices that are gendered, racialized, and classed, the chapters of this volume offer insights into conceptions of self-perception, belonging, and representation of urban Indigenous peoples in the cities of the world.

One of the greatest myths about Indigenous peoples is the inevitable loss of identity in favor of the majority when they move to cities. As Carey and Lyndon (2014) point out, these views rest on the notion of cultural change as acculturation and the appropriation of non-Indigenous ideas and practices as undermining Indigenous peoples' own identity. Stereotypically, Indigenous peoples are seen as either autochthonous and fixed or as displaced and inauthentic (Carey and Lyndon 2014). This has resulted in a conditioning of Indigenous peoples to live up to ideologies of authenticity from which the non-Indigenous society is excluded. Consequently, urban Indigenous people are perceived as less authentic and an even more dysfunctional people (Gagné 2016). As Māori scholar Linda Tuhiwai Smith (2012) maintains, this conception limits the agency of Indigenous people by establishing unrealistic expectations of authenticity combined with accusations of identity invention and illegitimacy. This, according to Carey and Lyndon (2014), is a form of racism and primitivism in disguise, working as a system of exclusion of indigeneity in cities.

Social and geographical orthodoxies, for different reasons, have been propagated by both Indigenous and non-Indigenous people alike. Usually, states tend to demand authenticity by recognizing the rights of Indigenous peoples who "have been relatively untouched by history" (Paradies 2006, 361); those who are able comply with social, political, and economic criteria required by states. Additionally, Indigenous people are at pains to distance themselves when they are being looked down upon by those living in the homeland and treated as not being Indigenous enough. As has been the case with the Māori in New Zealand, the Mapuche in Chile, and the Métis in Canada, for instance, discrimination is further accentuated for descendants of mixed marriages.

Throughout this volume, contributors focus on Indigenous identification as a process of construction and reconstruction inside and outside ethnic communities (Nagel 1994), given the porous nature of ethnic boundaries that separate different ethnic groups (Chandra 2006). While social relations become tangible in a geographical context in which individuals conceive sameness and otherness (Wade 2010), the adaptable nature of ethnic identities leads individuals to consider the milieu beyond its physical dimension. As a result, new environments such as cities can acquire symbolic meaning upon which Indigenous peoples can reconstruct their identity (Brablec 2020a). Cities are sites for the extraction of meaning par excellence (Tuan 1975) as they offer innumerable opportunities to elicit meanings from interactions among diverse individuals in different social contexts. That is, ethnicity not only is a fluid notion based upon internal reconfiguration processes but can also be externally shaped (Nagel 1994). One way this occurs is through the resignification of urban space for the creation of small places of cultural safety for Indigenous peoples to express their physical and spiritual relationship to their territories and communities. That is to say, urban spaces can be reinterpreted, challenging hegemonic constructions of space and identity that restrict Indigenous peoples to land outside of cities (Wilson and Peters 2005).

Living in cities has represented a series of challenges in the work of being and feeling Indigenous (Bastos and Camus 2000). Migration to cities involves a series of adaptations in the cultural, economic, and sociopolitical conceptions of life for urban Indigenous people. However, as maintained by

Clifford (2007), the source of Indigenous identities, cultures, and social networks is still the nonurban homeland: Indigenous people still maintain solid links with their ancestral territories and communities when living in cities, defining their own identity based on their ancestral homeland. However, these links are not necessarily material but can also be based on a spiritual connection. For some authors, the understanding of Indigenous homelands outside of cities is, in itself, a colonial invention (Peters and Andersen 2013). That is, the conception of ancestral homeland is not equivalent to the contained lands found in rural reservations and settlements but instead encompasses territories in which contemporary cities are situated. In turn, not all Indigenous peoples are chiefly dependent on land for their daily subsistence, meaning that their relations are recontextualized and revitalized to other aspects of their lives while living in cities.

Issues of Indigenous identity continuity remain especially troubled in cities. Several decades ago, scholars and activists challenged assumptions that maintained the impossibility of Indigenous survival in modern societies (de la Cadena and Starn 2007). Nowadays, we see similar attempts to defend the preservation of Indigenous identities in cities. Individuals and groups in cities can face challenges in defining and asserting Indigenous identities. As maintained by Peters and Andersen (2013), cultural re-creation practices in cities are often viewed as not central to the production of contemporary indigeneity. As Furlan (2017) asks in her book on urban indigeneity in the United States, one of the major issues facing twenty-first-century Indigenous peoples is how indigeneity can be retained while participating in a global society.

Indigenous people possess unique languages, knowledge systems, and beliefs and have their own diverse concepts of development based on their traditional values, visions, needs, and priorities. All these characteristic features do not vanish as if by magic when they move to cities. In contrast, various studies from around the world (Watson 2014; Warren 2017) have demonstrated that Indigenous people in cities are strongly oriented toward continuing their Indigenous identity collectively either with members of the same household or as part of larger organizations. As several of this volume's contributors illustrate, the incorporation of traditional knowledge and practice becomes a mode for belonging from both a personal and collective perspective while interacting, at the same time, with other urban cultures. An inclusive approach to indigeneity allows us to recognize the diversity of subjective positions and experiences while acknowledging the survival of indigeneity in cities as a result of people's historical ability to adapt and endure, for which collective action has been crucial.

Organizations and Collective Action

Urban Indigenous peoples have resisted expectations of assimilation by building communities in urban areas and by reformulating Western institutions and practices to support their Indigenous identities (Peters and Andersen 2013). Indigeneity survives, adapts, and innovates in modern cities, and collective action has been key for this to happen. Space is a fundamental element for collective activity to be materialized. Indigenous ceremonial sites, community centers, and markets have become integral elements of the world's cities, representing symbols of spatial appropriation and resignification for the development of urban indigeneity. In many cases, the urban space becomes a site of rearticulation of citizenship and belonging and a locus of political movements. While cities may be places where multifaceted injustices become manifest, they may also represent sites where transformative activism is possible and productive. Indigenous organizations worldwide have declared, embraced, and mobilized around their members' ethnicity, challenging any anachronistic perceptions in regard to this process (Yashar 1998). Tuhiwai Smith (2012) maintains that irrespective of their place of origin, Indigenous peoples tend to share a common collective memory of imperialism and colonization, leading to a similar sense of oppression and alliance, shaping contemporary identities, and promoting collective national and transnational activism. This similar experience has led to a growing identification under the rubric of *Indigenous peoples* by very different and dispersed communities in the world. Following a similar line, the chapters included in this volume reveal the diversity and fluidity of Indigenous organizations and movements in terms of internal structures, goals, and methods. At the same time, they uncover various resemblances of urban Indigenous collective action around the world.

Even in the core of capitalist societies, social movements led by Indigenous peoples in cities, such as the Red Power movement of the 1960s–1970s in the United States, suggest parallels to processes of historical domination and injustice in other regions of the world. Among these processes are the maintenance of material links to their lands, the revitalization of traditional cultures, and the opposition to capitalist social structures. Similarities to the Red Power movement are found in Latin American Indigenous social movements and bear remarkable similarity to Indigenous peoples' struggles around the globe (Hall and Fenelon 2016). In Latin America, Indigenous peoples were involved in many social movements throughout the twentieth and twenty-first centuries, as seen in the case of the Centros Culturales Mapuche, created in the city of Temuco in 1978 in opposition to the military regime of Pinochet in Chile; the 2003 gas struggle in the cities of La Paz and El Alto in Bolivia; and the urban Indigenous uprisings in 2000 in Quito. The demands articulated have been varied, ranging from the formal recognition of specific Indigenous rights around self-determination, prior consultation, and land ownership, to redistribution rights—that is, access to certain goods and services such as health care, housing, and education. With the increasing levels of rural-to-urban relocation, these Indigenous demands and organizational structures have changed significantly in recent decades.

As members of the urban landscape, the sociopolitical dynamics of Indigenous peoples are conditioned by the interactions that happen in the city, which may impact the way their ethnicity is performed. This does not result in imminent acculturation but rather in a constant process of reconfiguration for which collective work is relevant. In cities Indigenous organizations have tended to be bounded by a state bureaucratic framework, which implements external regulations that may influence ethnic identification (Nagel 1994). State policies designed for Indigenous peoples play a role in the development of reethnification processes. As maintained by De la Maza (2010), the state is a sociocultural construction based on a national project that impacts society through different mechanisms, thus shaping society's identity. Social systems of governance, local economies, and land tenure become arenas of conflict within individual states. They are often sites of resistance to structures of domination and the imposition of profit-driven value systems (Lewis 2019). While surrounded by the forces of the state and public policy, Indigenous organizations have still presented the space for social interactions to occur in an urban setting. The question for Indigenous organizations, as Hale (2002) asked for the Guatemalan case, is how to occupy the spaces opened from above while resisting the state's homogenizing logics when enacting an Indigenous identity in the city.

It is a common experience for Indigenous peoples to be looked down upon by public authorities who may simply not consider the housing, educational, health, and other needs of urban Indigenous residents. Even when

Indigenous peoples are in such vulnerable conditions, they have been able to organize some form of collective work to support new arrivals to the city, such as in the case of the Maasai in Dar es Salaam (Rakoff 2019). When access to resources is more secure, as in the case of the Māori in New Zealand, Indigenous peoples can develop very strong and efficient urban organizations (Gagné 2013). While from a different geographical region, the Mapuche people have also been actively creating Indigenous organizations, with more than 220 groups in Santiago de Chile, including profession-based, ethnic, and productive collectives (Brablec 2020b). For the Māori and the Mapuche, life in cities has thus come to form a platform for the articulation of Indigenous demands, in line with that of life in rural communities.

As attested by the work of our collaborators in various countries of the world, urban Indigenous organizations have played a key role in cultural recovery, political involvement, and economic participation of their members. In turn, country studies indicate that relations with the communities of origin are maintained and even strengthened with the help of ceremonial re-creation processes that are often promoted or developed by urban Indigenous organizations. From family-based groups to collectives created across cultural and tribal groupings, Indigenous organizations have been fundamental for the reinforcement of collective cultural identity traits and the articulation of strategies for ethnic demands (Maíz 2004). Through the collective preservation of historical memory, practice of a common culture, development of support networks, and protest against social, political, and economic marginalization, urban Indigenous organizations have established themselves as contexts in which identity can be reimagined and reshaped. By engaging in activities relevant to their members, organizations enable the collective operationalization of Indigenous traits that are otherwise historically loaded with racist conceptions. This allows a revalorization of these practices, thus enabling a sense of identification to be kept alive in the urban context.

Nonetheless, urban Indigenous collective action has not always had a straightforward trajectory (Carey and Lyndon 2014). Multiple shifting alliances can be formed over time. Some Indigenous networks have remained autonomous or exclusively family based, others have been defined in terms of the relationship established with the state, and others have built cooperation channels with other transnational Indigenous organizations, NGOs, and broader social movements. In turn, membership in urban Indigenous organizations and participation in the life of non-Indigenous urban communities are not mutually exclusive. As illustrated by our contributors, urban Indigenous peoples have memberships in multiple social and political communities, getting involved, at different levels of engagement, in the contemporary life of the cities of the world—that is, there is an evident cosmopolitanism in the lives of contemporary Indigenous peoples.

The cosmopolitanism of Indigenous art is a central theme in Borea's contribution (chap. 1, this volume) as she explores the place of Indigenous art, not only in Peru but also globally. Art is clearly an important medium of political expression as well as a powerful way of articulating an Indigenous presence that is both modern and urban—and even cosmopolitan, as the works circulate internationally, increasingly in prestigious art galleries in world capitals (see also Goodale 2006; Flores Silva 2022). Indigenous cosmopolitanism does not, however, simply lie in the realm of art; it also lies in the realm of politics, as Indigenous movements are increasingly interconnected globally, not least as we collectively face a climate crisis (Escárcega 2010; Adamson 2012). Indigenous cosmopolitanism takes a number of forms. As Ikemura Amaral (chap. 3, this volume) shows, Indigenous peoples travel to other countries where they settle and enjoy thoroughly cosmopolitan existences. But Indigenous cosmopolitanism is not just about Indigenous experiences in world cities but also about Indigenous experiences in their own villages. In his work in the apparently remote village of Wila Kjarka in highland Bolivia where a road only arrived in 2011, Andrew Canessa has seen the urban penetrate the lives of Indigenous peasants, both as the road and mobile telephones bring goods and images into the village and as villagers are in constant communication with partners and family members who live as far away as Spain. The road means that the trip to the city can be done in a matter of hours, without the need to walk down steep mountain paths and cross ravines; it also means that consumer goods are readily available. But more importantly it blurs the difference between urban and rural lives. So it is not just the artists that Borea describes who have one foot in the rural and the other in the global urban, but also the subjects themselves of such representation that are increasingly familiar with both urban and global lifeways.

These processes are not, however, neutral. The very idea of indigeneity in Western discourse arises out of the birth of the modern nation-state, and Indigenous peoples have long been considered as the antithesis of what is modern, national, and indeed the state (Canessa and Picq, forthcoming). It is thus impossible to discuss Indigenous life in the cities of the world without referring to the controlling processes involved in the historic, multisited, multipurposed, and continuing colonial projects of modern nation-states. Over hundreds of years, states have been successful in displacing, absorbing, incorporating, assimilating, or destroying Indigenous peoples. Yet despite myriad alarming predictions—and, more importantly, repeated military and social actions directed against them by states, sometimes in agreement with private firms—many Indigenous peoples have steadfastly resisted and survived attempts at total annihilation.

Even though Indigenous residence in cities is increasing, it is important to remember, as stated above, that it is not a new phenomenon. This is evidenced in Stevens's study on indigeneity in Fiji (chap. 2, this volume), in which urbanization appears to be an enduring aspect of the colonial and postcolonial experience of the Indigenous peoples of the Pacific. It is, however, not only in colonial cities that Indigenous peoples were present but also in precolonial ones. Even in the Amazon, Indigenous peoples were highly urbanized long before Europeans settled there (Peluso, chap. 6, this volume). It is as important to recognize the long history of Indigenous urbanization as it is to recognize the urban features of contemporary Indigenous life: in recent decades highly sustained migration rates have resulted in urban areas becoming home to large Indigenous populations.

Some Indigenous peoples are geographically dispersed in the world's cities, while others have suffered from sociopolitical invisibility. One of the key aims of this volume is to make visible Indigenous presence, lives, and contributions to urban life in the world's cities. Perhaps at least as importantly, we aim to reclaim the urban experience for Indigenous people and resist the notion that being urban makes one somehow less Indigenous: it is merely a different Indigenous experience. At root here is the question, Who has the power to decide who is—and is not—Indigenous?

Defining Indigeneity

Redefining oneself as part of an Indigenous group, or merely rediscovering one's Indigenous identity, can be an important step for marginalized groups to gain recognition from their corresponding states. As a response to the emergence of Indigenous peoples as contemporary actors in the sociopolitical scene, countries around the world started to face the dilemma of how to distinguish the Indigenous urban population from the non-Indigenous one.

Would this be a matter of state recognition based on the exercise or possession of certain traits like proficiency in an Indigenous language? Or, on the other hand, would the decision be delegated to the same Indigenous peoples based on their self-identification? Who, then, names Indigenous people? The power to decide who is or is not Indigenous is often guarded by a state actor whose interests may lie in systematically undercounting the Indigenous population. States try to monopolize the use not only of legitimate force but also of symbolic force. This, following a Bourdieusian approach, includes the "power to name, to identify, to categorize, to state what is what and who is who" (Brubaker and Cooper 2000, 15).

Given the diversity of Indigenous peoples, there is no widely accepted definition, yet some features have served to distinguish the urban Indigenous from other populations. Despite seemingly unifying characteristics, the UN stipulates that the most fruitful approach to the wide range of Indigenous cultures and ways of living is to identify rather than define them—that is, as Schkolink and del Popolo (2005) maintain, challenging top-down models of state control by empowering Indigenous peoples themselves with the faculty of deciding who can be a member to their own group. Inserted in a wider urban context, self-identification has operated as a crucial tool for those Indigenous residents, as cultural identifiers tend to be less evident than those of their rural Indigenous counterparts. Power struggles over the determination of Indigenous identities in cities are entangled with stereotypical expectations and a lack of awareness of the wide scope of the new modes of agency and community in cities (Howard and Proulx 2011). In this regard, as stated by del Popolo et al. (2007) in their work for the United Nations Economic Commission for Latin America and the Caribbean, Indigenous peoples in cities can be recognized by their origin but not necessarily by the possession or fulfillment of certain features, as can be seen in (1) those who resided in territories where cities were founded and who are still present in those areas; (2) Indigenous people who are first-generation, rural-to-urban immigrants; and (3) the descendants of previous generations of migrants or, in other words, those who were born in cities.

The Impact of Urbanization

The impact of urbanization is being deeply felt by Indigenous peoples across the world and carries both potential severe consequences for their culture, heritage, and connection to their traditional lands and socioeconomic opportunities. The incorporation of Indigenous peoples into cities has not necessarily been equivalent to progress from their poor rural living conditions. The joint consequences of poverty and racism have usually been translated into integration into the most deprived strata of the urban social scene. It may very well be that migration to urban areas increases their annual income, but it will also increase their housing and food costs. On the other hand, cities are not always synonymous with hostility; they are also spaces in which new social bonds with human and nonhuman entities can emerge. Migration can also provide more employment opportunities for Indigenous people, who can use the surplus earned to support their families and communities in their territories of origin. Also, in some instances, Indigenous rural-to-urban relocation may enable identity reaffirmation through new learning experiences, posing new challenges for the adaptation of Indigenous identities that are moving toward spaces of greater complexity. As Brablec maintains (chap. 4, this volume), urban migration may open possibilities for challenging traditional hierarchies and can provide a space for the empowerment of women.

Clifford (2013) notes that Indigenous peoples reemerged in public debates not as victims or as messengers from a utopian past, but as visible actors in the local, national, and global political arenas. Their claim for specific rights went hand in hand with the questioning of relations based on racial discrimination, ethnic intolerance, and the control of one culture over others. Over the years these demands have increased in complexity and vary widely from people to people, including areas such as autonomy, territoriality, self-government, and an extensive range of Indigenous rights. This reemergence led to a series of Indigenous demonstrations of cultural resistance and identity reconstruction. Yet in the social sciences, relatively little attention has been given to the historical and contemporary conditions of Indigenous peoples living in the world's cities (Howard and Proulx 2011; Peters and Andersen 2013; Horn 2019).

City, Life, Mobility, and Poverty Culture

Indigenous cultures have never been immobile; they have connected and adapted to many circumstances before their confrontation with colonizing powers. While homelands remain relevant for the re-creation of identities,

Indigenous bodies are not bound by state-imposed borders. At the intersection of the city's material and immaterial practices, interpretations, and lived experiences, Indigenous urban life is understood as dynamic and characterized by motion. Focusing on these multiple acts of traversing—both within the city and in relation to rural-to-urban and international migration—several chapters of this volume allow us to rethink notions of Indigenous belonging that are usually linked to rural ancestral territories, challenging traditional and essentialist constructions of indigeneity. In doing so, this volume addresses distinct forms of emplacement despite the difficulties Indigenous peoples find in cities.

Indigenous rural-to-urban migration needs to be understood beyond the explicit meaning of spatial mobility from an ancestral territory to a new milieu. This shift mirrors the intricacy of identity reconfiguration, which is deeply spiritually linked to the ancestral territory, and the new interactions in plural-heterogeneous settings circumscribed by always-evolving cities (Brablec 2022). The chapters in this volume reflect the diversity of reasons behind the decision to migrate to cities, either voluntary, involuntary, or indirectly forced by the circumstances. However, as noted by Furlan (2017), even those who have left their communities of origin by choice are affected by economic conditions that are a direct result of a history of colonialism or settler colonialism. In this sense, one of the common factors leading to migration throughout different regions is related to the precarious living conditions Indigenous peoples face in their territories of origin.

The World Bank (2019) reports that although Indigenous peoples make up 6 percent of the global population, they account for nearly 15 percent of the extreme poor. In addition, their life expectancy is twenty years lower than that of non-Indigenous people worldwide. Even in countries considered rich, Indigenous peoples seem to constitute islands of poverty within wealthy nations. Many factors contribute to this outcome. In the case of the Maasai in Tanzania, for instance, their traditional lands and livelihoods have been steadily diminishing due to unfavorable government policies. The same deplorable scenario can be seen among many other Indigenous communities in Africa, whose traditional lands are gradually being seized by other actors. With limited viable economic alternatives in rural areas, Indigenous peoples are drawn to urban settings by the prospect of job and education opportunities and economic security. Cities are widely perceived as cosmopolitan places with shifting borders and populations, with geographies that must be navigated and learned, sites that are markedly different from rural communities and towns, and economies dependent on the labor of the working classes (Furlan 2017). In cities, Indigenous livelihoods tend to improve in terms of access to services, jobs, and education. However, the urban milieu brings about several challenges. These challenges arise from "the need to speak a different language, to learn a different culture, or to negotiate a bureaucratic social system replete with differing spiritual values and expectations of the individual" (Watson 2010, 274). Indigenous people who migrate to urban areas often experience systemic racism and discrimination. Frequently they do not enjoy basic rights, being subjected to inadequate housing, unemployment, and limited access to health services and justice. As pointed out by Ijjasz-Vasquez and Hentschel (2017), one in three Indigenous people living in cities inhabit insecure, unsanitary, and polluted slums twice as often as non-Indigenous peoples. Indigenous peoples tend to be more exposed to disease outbreaks such as COVID-19, tuberculosis, and typhoid, which are exacerbated due to their poverty and overcrowding living circumstances (World Bank 2019). Additionally, their traditional knowledge and skills have less value in the urban job market, they tend to have enjoyed fewer years in formal education (and may not be fluent in the national language), and very often face systematic racism. A combination of all these factors means they tend to be relegated to low-paying tasks in the informal sector usually associated with precarious employment conditions, job instability, low wages, and lack of social protection.

They also have difficulties in sustaining their culture and identity, leading to the generations born in urban areas facing the complexities of loss of Indigenous heritage and values. Even when they are in the majority within the urban space, they can struggle to assert their cultural values and ways of being in the face of even well-meaning and outwardly benign outsiders when territorial sovereignty is abrogated by the state. Family separations caused by Indigenous migration can have a profound emotional effect on the individuals who migrate and on those family members left behind. In many cases, young Indigenous individuals are especially drawn to migrate in search of better opportunities for themselves and their families. As a result, rural communities and reservations face the challenge of losing part of their youth and, therefore, their main workforce. However, remittances sent by urban Indigenous people can provide support and contribute to the survival of rural communities. This process marks a new relational interaction based on cooperation at a distance. The exchange of goods and products between rural and urban areas is, thus, not an uncommon dynamic. It is important to highlight that migration is not necessarily unidirectional. Sometimes, Indigenous individuals work or study in cities and decide to return to the rural communities at some point in their lives, establishing an inverse migration process: urban to rural. Others choose to travel only occasionally to their communities to visit their relatives. Yet modern communications—especially cell phones—can reduce a sense of detachment, complicating notions of loss and distance.

The economic gap between Indigenous and non-Indigenous peoples is evident in regions such as Latin America and the Caribbean. The participation in the informal economy among Indigenous people is 82.6 percent, while that of non-Indigenous people is estimated at 51.1 percent. This rate is even higher among Indigenous women in the region, with a rate above 85 percent (ILO 2020). While migration often occurs under economic desperation, resettlement may represent an opportunity that empowers Indigenous women by providing the space in which they can set their own agendas, challenge specific oppressions in their own way, and mark new political trajectories in the new milieu (Brah 1996). As discussed by Course (2011) regarding the Mapuche in Chile and by Oelz and Kumar Dhir (2015) regarding the Scheduled Tribes in India, Indigenous women have been particularly drawn to the domestic service sector as a result of their unobstructed insertion into the urban labor market. However, Indigenous women in cities continue to be more exposed to a series of inequalities, vulnerabilities, violence, and sexual harassment than non-Indigenous women (see also Gill 1994). At the same time, the limited access to political decision-making processes means that Indigenous peoples are unable to use the political system to improve their position. This situation only contributes to the continued marginalization of Indigenous communities in urban centers. This disadvantage may be compounded by a denial of urban indigeneity by the national culture. For instance, Peluso (chap. 6, this volume) explores the struggles of urban Indigenous in Amazonia who face the dual pressure to assimilate and loss of "authenticity" in the eyes of neighbors and authorities as they do so. In a similar vein, del Valle Casals (chap. 7, this volume) demonstrates the ways in which Mapuche representation in mainstream film, even when sympathetically portrayed, stresses the unredeemable otherness of Indigenous people in the urban milieu where they are perpetually "out of place."

Nonetheless, as the number of urban Indigenous households is only likely to grow in the coming decades, governments—both local and national—need to understand their needs and potential. While the media and governments often portray urban Indigenous peoples as desperate for assistance, the precarious life they encounter in cities is often presented in a simplistic and misleading way, as if poverty is intrinsic to Indigenous cultures. To genuinely change the vicious cycle of inequality and discrimination, the chapters in this volume provide a diversity of viewpoints that engage with the structural factors that create this culture of poverty while proposing some policy solutions.

This Volume

This volume had its beginnings in a workshop at Cambridge University in late 2019 that brought together twenty-two speakers in different career stages whose research addressed crucial issues for the analysis of urban indigeneity around the world, from both practical and theoretical perspectives. The workshop sought to bring urban indigeneity to light by discussing the continued persistence of Indigenous identities in cities and the different ways in which Indigenous peoples have defied simplistic theoretical predictions about their disappearance by assimilation into the dominant non-Indigenous urban societies. Based on the interest generated after the event, the network of contributors was expanded to illuminate more fully the questions around Indigenous identities in the wake of urbanization. Inherent concerns of this volume are questions around gender, race, and collective resistance; the negotiation of otherness in terms of identity reconstruction, the shaping of borders, and a sense of belonging; the politics of urban Indigenous representation; and the unavoidable topic of environmental racism and the enforcement of urbanization. This project purposefully brings together interdisciplinary theoretical positions, including those from cultural studies, Indigenous studies, development studies, postcolonial studies, gender studies, and urban studies. The main questions that frame the chapters included here are, What does it mean to be Indigenous in the contemporary cities of the world? And how are Indigenous peoples challenging conceptions of belonging in the wake of increasing global urbanization? The volume takes on the ambitious task of removing the layers of invisibility that urban Indigenous peoples face, thus highlighting various aspects of their contemporary life in different cities around the world.

From an international perspective, this volume is timely: 2019 commemorated one of the most relevant landmarks on Indigenous affairs with the thirtieth anniversary of the ILO Convention 169 on Indigenous and Tribal Peoples. This mechanism remains the only legally binding treaty that promotes the interests of Indigenous and tribal peoples and fosters their rights worldwide. However, only about 15 percent of Indigenous people live in the twenty-three countries that have ratified the 169 Convention. This underlines an important challenge, as a majority of Indigenous peoples continue to fall outside the protection provided under the ILO Convention. Added to this, and what is of particular interest to this volume, is that there is still no reference to the increasing urbanization rates of Indigenous peoples and the consequent challenges they face in cities daily. Additionally, fewer than ten years separate us from the fulfillment of the goals stipulated in the UN 2030 Agenda for Sustainable Development, at the center of which is the principle that no one will be left behind. Indigenous peoples were actively involved in the principles of Agenda 2030 to ensure that their experiences with discrimination in national development and historical marginalization processes are tackled. However, and in reference to the goal of making cities inclusive, safe, resilient, and sustainable for Indigenous peoples (UN Sustainable Development 2015), we know that, up to now, their experience has been one of disproportional deprivation and multifaceted inequality compared to non-Indigenous urban residents.

One of the central claims of this volume is that Indigenous political agency and cultural preservation are indeed possible in the city. Our contributors demonstrate the persistence of community stories and identities regardless of geographic location. Urban Indigenous narratives are not solely about despair and dislocation; they imagine a cultural past identified with their ancestral lands and a present that requires the making and remaking of Indigenous bonds and communities. That is to say, Indigenous peoples' identities endure postmigration to cities while also resulting in changes to their social, political, and cultural landscapes. A common topic for the chapters included in this volume is the theoretical and practical relevance of borders in the conceptualization of indigeneity in the city. In this sense, borders refer not only to physical boundaries but also to the creation, imposition, and traversing of adaptable identity boundaries. As discussed in the volume, the construction and reconstruction of Indigenous identities in the cities of the world usually bring together experiences such as diasporic feelings in relation to the territories and communities of origin, the absence of support systems, racism, changes in citizenship rights, tensions between home and away, shaping of collective memory, and organizational rearticulation practices, among others. Our focus is not, however, on describing and comparing similarities and differences in the urban experiences of all the Indigenous cases presented in the volume; instead, we hope to identify key themes and insights that have broader application for the new generation of research and understanding on urban indigeneity. Therefore, the volume provides a baseline for future research on the processes of urban Indigenous identity elaborations and performances for the cases not covered here.

The studies of urban Indigenous lives in cities presented in this volume offer innovative perspectives on cultural transformation and continuity. They demonstrate how examinations of the diversity within and across urban Indigenous experiences contribute to broader understandings of the relationship between Indigenous peoples and their corresponding states, and address theoretical debates about power dynamics in the production of community and identity formation, with consideration of factors such as class, gender, and resistance to colonial structures. The contributors provide cutting-edge arguments for understanding Indigenous experiences in cities by challenging homogenizing conceptions of indigeneity as something eminently rural, while providing analytical tools for the understanding of the processes of rural-to-urban migration, identity construction, and sociopolitical participation, among many other topics. As maintained by Hall and Fenelon (2016), contemporary theory and practice should not continue to reflect the interpretations of colonial or even modern positions that neglect the continued presence of Indigenous peoples and their ways of life in cities. As our contributors argue, urban Indigenous voices, experiences, and actions have to be central to research in Indigenous studies beyond cultural essentialisms and represent the fluidity of the rural-to-urban migrant experience. As presented in this volume, this task requires a fundamental reconceptualization of imperial and colonial legacies, mobilities, and exchanges. We recognize the diversity of Indigenous populations reflected in cultural differences, varied histories, and relationships to the state. Some, such as the Māori, were recognized by the colonial state; others, such as those in Latin America, exist in a context where there is a strong ideology of redemptive racial mixing (*mestizaje*) that seeks to absorb an Indigenous past and erase its future; and many others, such as in Africa and Asia, were only recognized as Indigenous in the late twentieth or even twenty-first century. In fact, even when considering a single case study, there are multiple angles from which to contemplate different life experiences between first-, second-, and third-generation Indigenous migrants, between young and old, between men and women, and between rural and urban lives.

In this way, this volume engages with a critical approach to Indigenous urbanization (or "critical urban indigeneities," as further developed in Brablec, chap. 4, this volume). In more detail, we aim to reconsider postcolonial relations between Indigenous peoples, states, and societies at large, still very present around the globe, and highlight the agency Indigenous individuals and collectives actively exercise within established socioeconomic structures while examining the reshaping processes of their sense of being a people when living in cities. In doing this, we do not hope to extrapolate urban indigeneity as a phenomenon independent of other social realities (Andersen 2009). Such a task would be futile, as all identities are (re)produced by a matter of relations and tensions with each other. Instead, we seek to position indigeneity in light of processes that result from interactions based on complex mechanisms of power and differential social hierarchies, as in the case of whitening and *mestizaje*. As maintained by Porter and Yiftachel (2019), we acknowledge how urbanization continues to materialize Indigenous peoples' subaltern social position in cities and elsewhere. Nevertheless, by positioning urbanization at the center of the volume's discussions, we endeavor to analyze urbanization not as an infallible strategy of domination by postcolonial states but as an opportunity for sociopolitical, economic, and cultural rearticulation. Similarly, as Indigenous scholars Julieta Paredes (2017) and Ana Millaleo (2020) maintain about Indigenous feminisms, the chapters of this volume also endeavor to show how Indigenous peoples in different regions of the world, utilizing a wide range of sociopolitical and cultural strategies, are recovering, reappropriating, and reimagining the city to accommodate their old and contemporary experiences in the urban milieu. To accomplish this, our volume's contributors explore Indigenous urbanization in numerous ways. Some chapters epistemologically engage with Indigenous literatures as the producer of complex knowledges while establishing dialogues with the rich mainstream Western scholarship. Other chapters reflect on urban indigeneity from a first-hand account, articulating collaborative relationships with members of their own Indigenous communities. On the other hand, from a non-Indigenous position, other chapters have actively sought multiple forms of cooperation, establishing partnerships, engagements, and, especially, opportunities for academic, functional, and policy-level reciprocity with the Indigenous communities represented here. In many cases our contributory authors draw on many years of advocacy and political engagement with Indigenous peoples.

Moreover, our purpose is not to create a simplistic divide between allegedly distinct urban and rural identities as we recognize how the multiple exchanges nurture each of these realities, but rather to consider, from a multisited, interdisciplinary, and predominantly ethnographic perspective, Indigenous lives adapting to changing circumstances and environments. While our objective was to be as inclusive as possible in terms of geographical coverage, we cannot claim comprehensiveness in including the full diversity of Indigenous experiences across different regions. Instead, with a wide range of diverse cases, the volume aims to reveal that, while there is no single way of being urban Indigenous, Indigenous peoples in cities often face similar challenges, even considering the historical, sociocultural, political, and economic circumstances of the countries they inhabit. *Urban Indigeneities* delves into and goes beyond these commonalities by bringing together a series of histories and geographies to propose a way of thinking about and discussing the extent of evolving urban indigeneity today.

References

Adamson, Joni. 2012. "Indigenous Literatures, Multinaturalism, and Avatar: The Emergence of Indigenous Cosmopolitics." *American Literary History* 24 (1): 143–62.

Andersen, Chris. 2009. "Critical Indigenous Studies: From Difference to Density." *Cultural Studies Review* 15 (2): 80–100.

Bastos, Santiago, and Manuela Camus. 2000. "Los Indígenas de La Capital. Informe Etnográfico Comisionado Por CIRMA Para El Proyecto '¿Por Qué Estamos Como Estamos?'" http://lanic.utexas.edu/project/laoap/cirma/biblioteca/capital.pdf.

Brablec, Dana. 2020a. "Indigenising the City Together: Ethnic Place Production in Santiago de Chile." *Journal of Ethnic and Migration Studies* 49 (3): 892–908. https://doi.org/10.1080/1369183X.2020.1814711.

———. 2020b. "The Mapuche and the City: Ethnicity (Re)Creation within Indigenous Associations in Santiago de Chile." Doctoral thesis, University of Cambridge. https://www.repository.cam.ac.uk/handle/1810/298812.

———. 2021. "Who Counts as an Authentic Indigenous? Collective Identity Negotiations in the Chilean Urban Context." *Sociology* 55 (1): 129–45. https://doi.org/10.1177/0038038520915435.

———. 2022. "Indigenous Language Revitalisation: Mapuzungun Workshops in Santiago de Chile." *Bulletin of Latin American Research* 41 (1): 69–84. https://doi.org/DOI:10.1111/blar.13291.

Brah, A. 1996. *Cartographies of Diaspora: Contesting Identities*. London: Routledge.
Brubaker, Rogers, and Frederick Cooper. 2000. "Beyond 'Identity.'" *Theory and Society* 29 (1): 1–47.
Canessa, Andrew. 2012. *Intimate Indigeneities: Race, Sex, and History in the Small Spaces of Andean Life*. Durham, N.C.: Duke University Press.
———. 2018. "Indigenous Conflict in Bolivia Explored through an African Lens: Towards a Comparative Analysis of Indigeneity." *Comparative Studies in Society and History* 60 (2): 308–37. https://doi.org/10.1017/S0010417518000063.
Canessa, Andrew, and Manuela Picq. Forthcoming. *Savages and Citizens: Indigenous People and the Nation State from Thomas Hobbes to Evo Morales*.
Carey, Jane, and Jane Lyndon. 2014. *Indigenous Networks: Mobility, Connections, and Exchange*. New York: Routledge.
Chandra, Kanchan. 2006. "What Is Ethnic Identity and Does It Matter?" *Annual Review of Political Science* 9 (1): 397–424. https://doi.org/10.1146/annurev.polisci.9.062404.170715.
Clifford, James. 2007. "Varieties of Indigenous Experience: Diasporas, Homelands, Sovereignties." In de la Cadena and Starn 2007, 197–224.
———. 2013. *Returns: Becoming Indigenous in the Twenty-First Century*. Cambridge, Mass.: Harvard University Press.
Course, Magnus. 2011. *Becoming Mapuche: Person and Ritual in Indigenous Chile*. Interpretations of Culture in the New Millennium. Urbana: University of Illinois Press.
Cruz Manjarrez, Adriana 2013. *Zapotecs on the Move: Cultural, Social, and Political Processes in Transnational Perspective*. New Brunswick: Rutgers University Press.
de la Cadena, Marisol, and Orin Starn, eds. 2007. *Indigenous Experience Today*. 1st ed. London: Bloomsbury Academic. https://doi.org/10.5040/9781474214933.
De la Maza, Francisca. 2010. "Aportes de La Etnografía Del Estado Para El Estudio de Las Interacciones Interculturales Locales Región de La Araucanía." In *VII Congreso Chileno de Antropología*. San Pedro de Atacama, Chile: Colegio de Antropólogos de Chile. https://www.aacademica.org/vii.congreso.chileno.de.antropologia/64.pdf.
del Popolo, Fabiana, Ana María Oyarce, Bruno Ribotta, and Jorge Rodríguez. 2007. *Indigenous Peoples and Urban Settlements: Spatial Distribution, Internal Migration and Living Conditions*. Población y Desarrollo 78. Santiago, Chile: CEPAL. https://repositorio.cepal.org/bitstream/handle/11362/7219/1/S0700810_en.pdf.
Escárcega, Sylvia. 2010. "Authenticating Strategic Essentialisms: The Politics of Indigenousness at the United Nations." *Cultural Dynamics* 22 (1): 3–28. https://doi.org/10.1177/0921374010366780.
Flores Silva, Fabian. 2022. "Cosmopolitanism, Cosmopolitics and Indigenous Peoples: Elements for a Possible Alliance." *Alternautas* 4 (1): 10–20.
Foxen, Patricia. 2007. *In Search of Providence: Transnational Mayan Identities*. Nashville: Vanderbilt University Press.

Furlan, Laura. 2017. *Indigenous Cities: Urban Indian Fiction and the Histories of Relocation*. Lincoln: University of Nebraska Press.

Gagné, Natacha. 2013. *Being Maori in the City: Indigenous Everyday Life in Auckland*. Toronto, Ontario: University of Toronto Press.

———. 2016. "The Waxing and Waning of the Politics of Authenticity: The Situation of Urban-Based Māori through the Lens of Municipal Politics." *City & Society* 28 (1): 48–73. https://doi.org/10.1111/ciso.12073.

Gill, Lesley. 1994. *Precarious Dependencies: Gender, Class, and Domestic Service in Bolivia*. New York: Columbia University Press.

Goodale, Mark. 2006. "Reclaiming Modernity: Indigenous Cosmopolitanism and the Coming of the Second Revolution in Bolivia." *American Ethnologist* 33 (4): 634–49.

Hale, Charles R. 2002. "Does Multiculturalism Menace? Governance, Cultural Rights and the Politics of Identity in Guatemala." *Journal of Latin American Studies* 34 (3): 485–524.

Hall, Thomas, and James Fenelon. 2016. *Indigenous Peoples and Globalization: Resistance and Revitalization*. New York: Routledge.

Haynes, Nell. 2013. "Global Cholas: Reworking Tradition and Modernity in Bolivian Lucha Libre." *Journal of Latin American and Caribbean Anthropology* 18 (3): 432–46. https://doi.org/10.1111/jlca.12040.

Hodgson, Dorothy. 2011. *Being Maasai, Becoming Indigenous: Postcolonial Politics in a Neoliberal World*. Bloomington: University of Indiana Press.

Horn, Philipp. 2019. *Indigenous Rights to the City: Ethnicity and Urban Planning in Bolivia and Ecuador*. New York: Routledge.

Howard, Heather, and Craig Proulx, eds. 2011. *Aboriginal Peoples in Canadian Cities: Transformations and Continuities*. Waterloo, Ontario: Wilfrid Laurier University Press.

Ijjasz-Vasquez, Ede, and Jesko Hentschel. 2017. "Urban Indigenous Peoples: The New Frontier." *World Bank Blogs*. https://blogs.worldbank.org/sustainablecities/urban-Indigenous-peoples-new-frontier-argentina.

International Labour Organization (ILO). 2020. "Pueblos Indígenas y Tribales: Más de La Mitad de Casi 55 Millones de Personas Indígenas En América Latina y El Caribe Viven y Trabajan En Ciudades." International Labour Organization. https://www.ilo.org/americas/sala-de-prensa/WCMS_735914/lang--es/index.htm?fbclid=IwAR30FgBcOLtvQLki5MVBC_aeTnfuO56SksKFuepKu_Q_2d877XESbvHie3Y.

Laruelle, Marlene. 2019. "The Three Waves of Arctic Urbanisation: Drivers, Evolutions, Prospects." *Polar Record* 55 (1): 1–12.

Lewis, Courtney. 2019. *Sovereign Entrepreneurs: Cherokee Small-Business Owners and the Making of Economic Sovereignty*. Chapel Hill: University of North Carolina Press.

Maíz, Ramón. 2004. "El Indigenismo Político En América Latina." *Revista de Estudios Políticos (Nueva Época)* no. 123, 29–174.

Millaleo, Ana. 2020. "Resistencia Desde El Fogón: Pensando Un Feminismo Mapuche." *Mapuexpress*. https://www.mapuexpress.org/2020/09/07/resistencia-desde-el-fogon-pensando-un-feminismo-mapuche/.

Nagel, Joane. 1994. "Constructing Ethnicity: Creating and Recreating Ethnic Identity and Culture." *Social Problems* 41 (1): 152–76.

Oelz, Martin, and Rishabh Kumar Dhir. 2015. *Indigenous Peoples in Domestic Work: Facing Multiple Discrimination and Disadvantage*. ILO's Work in Progress. http://oit.org/wcmsp5/groups/public/---ed_protect/---protrav/---travail/documents/publication/wcms_389240.pdf.

Paradies, Yin C. 2006. "Beyond Black and White: Essentialism, Hybridity and Indigeneity." *Journal of Sociology* 42 (4): 355–67. https://doi.org/10.1177/1440783306069993.

Paredes, Julieta. 2017. "El Feminismocomunitario: La Creación de Un Pensamiento Propio." *Corpus* 7 (1): 1–10. https://doi.org/10.4000/corpusarchivos.1835.

Pelican, Michaela. 2009. "Complexities of Indigeneity and Autochthony: An African Example." *American Ethnologist* 36 (1): 52–65.

Permanent Forum on Indigenous Issues (UNPFII). 2007. *Urban Indigenous Peoples and Migration: Challenges and Opportunities*. United Nations. https://www.un.org/esa/socdev/unpfii/documents/6_session_factsheet2.pdf.

Peters, Evelyn, and Chris Andersen, eds. 2013. *Indigenous in the City: Contemporary Identities and Cultural Innovation*. Vancouver: University of British Columbia Press.

Porter, Libby, and Oren Yiftachel. 2019. "Urbanizing Settler-Colonial Studies: Introduction to the Special Issue." *Settler Colonial Studies* 9 (2): 177–86. https://doi.org/10.1080/2201473X.2017.1409394.

Rakoff, Elise. 2019. "Labor Migration and Social Networking: Maasai Labor Migrants in Dar Es Salaam, Tanzania." Undergraduate honors thesis, William & Mary. https://scholarworks.wm.edu/honorstheses/1344/.

Runnels, Daniel. 2019. "Cholo Aesthetics and Mestizaje: Architecture in El Alto, Bolivia." *Latin American and Caribbean Ethnic Studies* 14 (2): 138–50. https://doi.org/10.1080/17442222.2019.1630059.

Schkolink, Susana, and Fabiana del Popolo. 2005. "Los Censos y Los Pueblos Indígenas En América Latina: Una Metodología Regional." In *Pueblos Indígenas y Afrodescendientes de América Latina y El Caribe: Relevancia y Pertinentica de La Información Sociodemográfica Para Políticas y Programas*, 101–32. Los Censos y Los Pueblos Indígenas En América Latina: Una Metodología Regional Santiago, Chile: CEPAL. https://repositorio.cepal.org/bitstream/handle/11362/12769/np79101132_es.pdf?sequence=1&isAllowed=y.

Simpson, Audrey. 2014. *Mohawk Interruptus: Political Life across the Borders of Settler States*. Durham, N.C.: Duke University Press.

Swineheart, Karl 2012. "Tupac in Their Veins: Hip-Hop *alteño* and the Semiotics of Urban Indigeneity." *Arizona Journal of Hispanic Cultural Studies* no. 16, 79–96.

Tuan, Yi-Fu. 1975. "Place: An Experiential Perspective." *Geographical Review* no. 65, 151.

Tuhiwai Smith, Linda. 2012. *Decolonising Methodologies: Research and Indigenous Peoples*. London: Zed Books.

UN Habitat. 2010. *Urban Indigenous Peoples and Migration: A Review of Policies, Programmes and Practices*. United Nations Housing Rights Programme, Report No. 8. https://unhabitat.org/sites/default/files/download-manager-files/Urban%20Indigenous%20Peoples%20and%20Migration%20A%20Review%20of%20Policies%2C%20Programmes%20and%20Practices.pdf.

UN Sustainable Development. 2015. *Indigenous Peoples Major Group Policy Brief on Sustainable Development Goals and Post-2015 Development Agenda: A Working Draft*. https://sustainabledevelopment.un.org/content/documents/6797IPMG%20Policy%20Brief%20Working%20Draft%202015.pdf.

Wade, Peter. 2010. *Race and Ethnicity in Latin America*. London: Pluto Press.

Warren, Sarah D. 2017. "Indigenous in the City: The Politics of Urban Mapuche Identity in Chile." *Ethnic and Racial Studies* 40 (4): 694–712. https://doi.org/10.1080/01419870.2016.1181772.

Watson, Mark. 2010. "Diasporic Indigeneity: Place and the Articulation of Ainu Identity in Tokyo, Japan." *Environment and Planning A: Economy and Space* no. 42, 268–84.

———. 2014. *Japan's Ainu Minority in Tokyo: Diasporic Indigeneity and Urban Politics*. New York: Routledge.

Wilson, Kathi, and Evelyn J Peters. 2005. "'You Can Make a Place for It': Remapping Urban First Nations Spaces of Identity." *Environment and Planning D: Society and Space* 23 (3): 395–413. https://doi.org/10.1068/d390.

World Bank. 2019. *Indigenous Peoples*. https://www.worldbank.org/en/topic/Indigenouspeoples.

Yashar, Deborah J. 1998. "Contesting Citizenship: Indigenous Movements and Democracy in Latin America." *Comparative Politics* 31 (1): 23–42. https://doi.org/10.2307/422104.

CHAPTER ONE

The Making of an Urban Indigenous Community

Shipibo Art and the Battles for Place, Dignity, and a Future

GIULIANA BOREA

This chapter explores the ways in which Shipibo artists have reflected upon their own experience of migration and their battle to establish an Indigenous community, the Shipibo community of Cantagallo, in Peru's capital city, Lima.[1] Lima is a city that until 2010 was represented only by its white colonial past, and an ongoing racism exists despite it being Peru's region with the largest Indigenous population—22.5 percent.[2] This racism was fully exposed during the presidential elections of 2021, when Lima's elites in particular, many of whom have lately been haranguing Indigenous art on a cultural, national, and global level, called for several rural Indigenous votes to be disregarded. With a focus on the work of Elena Valera (or, in Shipibo, Bahuan Jisbë) and Harry Pinedo (in Shipibo, Inin Metsa), it is my contention that Indigenous art practices have become central players in the politics of place and dignity. I show how their artworks shed light on spatial politics and practices, mobility, and sense of belonging, and become agents in the claims and strategies to achieve a *vida digna* (dignified life). *Vida digna* is a notion that circulates widely in the demands of the Indigenous, the poor, and other excluded people in Latin America. This notion integrates the rights of life with quality of life: the state has the duty to provide the conditions to attain the basic necessities of life such as drinking water, food, sanitation, health care, and housing.[3] For Indigenous peoples, their original territories are a condition for their life and future; for some urban Indigenous people, living in an Indigenous community creates the possibility for attaining a *vida digna* in the city, as Harry Pinedo clearly states and I demonstrate in this chapter. Moreover, Valera's and Pinedo's artworks highlight how the making of the urban Indigenous community relates to Amazonian rural communities as well as to the larger city through what I call a triangulation of Indigenous practices of urban place making. Looking at the connections between place making and art, I also argue that the Shipibos' struggles, achievements, and dreams of an urban Indigenous community have had a direct impact on the strengthening of Amazonian Indigenous contemporary art. Central to this chapter are the paradoxes that arise from the current public and private fostering of Indigenous art and culture, and the rural and urban Amazonian peoples' still precarious living conditions.

Migration: From the Amazon to a Derelict House in the Center of Lima

A Shipibo couple look at one another (fig. 1.1). In front of them a vast scene speaks of the geographical trajectory experienced by the Shipibo people who migrate from the communities of Ucayali in Peru's Central Amazon to the coastal region, and specifically to Lima. The composition shows the importance of the bodies of water: Peru's Amazonian rivers that begin in the high Andean mountains, and the Pacific Ocean behind those mountains. The animals, with their agencies, are also central in this work. Orange and black jaguars, the guardians of the forest, are close to the couple. Monkeys and sloths hang from the trees. In the river are red dolphins, and a big powerful anaconda is emerging from the water to look at the coming migratory enterprise. The anaconda is the mother of the river and of the Shipibo *kené* identity designs. The anaconda's tongue touches the face of a mountain. This mountain is the San Cristóbal Apu, at the foot of which the Shipibo urban community will develop. *Apu* is a Quechua name given to mountains with power and agency, and in the Amazon it is sometimes used to name the community authority. It is important to mention the historical relationship between the Shipibo people and the Incas, which receives much attention in Shipibo mythology.[4] Apu San Cristóbal has become a landmark and an agent in the representation of the urban Shipibo community of Cantagallo, and a sign of Shipibos' attachment to that place. The painting is titled *Migra-*

FIGURE 1.1 Harry Pinedo / Inin Metsa, *Migration III*, 2020

tion III and is Pinedo's third version on this theme. While the earlier versions represent the San Cristóbal Apu as a male Andean entity, in this painting it is in the form of an Amazonian female Apu, showing Pinedo's reassessment of symbols of power and the key role of women in the making of the community.[5] On the central axis, a bridge covered with Shipibo patterns reinforces how migration connects Peru's territory despite its difficult geography.

Pinedo's paintings show many Shipibo people's dreams and experiences of migration, including those of his parents, who took him to live a new urban Shipibo life in Lima when he was a child.

Amazonian people's migration to Lima is a recent story compared to their migration from the Andes, which began in the 1930s. The Shipibo have been migrating more permanently to Lima only since the 1990s, looking for better opportunities for education, employment, and peace, leaving behind the terrorist incursions and drug trafficking in the Amazon.[6] Among the first migrants were young people seeking to enroll in the new intercultural higher education program and women migrating temporarily or permanently to sell their products—their *artesanías*—such as seed necklaces, bracelets, and textiles to tourists and local passersby. Women and their children continuously cross Peru's territory.

An anecdote: My first anthropological fieldwork, in 1998, was in the San Francisco Shipibo community. I stayed with the Roque Agustin family, and before I left, I gave them my address in Lima. Some months later, I received a visit from my female Shipibo friends, and a year later another, and later another, and so on. Their constant mobility always surprised me. They travel to Lima and other cities to sell their handicrafts at least once a year, generating paths and connections, experiences, knowledge, and a living from this constant labor mobility. However, in the early 2000s it was not easy for them to be in Lima: there was even more explicit discrimination in the capital than there is today, and the Shipibo selling their wares were evicted from the plazas. Being permitted to sell in the plazas has been a gradual achievement for these women. But despite the fact that their wanderings in the city are an important tactic in terms of work and of apprehending and appropriating the city, following Michel de Certeau (2008), these wanderings are also physically consuming, as women artisans told me in our conversations.

The work of the artist Elena Valera / Bahuan Jisbë presents a compelling focus on the women's migration and gendered geography. Her work *Women Shipibo Migrants in Cantagallo* (fig. 1.2) is composed with only female agents, including the Apu. The artist explores the mobility of women from the rural Amazonian communities to the Amazonian city of Pucallpa—which, due to its proximity, is the first city where the Shipibo people migrated and has a large Shipibo population—and to the urban community of Cantagallo in coastal Lima. Valera shows a transversal mobility that links Peru's east (the Amazon) to the west (the coast) and west to east in a vivid map that connects

FIGURE 1.2 Elena Valera / Bahuan Jisbë, *Women Shipibo Migrants in Cantagallo*, 2010

geographies including the Andes. In the diverse geographical scenarios that Valera shows, women are engaging in different activities: making pottery, cooking, taking care of children, teaching in their Amazonian rural communities, reading, and undertaking other jobs in the city. The female Shipibo Apu points to a computer with "Google" displayed on the screen. Valera has produced a series of these works showing an Indigenous, and female, mapping practice, based on women's experience, that records and expresses mobility between urban and rural settings, relations among places and their relationship to each place, their diverse activities, and the expansion of their ontologies. In another work, *Shipibo Women Selling Handicrafts in Lima* (fig. 1.3), Valera focuses on the women's activity of selling *artesanías* and on their right to pursue their work in their traditional dress in Lima's main plaza. This painting was produced in 2013 as Lima's municipality began to promote cultural diversity as part of its creative city policy (Borea 2021, chap. 6; Cánepa and Lossio 2019). In a row at the back, Valera shows the government palace, representing national power; Lima's municipal building, representing local urban power; and the Ministry of Tourism, representing

FIGURE 1.3 Elena Valera / Bahuan Jisbë, *Shipibo Women Selling Handicrafts in Lima*, 2013

Peru's campaign of cultural diversity. The artists represent these institutions as they call them to support the sale of *artesanías*. This and many other paintings include the Peruvian flag, making the work itself an active agent for Indigenous demands and aspirations.

But let's go back in time. The first Shipibo people in Lima lived in overcrowded derelict buildings in Lima center, many in a property in legal dispute known as Tarata House. In 2000 the owner of the house told the Shipibo they must leave. There were two ways they could leave the house and look for a new place: individually or collectively. They decided to find a new place collectively with the guidance of the Amazonian leaders in Lima who were rising in prominence. This was the time of protests against President Alberto Fujimori's authoritative regime and political leader Alejandro Toledo's Marcha de los Cuatro Suyus (The March of the Four Suyus)[7]—an intercultural political protest march in which millions of people from all over Peru participated. The Amazonian leaders played an active role in these protests. When Toledo—who was born in an Andean rural community, migrated to the coast as a child, and then studied economics at Stanford University—assumed the presidency, the Shipibo in Lima and their leaders became his strategic allies. Toledo's government with his wife, the anthropologist Eliane Karp, took a neoindigenist approach that provided greater visibility and political maneuverability for Indigenous leaders and associations.[8]

"Raising the Hut": From an Artisanal Fair to a Place for Living; The Making of Amazonian Contemporary Art

As I have explained elsewhere (Borea 2021), Peru's recovery of democracy opened up a time of hope in Peru for political, social, cultural, and material redefinition. Previously the Amazon had not been included in the representation of Peru, which only encompassed the coast through notions of modernity and the Andes through notions of tradition with the Inca past. This new period saw key exhibitions of Amazonian art with the participation of Indigenous Amazonian movements, the government with its new *indigenista* interest, and new curators with a wider perspective. A series of events and agents boosted a vibrant period of experimentation, and the limits of art gradually expanded. The Shipibo artists Elena Valera and her then husband, Roldán Pinedo / Shoyan Sheca, were key actors in the process of redefining Indigenous art and art at large with curators who resituate their work in the art scene.[9] Valera and Pinedo were also community leaders. Both started to paint for the historian Pablo Macera's project in 1997, which promoted the use of paintings to explain oral traditions. The project offered Shipibo people the opportunity to explore another type of media, painting on canvas and paper—expanding their already rich artistic repertoire of designed painted pottery, embroidered textiles, and body painting—and to embrace another style, figurative motifs that intersect with Shipibo traditional identity *kené* designs. It also offered men the opportunity to paint. As María Eugenia Yllia points out, it is the use of a Western format—painting—that allowed Amazonian artists to gradually enter in the artistic circuits (Yllia 2017). In Elena Valera and Roldán Pinedo's first exhibition in 1999, their work was labeled *popular art* (*arte popular*) and they themselves were labeled *artisans*. But by 2005, with the curator Gredna Landolt, they were participating as *artists* in the important *Uncovering Amazonia* exhibition of contemporary art. The understanding of their work started to transition from *arte popular* to *art* at a moment of Peru and Lima's redefinition and at the time of spatial transformation of the living conditions of urban Shipibo people.[10]

Under Toledo's policy, and as a mechanism to maintain this support for Indigenous peoples, the new government organized an intercultural artisanal fair in 2001 that included Indigenous groups from the Andes, the Amazon, and the coastal region.[11] The urban Shipibo people were invited to participate. The fair was held in a large and almost empty flat cemented area next to an impoverished black market, in a place called Cantagallo in Lima. The fair was held at Cantagallo in what is called Level 2. Mestizo people, many of whom work at the market and some of whom migrated from the Andes, live on Level 1 and 2. The Artisanal Fair lasted a week, during which Shipibo leaders investigated the area and found it a perfect place to live. They organized and acted fast, raising huts as soon as the fair was over. Their political relationship with the government facilitated this invasion. To Cantagallo came not only people from the overcrowded Tarata House but also other Shipibo in Lima who had been longing to live with their own people as a community, because this was what Cantagallo was going to be—an urban Shipibo community in Lima. As the anthropologist Oscar Espinosa writes, it offered the opportunity "to be able to be Indigenous in the city" (Espinosa 2019). One Shipibo longing to live with other Shipibo people was today's celebrated artist Olinda Silvano. In an interview she explained:

> I was looking for Shipibos everywhere, I was crying. I once saw a Shipibo on the street, so I jumped off the bus and hugged him, crying. I told him to take me to where they lived, but they were like me, in a small room. But at least I already contacted these people until I found Tarata House, which was full of Shipibo people. There was no space and I returned sadly to my room. Until one day my cousin told me "Olinda, we are going to make a community in Cantagallo." And I said . . . "Come on!" . . . There was land to build houses, but there was no money for the materials. . . . People kept coming. So in 2001 we consolidated as an association with Gustavo Ramírez as president. . . . I no longer cried, I was happy, happy, happy because this was my family. They were not from my community, but they were Shipibo. I brought my parents and then took up the presidency of Cantagallo. But one day someone knocked on my father's door and they beat him, bad people. Six months later he died. We didn't even report it because we knew almost nothing, and nobody. We were very discriminated against. They said to us: "Why have you come to live here? Go to your own land."[12]

The Shipibo wanted to live together to keep their identity and traditions and to feel safe and accepted, at least in that part of the huge city of Lima. However, territorial and cultural tensions arose with the mestizo people living on Levels 1 and 2 and grew over the following five years. The Shipibo leaders wanted to build a community that expressed their lifestyle and was free of territorial and cultural disputes. Finding a suitable new place—which for them meant flat and cemented—in overcrowded Lima was impossible: poor newcomers tend to live in derelict buildings in the center and on Lima's surrounding mountain slopes. The Shipibo leaders analyzed the landscape: there was an immense landfill site just next to them. Nobody wanted this land, so a waste site became a possible site for dwelling.

Creating a Community: A Landfill Site Becomes Home; Art and Reflexivity in Imagining Cantagallo

A big unwanted space became a possibility as a site of habitation for the urban Indigenous. They decided to take over the area, clean it, and raise their homes and their community. They built their huts of plywood, cardboard, and other found materials in what is Cantagallo Level 3, which became home of most of the artists, while other people stayed in Cantagallo Level 2.[13] There were no basic services to start with: electricity would come, while water supply and sanitation are still pending. An intercultural school was one of the first projects; it was built in the cemented Level 2 along with the football pitch and local groceries. The community did not want their children to fall behind and face discrimination at a regular Spanish-speaking mestizo school, and they wanted them to learn and value Shipibo culture. Beyond the precarious living situation and constant stomach infections, skin problems, and other health conditions, Cantagallo has become a place where they feel more accepted, safer, and happier; are able to retain their identity and practice their traditions, including their own language, medicine, food and cooking, celebrations, clothing, and education; and can offer their healing practices and art production to the tourists and, at the same time, be part of Lima as the first Indigenous urban community in the capital, at least on a practical level.

Andean migration to the capital challenged the image of an ethno-racial fixed geographical map that anchored Andean Indigenous people living only in the Andes, Native people living only in the Amazon, and the whiter Spanish descendants living only in—and owning—the coastal region. Migration challenged this fictional construction and racialized geography (Cánepa 2007). However, the migration from the Andes followed a strong process of assimilation to urban practices: the word *cholo* refers to the Andean migrant as a new actor who transits from the "traditional" to a "modern" urban society but was also seen as an actor that polluted the white cities. The battles of Andean people for owning a space for housing and services—with strong grassroots community organizations linked to the organizational forms of Andean communities—were based on issues of citizenship; for the Shipibo people, this was also based on issues of identity and on the need of establishing a community.

The formation and consolidation of Cantagallo as an urban Indigenous community in Peru's capital has challenged national laws on community recognition and land tenure. Peruvian law recognizes peasant and Native communities—being peasant not always equating with Indigenous communities—in rural areas of the Andes, the coastal region, and the Amazon, but does not recognize the possibility of urban communities, as this goes beyond housing issues to include territorial rights and other forms of traditional government in the city. This is a situation that happens in other Latin American countries, even those in which national legislations are more responsive to Indigenous rights, as Philipp Horn (2019) shows in his book on ethnicity and urban planning in Ecuador and Bolivia. While people's mobility challenges the racialized map, Indigenous urban communities challenge the racialized political-territorial map that recognizes only rural Indigenous communities in their original lands. Let us look at this more closely.[14]

Peru has two sets of legal instruments that apply to Indigenous peoples and their land, which do not always overlap, and that are overseen by two different ministries. One is the recognition of Indigenous peoples based on the International Labour Organization (ILO) 1989 Indigenous and Tribal Peoples Convention (C169), the main international, legally binding instrument regarding the key rights to Indigenous self-determination and prior consultation. C169 was reinforced by the United Nations Declaration on the Rights of Indigenous Peoples (UNDRIP) in 2007, which "establishes a universal framework of minimum standards for the survival, dignity and well-being of the Indigenous peoples of the world."[15] Peru ratified the ILO's C169 in 1993 and the UNDRIP in 2014. Peru's Ministry of Culture is in charge of the formal identification of Indigenous peoples based on four principles: historic continuity (groups that originated before the state); territorial connection (groups whose ancestors inhabited the country or a region thereof); distinctive institutions (groups retaining all or part of their distinctive institutions); and self-identification (groups that self-identify with an Indigenous or original identity). The Ministry of Culture's Database of Indigenous Peoples has identified fifty-five such groups to date, four from the Andes and fifty-one from the Amazon, among which are the Shipibo people. The introduction to the Shipibo's informative file states:

> The Shipibo-Konibo have been known for their great mobility and their ability to organize conglomerates of Indigenous populations in urban areas, an example being the Community of Cantagallo, which is the best-known and most populous Amazonian Indigenous settlement in Metropolitan Lima, located in the Rímac district. . . . On the other hand, the craft and textile production of the Shipibo-Konibo people is one of the most famous in the Peruvian Amazon due to its typical designs. . . . Currently there are Shipibo-Konibo communities in the departments of Ucayali, Madre de Dios, Loreto and Huánuco.[16]

It is important to notice the change in concept: the text refers to Indigenous people living in Lima as an Indigenous settlement (*asentamiento indígena*) rather than as community, apart from the name itself.

The second set of legal instruments is related to this issue and has a longer existence in the Peruvian law. This legislation is about the recognition of Native and peasant communities and land tenure. In Peruvian law, Native communities "originate in the tribal groups of the Amazon [Selva and Ceja de Selva] and comprise groups of families linked by the following main elements: language or dialect, cultural and social characters, common and permanent possession and use of the same territory, with settlement nucleated or dispersed."[17] This requires evidence of common use and possession of the same territory, and this why Cantagallo is recognized as a settlement of Indigenous peoples but not formally acknowledged as a Native community. On the other hand, an *asentamiento humano* (a human settlement) is understood as a group of families established without legal title and that lack some of the basic services (water, sewage, electricity, tracks, sidewalks, etc.). Shipibo Cantagallo is recognized and recognizes itself as part of the Shipibo peoples and classified as *asentamiento*. Shipibo Cantagallo, as a spatial urban practice and planning from below, leads us to think about how indigeneity and community making are deployed in and shape the city, and about the need to develop new legal instruments and public policy that answer to this new condition, which is expected to increase with social, economic, and ecological migration in the coming years. The establishment of Indigenous urban communities challenges the national politics of community recognition and the urban landscape by imprinting diversity and interculturality in terms not only of multicultural branding but also of spatial planning.

During Susana Villarán's leadership of Lima's municipal government from 2010 to 2014, culture and diversity were central elements of her urban policy, linked to an aesthetic celebration of the creative city. Mural paintings reinforcing colorful multicultural diversity were promoted. In 2011 Cantagallo was selected as one of the settings for a festival of mural painting. The community gained media and art visibility. Urban street artists painted the murals alone or in collaboration with the locals, aiming to capture Amazonian urban culture. Shipibo artists were not yet working on mural projects, as they did not know this technique. Cantagallo was aesthetically transformed. The Shipibo people had their living/workshop space for making and selling their art and handicrafts, offering ayahuasca rituals and playing music to attract visitors. Mural painting added to the uniqueness of these offers. Many contemporary artists sought to engage with local communities in participatory projects, as they still do. During 2014 and 2016, the artist Alejandra Ballón worked with a group of Shipibo women artists such as Olinda Silvano, Silvia Ricopa, and Wilma Maynas to transfer the Shipibo *kené* identity designs traditionally embroidered on textiles and painted on pottery and the body to larger formats, particularly murals.[18] Shipibo women began to participate in street art promoted by the municipality. The Shipibo artists, first with Alejandra Ballón and later by themselves, painted murals in different parts of the city, such as on the Lima metro's cement structures, captivating the view and imagination of many of Lima's inhabitants. Mural painting became a mechanism for participating in designing the city, at least in visual terms, and developing a new sense of pride in being a Shipibo Limeño.

Between 2010 and 2015, many painters, filmmakers, and musicians emerged in Cantagallo who began to narrate, imagine, and reinforce Cantagallo itself. For instance, the Shipibo documentary filmmaker Ronald Suárez, in a collaborative project, launched the film *LimaShipibo* (2013), which offers an insider view, in both Shipibo and Spanish language, of how Shipibo people live in Cantagallo. It focuses on how people (working as artisans, chefs, teachers, etc.) pursue their livelihoods in the community and the city while retaining their identity: "I'm a chef and I'm a Shipibo"; "I'm a teacher and I'm a Shipibo." As Quinteros, Vailati, and Zamorano (forthcoming) affirm, Suárez is producing not only for the Shipibo people but also for a larger Limeño audience, highlighting the Shipibo people's contributions to Lima. The film also questions the constant reference to poverty in relation to the community, mobilizing a positive view of Cantagallo that combines culture and creative entrepreneurship in connection with Lima's cultural policies and Peru's Marca País; both urban and national policies provide the atmosphere for this production and fuel its circulation. In general, it is both with and through this Marca País branding public project that many Shipibo urban artists have engaged to build their narratives and mobility. Suárez stopped producing documentaries to participate more actively as a Shipibo political leader. During this time, Olinda Silvano became a branded national icon for the *kené* as a form of public art, while her sister Sadith Silvano expanded the use of *kené* designs from women's traditional skirts to other items of urban clothing, such as trousers, tube skirts, and swimwear. Both have a strong public profile and work with women artisans and with NGO and governmental empowerment projects. Other artists emerged, including the Ramírez brothers and Harry Pinedo, the son of Elena Valera and Roldán Pinedo. César Ramos, an anthropologist, art promoter, and cultural municipal worker in Villarán's government, became a key agent for the visibility and circulation of these urban Shipibo cultural production, and Lima's municipal gallery, Pancho Fierro, became the platform for important exhibitions.

In 2014 the exhibition *Buscando el Río: Estéticas de los Pueblos Indígenas Amazónicos en Lima* (Looking for the River: Aesthetics of the Amazonian Indigenous Peoples in Lima) was launched at Pancho Fierro gallery. Curated by the art historian María Eugenia Yllia, who has long been committed to Indigenous art, *Buscando el Río* featured work of Amazonian artists working in Lima with a wide range of topics. The aim of the exhibition was "to contribute to the visibility, participation and political representation of the Amazonian Indigenous peoples in Lima, and to establish a democratic and intercultural management model that considers the capital's cultural diversity."[19] This show was part of the broader project Rights, Inclusion and Participation: Amazonian Indigenous Peoples in Metropolitan Lima, conducted by the Metropolitan Municipality of Lima, the Amazonian Center for Anthropology and Practical Application (CAAAP), and Terra Nuova. Another outcome of this project was CAAAP anthropologist Ismael Vega Diaz's 2014 book, *Buscando el Río: Identidad, Transformaciones y Estrategias de los Migrantes Indígenas Amazónicos en Lima Metropolitana* (Looking for the River: Identity, Transformation and Strategies of Amazonian Indigenous Migrants in Lima).[20] This important book provides an analysis of the migration of Indigenous Amazonians to Lima, and on its cover is Harry Pinedo's first Cantagallo artwork, *Amazonia in the Rimac* (2013): a Shipibo woman and her child stand in colorful Cantagallo looking toward the San Cristóbal Apu; to one side are the painted houses of Rimac, to the other the modern buildings, and there is a big tree in the top right-hand corner.[21]

Reflections of Cantagallo itself were central in the works of the Cantagallo Shipibo artists Elena Valera, Harry Pinedo, and Julio Maldonado-Shawa in the *Buscando el Río* exhibition. Other artists such as Olinda Silvano, Roldán Pinedo, David, Demer, and Pedro Ramírez Nunta, and Sadith Silvano started to explore this topic too. Through a process of reflexivity, the artists focus on Cantagallo, the place that they live, making it a protagonist in their visual-political narratives. Their artistic and visual narration of Cantagallo reinforced Cantagallo itself both for the people of the community and for other Limeños who saw it via the circulation of these works and exhibitions. With the impactful *kené* murals in different parts of Lima and the artworks of Shipibo Cantagallo, artists have located Cantagallo in Lima's imagination—an important task in their dreams of a real respect and dialogue as an intercultural Lima. Moreover, I argue that the Shipibo Cantagallo artists have developed a type of composition of Cantagallo, which I call triangulation, that includes three specific elements: the San Cristóbal Apu and Cantagallo; the Amazonian communities; and Lima city. This art production is a self-representation of urban indigeneity and community making, and gives an insight into the Shipibo sense of place. Harry Pinedo / Inin Metsa's *Intercultural Immigration Community* (fig. 1.4) is one such artwork that explores and imagines the community of Cantagallo, expressing this triangulation and its negotiations. Standing together in front of his painting in an exhibition in 2019, Harry explained it to me, combining the past and the present tense:

> Here I wanted to capture life, the houses of Cantagallo, under a hill called the San Cristóbal Apu. Cantagallo has always been very happy and colorful, for its design and painted houses, where we received tourists who went there to learn about medicine, painting, food, and ayahuasca sessions. The community was very welcoming. This scene—this image—continued for more than fifteen years; it was very intercultural. And beyond is the city, for education, work, health—the reasons for which we migrated. Since Shipibos have settled in Lima, Lima has changed. It has seen a type of worldview that transmits energy. At the top, smoking tobacco, it is the moon, who observes. The birds are messengers from the Shipibo people. The anaconda is one of the guardians that gives us food.

Like the documentary filmmaker Ronald Suárez, Harry Pinedo stresses the Shipibo people's contribution of color and diversity to the capital. Harry Pinedo's work also reflects on how the making of Cantagallo is in constant relationship with the Shipibo communities in the Amazon. At the right of the painting, a tree marks the space between the urban and the rural setting, with a canoe moored next to it by a rope tied to a tree, which becomes the San Cristóbal Apu's headband and the city roads. The urban and rural communities are linked, shaping each other through the mobility of people, culture and resources, and through the arts (see Figs. 1.1, 1.2, and 1.4). An-

FIGURE 1.4 Harry Pinedo / Inin Metsa, *Intercultural Immigration Community*, 2016

thropologists have focused on this Amazonian rural-urban mobility. Miguel Pinedo and Christine Padoch have analyzed the rural-urban multisited and multihousehold life in Brazil and Peru, and Miguel Alexiades and Daniela Peluso have focused on Indigenous urbanization and rural-urban linkages, analyzing how notions of the self and place are transformed by these urban-rural flows, which challenge dichotomic visions of the urban/rural, nature/culture, and modernity/tradition (Alexiades and Peluso 2015; Peluso 2015; Pinedo Vasquez and Padoch 2009). In addition to this urban-rural nexus, art production comments on other nexuses and tensions within the city. Next to the canoe is a blue bus on which Pinedo appropriates the Lima municipal government's slogan, changing "Lima, the City for All" to "Lima-Shipibo, City for All." However, a closer look at this painting and deeper conversation with the artist reveals other complexities. Harry Pinedo told me:

> Lima received us by separating us from the city due to the ongoing inequality. This is a life-story. At the back is a modern city, apart [without color]. We are in the city, but we are excluded. The reality is that we are excluded in the same place.

Thus, this colorful, apparently harmonious painting also alludes to and questions social exclusion and speaks about mobility, negotiations, and appropriations aspiring to a "Lima-Shipibo for All": to an intercultural city. The triangulation that the artists express implies a construction of identity and space in relation to and negotiation across these spheres—San Cristóbal Apu and Cantagallo, Amazonian communities, and larger Lima city—which at the same time are transforming all three.

Let us consider another, more recent painting by Elena Valera (fig. 1.5), *Comunidad JONI Cantagallo*.[22] In this work Valera clearly expresses the triangular composition that alludes to the constant negotiation involved in being Indigenous, particularly urban Indigenous, and in place making. At the center stands the San Cristóbal Apu, creating three sections in the painting. The Apu is covered with Shipibo designs. In the middle is an Inca, and at the top a cross that also comprises part of the body of a big traditional Shipibo pot, the *chombo*, crowning the Apu. This central image, now an Andean-Amazonian mountain located in the coastal capital, becomes a powerful symbol of diverse epistemologies, negotiation, and interculturality. On one side of the Apu is a rural Amazonian community with people,

FIGURE 1.5 Elena Valera / Bahuan Jisbë, *JONI Cantagallo Community*, 2019

houses, animals, and trees, and the other side shows buildings and the governmental palace with its Peruvian flag. Modern Lima or traditional Lima with its governmental offices occupies this third space, which also alludes to equating Lima with the government in reference to Peru's centralization. At the bottom of San Cristóbal Apu lies Cantagallo, with the sign *JONI Cantagallo Community*, which translates as "The people's community of Cantagallo," announcing in capital letters the artist's preference to be known as Joni, meaning "the people," rather than as Shipibo, a name given by outsiders that refers to a type of monkey. These Shipibo-Jonibo Cantagallo paintings and exhibitions are important arenas for the analysis of Shipibo identities and place-making projects, and most importantly are powerful agents of reflexivity, self-representation, and activism to claim their Indigenous rights in an intercultural city.

Cantagallo on Fire: From the Ashes to the Art Market

Traffic in Lima is a huge problem that disrupts the image of Lima as a modernizing city. To solve this problem, the Metropolitan Municipality of Lima proposed the Yellow Line, a new megatransit project authorized in 2009 by Mayor Luis Castañeda Lossio. Work started under the next mayor, Susana Villarán, who renamed the project Rimac Parkway. The project was to include the Yellow Line expressway that would connect eleven districts, with a new tunnel beneath the Rimac River and green areas alongside the parkway, revitalizing the Rimac area. The project maps the Cantagallo area as green space, and the Cantagallo Shipibo were therefore to relocate, initiating a long process of dialogue, tension, and promises. In the end, after living in Cantagallo for fifteen years and establishing crucial connections with its geography, including the San Cristóbal Apu, the Shipibo people accepted their relocation to a new settlement in Campoy, which included a housing project with all the basic services, conditions, and help to own the property. A municipal budget was allocated for this. However, Susana Villarán's government came to an end before the relocation had begun, and Lima's next mayor, Luis Castañeda Lossio, reversed many of Villarán's policies; for instance, he cancelled Villarán's mural project and erased the Lima center murals that offered a broader approach to art and Lima's cultural diversity. Castañeda also canceled the relocation of the Shipibo people to Campoy, while the Yellow Line project continued.

On November 4, 2016, at the peak of the struggle between the Indigenous people and the municipality, an enormous fire destroyed Cantagallo, and the Shipibo people lost their houses, their workshops, their clothes, their art, and their intercultural school, and one child lost his life. They lost everything they had created in Lima. Suspicion of the municipality circulated. The fire in Cantagallo brought diverse reactions from Lima's white mestizos. Many felt strong empathy for the Shipibo people and created networks of collaboration for food and other assistance, promoted by artists, filmmakers, and other cultural agents. Facebook became a platform for images and the mobilization of aid. It also became a platform for racist comments: "Why do they live in Lima? They should go back to the Amazon"; "In the Amazon they have better living conditions, they'll be happier," and so on. Lima was thus affirmed only for white mestizos, with comments that restricted free movement and free choice of residence for citizens of the same country, and once again highlighting substantial problems of Peruvian-ness and citizenship, beyond the celebration of diversity. The third reaction was that of the Shipibo people, and here again the arts played a leading role. The Cantagallo Shipibo people organized an exhibition to show who and what the Shipibo people and Cantagallo were, selling the works to benefit the community in crisis.

This painful and frustrated moment for the Shipibos is recorded and expressed in one of Harry Pinedo's paintings, *Cantagallo on Fire* (fig. 1.6), which he produced only a few days after the fire. This painting was not included in the exhibition, and it was not made public until 2019. I remember that when I asked Harry for this painting, which he put up on Facebook and which then went off the radar, he asked me, "How do you know about that painting? I've never shown it!" He almost seemed to excuse himself saying, "I was very upset when I did it." He was worried, as Indigenous artists are still expected to follow the celebratory mode of the city and the country. Standing at the exhibition in front of his painting, he told me:

> I wanted to register what had happened and wanted to do a painting about that. Because the Shipibo people had lived in Cantagallo for twenty years, and they wanted to throw us out like dogs. So unfair. I painted that. They were guilty; they did not keep their promise about giving us a new place. We are a culture. The leaders had fought to give us title deeds, and the municipality had already given us a place, and then when Castañeda became mayor he didn't pursue it. They spent it

FIGURE 1.6 Harry Pinedo / Inin Metsa, *Cantagallo on Fire*, 2016. Acrílico sobre tela, 100 × 149 cm. Colección Miguel A. López. Photo: Juan Pablo Murrugarra

> all. They wanted to kill us, as they did in the past—and we are in the twenty-first century! That is why the century is highlighted. The Apu, as ancestor, was looking at the people, but he could not do much. On one side is the Municipality of Lima with a pirate flag, on the other is the Palace of Justice.
>
> This work shows the Shipibo *en la calle* [on the street, homeless] and a wall dividing us as if we do not have the right to a dignified life [*una vida digna*]. *Lima Riki Jatibina*, "Lima is for Everyone" is written in the Shipibo language. This is a Shipibo family and an Andean woman who are calling for help. This painting is strong. What I did with this painting is to protest.

After the fire the Shipibo people dispersed and rented rooms outside Cantagallo or in other parts of Lima. The possibility of living together as a community had been taken away from them. Paradoxically, this time saw growing interest in Indigenous art, not as a result of national policy, but from the global art world. Amazonian Indigenous art became an asset, and Peruvian museums such as the Museo de Arte de Lima (MALI) that respond to global tendencies now turned to look at Amazonian art, including Shipibo art. Yet the living conditions of urban Shipibo people were worse than ever. In 2019 Peru was invited to participate in the Madrid Contemporary Art Fair (ARCO) as the guest country. This event provided more visibility for Shipibo art, particularly that of the female Shipibo artists Olinda Silvano and Wilma Maynas, who painted a mural in Madrid, supported by the government, as part of ARCO's parallel events. The Cantagallo Shipibo artists were at the center of Peru's promotional images. If in 2000 the Amazon was not included in the image of Peru, in 2019 Peru represented itself through the Amazon. In addition, the MALI organized the exhibition *Amazonías* in Madrid. However, while this mobilized Indigenous art, most of the Amazonian artists were not funded to attend—raising Indigenous claims.[23]

Two months after the Shipibo artists' participation in ARCO, I was back in Lima for a medical test, and as I left the hospital, which is next to the Ministry of Housing, I saw a protest and recognized Shipibo people by their clothing. I paid the taxi. The Shipibo were demanding that the government fulfill its promises of relocation and housing; it was almost three years since the fire, and they were still living dispersed, and in even worse conditions. They shouted, "We have never been this bad!" and "Government, build the houses!" Although the national government and museums were promoting their art, respect for the people and their living conditions were not seen as important.

Lima elected a new mayor, Jorge Muñoz, who seemed less evasive to the Indigenous demands. In August of that year, the Pancho Fierro Municipal Gallery inaugurated the exhibition *A Less Gray Lima, The Indigenous Urban Community of Cantagallo: Colors, Dreams and Battles*, coordinated by the Shipibo associations in Lima (ASHIREL, AVSHIL, ACUSHIKOLM, and the Cantagallo Shipibo Konibo Community Association), the CAAAP, and curated by María Eugenia Yllia. It is in this exhibition that Harry Pinedo's *Cantagallo on Fire*, mentioned before, was shown for the first time.

Back to Cantagallo, COVID-19, and the Paradoxes of the Rise of Amazonian Art

After meetings and negotiations with national and local government officers and endless waiting—in what Arjun Appadurai calls the "politics of waiting" as a strategy of the poor in relation to "the politics of hope" (2013, 126)—at the end of 2019 the Shipibo people decided to go back to Cantagallo and rebuild their community. COVID-19 reached the community living in poorer conditions than before the fire, not only lacking running water and drains but also having to rebuild their houses. Harry Pinedo's work (fig.1.7) offers a glimpse of these last years of catastrophe, protests, negotiations, and patience: at the top is the fire of 2016; at the middle are the Shipibo protesting with banners demanding, "Stop racism!," "Shipibo people offer art and culture," and "The Shipibo Conibo community demands respect according to the ILO convention 169: Housing, Healthcare and Education." At the bottom Pinedo includes the last negotiations between community leaders and government officers during the pandemic, framed by the Tahuantinsuyo flag as a symbol of the original nations, and the Peruvian flag, in a work that expresses Indigenous agency and the battles for housing, citizenship, and equality.

Only a few months before the effects of COVID-19 were being experienced worldwide, the Shipibo leaders asked the government for portable toilets. The government refused. Cantagallo's precarious conditions with limited running water and drains—only a twenty-minute walk from the government palace—had a direct effect on the spread of the pandemic: in Cantagallo 80 percent of the population were infected with the virus. This time the government delivered a prompt and excessively repressive response: the police surrounded Cantagallo and blocked Shipibos' mobility, leaving the rest of Lima free to continue as normal. Nobody could go in or out without a permit. The government created a territorial boundary, but by strict policing and not by policies of recognition. Surrounded by the police, the Shipibo were supported by networks of friends and collaborators, including a strong contribution from art agents, who brought food, clothing, and other aid to the community. Urban and rural Amazonian settings activated their linkages as shamans investigated which plants could help in the pandemic, identifying eucalyptus and the Amazonian *matico*, which was brought from the Amazon to the coast by young Indigenous residents of rural communities and the Amazonian city of Pucallpa.[24] In a more recent work, Harry Pinedo shows Cantagallo fighting COVID-19 with the protection of the San Cristóbal Apu, the shamans, and the plants. Reflecting on the power of Amazonian knowledge and of being together again, the painting announces: "*Cantagallo, renace luchando*" ("Cantagallo reborn fighting"). At the same time, and activating the triangulation I have explained, when Minister of Culture Alejandro Neyra visited Cantagallo during the pandemic, the artist and leader Olinda Silvano advised him to also visit and support the Indigenous communities in the Amazon:

> It is not only Cantagallo. Go to the Ucayali, go to the Amazon, the biggest communities, also like us, are there. It would be the first time you set foot in the Indigenous communities there, because no one has been there before.
>
> We as Shipibo artists have made a donation with our art, and that is what we are sending, but it's not enough: we need action from the state. I ask this on behalf of all artisan mothers.

Art, Urban Indigenous Community, and Dignity

It has been my intention to show how Shipibo art practices are a central player in the politics of urban place and dignity. As I have explained, art is constitutive to the foundation and development of Shipibo Cantagallo. It is an important means of income for the Shipibo people and a medium through which they have expressed and represented their experiences of migration, their sense of mobility and place, their battles of making an urban commu-

FIGURE 1.7 Harry Pinedo / Inin Metsa, *Cantagallo and Our Battles for Housing, Healthcare, and Education*, 2020

nity, and their hopes of a dignified life. Following Appadurai's (2013, 120) call for "the need to re-examine the basic links between housing, citizenship and dignity," I have shown—intersecting analysis on indigeneity, art, and place—how for the Shipibo people a dignified life in the city requires not only housing but also a community to allow them to develop their full citizenship and Indigenous rights.

Taking art seriously has allowed me to envision and analyze the Indigenous spatiality that is explored and expressed in the arts, and to show how art practices themselves are actors in the making of place. Art makes the Shipibo Cantagallo people's sense of place and claims of belonging visible to the Shipibos, reinforcing their attachment to the space and to the larger Lima and national authorities. Moreover, I have identified that the Cantagallo artists have created a triangular type of composition that shows the processes and sense of community-making constructed in relation to the local community and the San Cristóbal Apu, to the Amazonian rural communities, and to the wider Lima. Through their paintings, Indigenous Cantagallo artists explain and mobilize their spatial practices and urban planning from below in the ongoing racist Lima, with the hope that their community will be recognized and the basic services will arrive, achieving a *vida digna* in the city.

Acknowledgments

My gratitude to Elena Valera, Harry Pinedo, Roldán Pinedo, and Sadith Silvano for sharing their art, knowledge, and time with me; and my admiration to the work and energy of my colleague César Ramos, who sadly died in 2017. This research is part of the Amazonart Project (Marie Skłodowska-Curie Individual Fellowship of the European Union's Horizon 2020 research and innovation program, 844895).

Notes

1. This research is part of the AmazonArt Project hosted at the University of Essex and supported by the Marie Skłodowska-Curie Individual Fellowship of the European Union's Horizon 2020 research and innovation program (844895). See website: http://amazonart-project.com/.
2. According to Peru's Ministry of Culture based on the 2017 National Census: "Ministerio de Cultura: Lima es el departamento con mayor población que se considera indígena - Noticias - Ministerio de Cultura - Gobierno del Perú,"

May 21, 2019, https://www.gob.pe/institucion/cultura/noticias/28611-ministerio-de-cultura-lima-es-el-departamento-con-mayor-poblacion-que-se-considera-indigena.

3. Jo Pasqualucci explains that the Inter-American Court of Human Rights has been a pioneer in recognizing "that the right of life is not merely a civil and political right, but also includes the economic and social rights necessary for an individual to have a dignified existence" (2008, 4); the state has the duty to provide basic services, otherwise this would constitute discrimination. The integration of these two types of human rights in the comprehensive notion of a dignified life is crucial and responds to the structural inequity in Latin America. See Pasqualucci (2008).
4. About the power and agency of Apus, see Marisol de la Cadena (2015); about Shipibo mythology and their relationship to the Incas, see Pierrette Bertrand-Rousseau (1984).
5. Painter Elena Valera, Pinedo's mother, expressed the gender and ethnic conversion of the Apu in earlier works.
6. As Ismael Vega Diaz (2014) explains, the presence of Amazonian Indigenous in Lima dates back to 1980, when the national Indigenous associations AIDESEP (Asociación Interétnica de Desarrollo de la Selva Peruana, or Interethnic Association for the Development of the Peruvian Rainforest) and CONAP (Confederación de Nacionalidades Amazónicas del Perú, or Confederation of Peru's Amazonian Nations) were created and leaders needed to negotiate and attain public visibility in Lima.
7. The Inca empire was divided into four *suyus*, representing the ecological and ethnic difference that made up the Inca empire, which was referred to as the Four Suyus, or *Tawantinsuyu*.
8. *Indigenismo* is a political and cultural movement that recognizes the Indigenous legacies as part of the nation-state building projects. It emerged in Latin America between 1920 and 1950 and was particularly strong in Mexico and Peru. It was composed by politicians, artists, and intellectuals of affluent sectors who talked about and represented the Indigenous people, although through an idealized and paternalistic gaze and without Indigenous participation.
9. Bora and Uitoto Amazonian artists have also been key in the redefinition of contemporary art. However, they have a different circulation in the art circuit and their forms of living in the city are not based on community but on the individual and their connections. See Borea (2010).
10. To explore more about this transition, see Borea (2017, 2021), Castillo (2017a, 2017b), Yllia (2017) and Rubio (2017).
11. According to the information collected by the layer and anthropologist Adriana Arista, this was a Christmas art fair organized by the mayor Alberto Andrade. Arista (2011) explores the precarious condition of living in Cantagallo. Anthropologist Óscar Espinosa (2019) offers other, but similar, narratives about the creation of Cantagallo.

12. Interview of Olinda Silvano by Beatriz García, CAAAP, November 7, 2019, https://www.caaap.org.pe/2019/11/07/debemos-sentirnos-orgullosas-de-quienes-somos-migramos-a-la-ciudad-pero-sin-olvidar-nuestras-raices-ni-nuestra-cultura-debemos-difundirla-para-derribar-la-discriminacion-porque-ensenando-l/.
13. The first article of the statutes of the Shipibo Residents in Lima Association (ASHIREL) says that most of Cantagallo's first inhabitants were Shipibo artisans from the Ucayali River basin (Arista 2011) and most of them would live in Level 3. The other Cantagallo Indigenous organizations are AVSHIL (Housing Association of Shipibos in Lima) and ACUSHIKOLM (Shipibo-Konibo Urban Community of Metropolitan Lima Association). See Castillo 2017b for more information about ASHIREL and AVSHIL.
14. The predicaments of Peru's legislation about the recognition of Cantagallo as an urban Indigenous community and its relation to Indigenous rights have received attention from law scholars such as Alvaro Másquez Salvador (2015), and A. Gonza (2019).
15. In United Nations Declaration on the Rights of Indigenous People, https://www.un.org/development/desa/Indigenouspeoples/declaration-on-the-rights-of-Indigenous-peoples.html.
16. In https://bdpi.cultura.gob.pe/pueblos/shipibo-konibo.
17. "Ley de Comunidades Nativas y de Desarrollo Agrario de la Selva y de Ceja de Selva," D.L. no. 22175, Art. 8, https://www2.congreso.gob.pe/sicr/cendocbib/con3_uibd.nsf/0D41EC1170BDE30A052578F70059D913/$FILE/(1)leydecomunidadesnativasley22175.pdf. Peasant communities are not always—and not always self-recognized as—Indigenous communities, as is the case with Native communities.
18. In 2008 the *kené* was recognized as part of Peru's national heritage. The anthropologist Luisa Elvira Belaunde wrote the project for this recognition and has been a key promoter of the *kené* with a patrimonial perspective. See Belaunde (2012).
19. In "Buscando el río. Estéticas y representaciones de los pueblos indígenas amazónicos en Lima – Perú," March 6, 2014, https://crespial.org/buscando-el-rio-esteticas-y-representaciones-de-los-pueblos-indigenas-amazonicos-en-lima-peru/.
20. It is important to mention that a year later, *The Journal of Latin American and Caribbean Anthropology* dedicated a Special Issue on Indigenous Urbanization in Lowland South America (2015) with Miguel Alexiades and Daniela Peluso as editors.
21. The making of Cantagallo is one the main topics that the artist has developed until today, as can be seen in the exhibition and catalog *Place-Making, World-Making: Three Amazonian Indigenous Artists*, which I curated at Art Exchange, University of Essex (Jan–March 2021). https://amazonart-project.com/place-and-world-making-exhibition/.
22. This work is part of the Museo de Arte de Lima collection of contemporary art.
23. For more information about this debate, see Borea (2021) epilogue.

24. Rember Yahuarcani and I curated the exhibition *Ite/Neno/Here: Responses to Covid-19* (Lima, Crisis Nov–Dec, 2020), in which the work mentioned before was shown along with other works of Harry Pinedo and Santiago Yahuarcani reflecting on the pandemic in the urban and rural Amazonian communities. About the *matico* plant and its circulation, see L. E. Belaunde: https://luisabelaunde.lamula.pe/2020/08/09/comando-matico-en-pucallpa-desafia-la-interculturalidad-inerte-del-estado/luisabelaunde/.

References

Alexiades, Miguel, and Daniela Peluso. 2015. "Introduction: Indigenous Urbanization in Lowland South America." *Journal of Latin American and Caribbean Anthropology* 20 (1): 1–12.

Appadurai, Arjun. 2013. "Housing and Hope." Chap. 6 in *The Future as Cultural Fact: Essays on the Global Condition*. London: Verso.

Arista, Adriana. 2011. "Pobres y excluidos en la selva de cemento: Los nativos shipibo de Cantagallo en Lima Metropolitana." In *Pobreza urbana en América Latina y el Caribe*, edited by M. Di Virgilio, 317–45. Buenos Aires: CLACSO.

Belaunde, Luisa Elvira. 2012. "Diseños materiales e inmateriales: la patrimonialización del kené shipibo-konibo y de la ayahuasca en el Perú." *Mundo Amazónico*, no. 3, 123–46.

Bertrand-Rousseau, Pierrette. 1984. "A propósito de la mitología Shipibo." *Anthropológica*, no. 2, 209–32.

Borea, Giuliana. 2010. "Personal Cartographies of a Huitoto Mythology: Rember Yahuarcani and the Enlarging of the Peruvian Contemporary Art Scene." *Revista de Antropologia Social do PPGAS-UFSCar* 2 (2): 67–87.

———, ed. 2017. *Arte y Antropología: Estudios, Encuentros y Nuevos Horizontes*. Lima: PUCP.

———. 2021. *Configuring the New Lima Art Scene: An Anthropological Analysis of Contemporary Art in Latin America*. London: Routledge.

Cánepa, Gisela. 2007. "Geopoética de identidad y lo cholo en el Perú: Migración, geografía y mestizaje." *Crónicas Urbanas*, no. 12, 29–42.

Cánepa, Gisela, and Félix Lossio, eds. 2019. *La nación celebrada: Marca país y ciudadanías en disputa*. Lima: Fondo Editorial Universidad del Pacífico, PUCP.

Castillo, Daniel. 2017a. "Las pinturas y los artistas amazónicos que viven en Cantagallo: El caso de Roldán Pinedo." In Borea 2017, 397–403.

———. 2017b. "El reconocimiento del Arte Amazónico de y en Cantagallo: Los casos de Roldán Pinedo y Guímer García." In *En busca de reconocimiento: Reflexiones desde un Perú diverso*, edited by M. E. Ulfe and R. Trinidad, 217-249. Lima: PUCP.

De Certeau, Michel. 2008. *The Practice of Everyday Life*. Berkeley: University of California Press.

De la Cadena, Marisol. 2015. *Earth Beings: Ecologies of Practices across Andean Worlds*. Durham: Duke University Press.

Espinosa, Oscar. 2019. "La lucha por ser indígena en la ciudad: el caso de la comunidad shipibo-konibo de Cantagallo en Lima." *RIRA* 4 (2): 153–84.

Gonza, A. 2019. "Situación de los derechos indígenas en la comunidad indígena urbana Cantagallo, Rímac." *Rev. Hacedor* 3 (1): 15–29.

Horn, Phillip. 2019. *Indigenous Right to the City: Ethnicity and Urban Planning in Bolivia and Ecuador*. London: Routledge.

Másquez Salvador, Álvaro. 2015. "El reconocimiento indígena de la comunidad shipibo-conibo de Cantagallo." *Themis*, May 4, 2015.

Pasqualucci, Jo M. 2008. "The Right to a Dignified Life (*Vida Digna*): The Integration of Economic and Social Rights with Civil and Political Rights in the Inter-American Human Rights System." *Hasting International and Comparative Law Review*, 31 (1): 1–32.

Peluso, Daniela. 2015. "Circulating between Rural and Urban Communities: Multisited Dwellings in Amazonian Frontiers." *Journal of Latin American and Caribbean Anthropology*, 20 (1): 57–79.

Pinedo Vasquez, M., and C. Padoch. 2009. "Urban, Rural and In-between: Multi-Sited Households, Mobility, and Resource Management in the Amazon Flood Plain." In *Mobility and Migration in Indigenous Amazonia: Contemporary Ethnoecological Perspectives*, edited by Miguel Alexiades, 86–96. New York: Berghahn Books.

Quinteros, Alonso, Alex Vailati, and Gabriela Zamorano. Forthcoming. "Producción documental en Latinoamérica." In *Trazando las Antropologías Visuales en América Latina*, edited by Gisela Cánepa, Giuliana Borea, and Alonso Quinteros.

Rubio, Brus. 2017. "Arte y Antropología." In Borea 2017, 317–18.

Vega Diaz, Ismael. 2014. *Buscando el Río: Identidad, transformaciones y estrategias de los migrantes indígenas amazónicos en Lima Metropolitana*. Lima: CAAAP, Terra Nuova, Munincipalidad de Lima.

Yllia, M. E. 2017. "Antropófagos contemporáneos: paradojas y lógicas visuales en la pintura amazónica contemporánea peruana." In Borea 2017, 387–95.

CHAPTER TWO

Roots in the City, Routes to the City

Suva, Fiji, as Indigenous Space

KATE STEVENS

Introduction

Fiji is an urban nation. The majority of the population—51 percent in 2007—live in urban areas, most in greater Suva, the capital (see map, fig. 2.1; UN Habitat 2012). Yet Pacific Island cities are often absent in the wider global literature on urbanization. Indeed, the common Asian-Pacific grouping can subsume the specific experiences of urban life and history in these islands into those of more prominent Asian megacities. Though the islands are much smaller in absolute population than these cities, this chapter argues that urbanization has been a significant and distinct aspect of the Pacific colonial and postcolonial experience. Colonial policies in Fiji reified racially based spatial and economic division of the islands and communities and emphasized that the "proper" place for Indigenous Fijians, or iTaukei, was in rural villages. Consequently, urban indigeneity in Fiji, and the region generally, is frequently viewed as a new phenomenon. The longevity of these imposed ideas of appropriate, authentic indigeneity located in villages in the Pacific continue in tension with, and often obscure, histories of urban life, migration, and rural-urban interconnections.

This chapter focuses on Suva as an example of Pacific urban space and the contested ideas of indigeneity and urban life shaping the city from its foundation as the colonial capital in the late nineteenth century. I argue that urban indigeneity in Suva was well-established and long-standing, rather than recent, despite enduring colonial and contemporary narratives that exclude

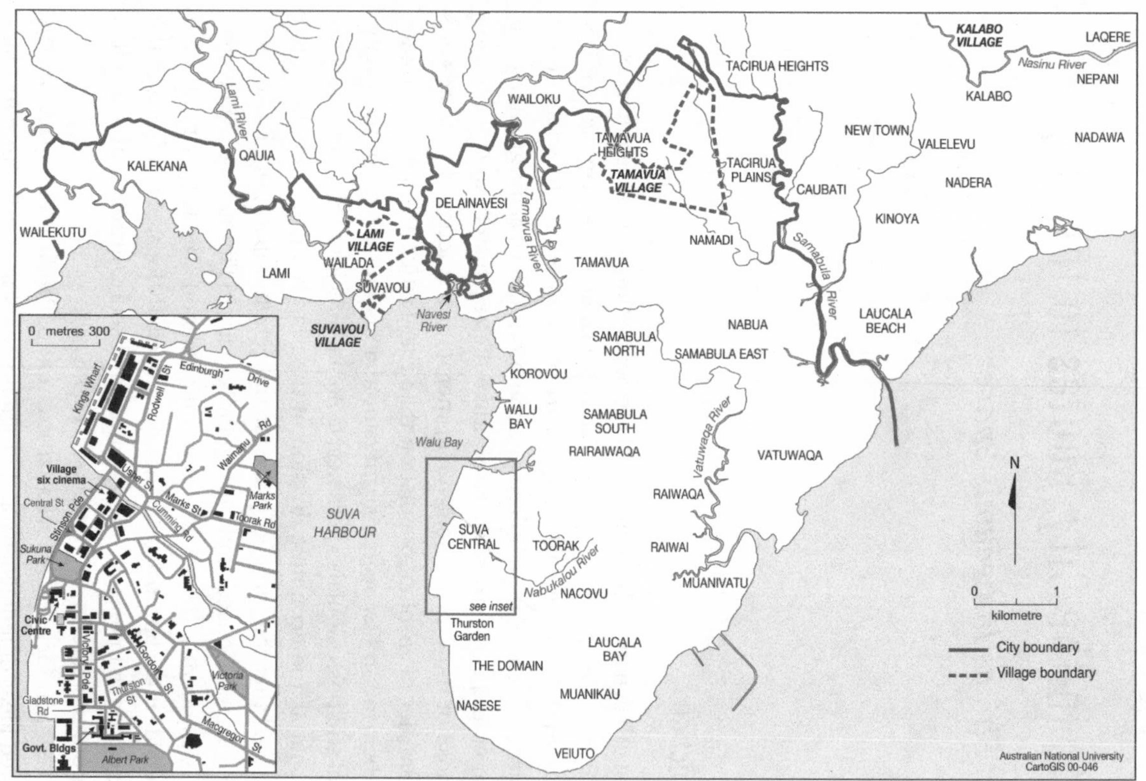

FIGURE 2.1 Map of Suva. Map reproduced with the permission of CartoGIS Services, Scholarly Information Services, The Australian National University.

and erase the significance of varied iTaukei histories in the city. In taking a historical view, this chapter highlights the ways in which urban life has been incorporated and adapted by Indigenous Islanders since the nineteenth century. Indeed, I also emphasize the continuities in how officials and outsiders have framed Indigenous presence in the city as out of place from foundation to present. As Daniela Peluso argues (chap. 6, this volume), Indigenous urban residents faced—and continue to face—questions about their authenticity and identity in the city, reflecting perceived binaries between tradition/modernity and rurality/urbanity imposed on Indigenous communities.[1] These divisions and related narratives serve to efface the ongoing nature of Indigenous life in urban places and the idea that urban sites remain Indigenous spaces despite the layers that hide these histories. As Rebecca Kiddle (2021) states for Aotearoa, cities were and are always Indigenous places, a point worth reiterating that applies across the case studies in this volume.

Like many Pacific cities, Suva emerged out of British colonization, and these roots can hide the long significance of urban indigeneity.[2] Nevertheless, today Fiji is one of the most urbanized nations in the Pacific region, with the urban population expected to increase to over 60 percent by 2030.[3] While Suva's rapid growth in recent decades dominates policy and development discussions, there are multiple palimpsests of Indigenous history in Fiji's urban spaces, from original settlement through generations of migration to the city to the continuation of Indigenous spiritual and ceremonial authority over the urban environment. This chapter aims to highlight the entanglement of Indigenous and urban space at various historical moments, and how these continue into the contemporary city.

The ongoing negotiation of Indigenous belonging and identity in Suva is exemplified through an examination of the changing use and depiction of two different areas in the city: the site of the original Suva village, now government district and botanic gardens, and the streets and markets surrounding Cumming Street and Nubukalou Creek. The latter area forms the heart of Suva's more diverse commercial district, while the government buildings and administrative center lie further south of the creek. These sites both sit within the original one-square-kilometer boundaries of the town, though the boundaries were expanded considerably in the 1950s when Suva officially became Fiji's first city.

Traced from the 1880s to the late twentieth century, these areas highlight the changing nature of Indigenous cosmopolitan life and representation in

Suva. The focus on part of the city's business district also challenges the separation of Indigenous and commercial life in Fiji. The chapter presents three periods of indigeneity in this space across time: from a place of precolonial mobility and conflict to colonial dispossession, to the so-called All Nations Street of the early twentieth century, and to the rise of urban tourism and development narratives from the postwar period where Indigenous permanence in the city is acknowledged. These examples demonstrate the need and possibility for Pacific urban histories that move beyond the current development narratives, and the potential for more research into the cultural and social meanings of urban life in the Pacific across time. Tracing indigeneity in the city across generations and in the face of colonial erasure demonstrates the book's argument that "Indigenous political agency and cultural preservation are indeed possible in the city" (Brablec and Canessa, introduction to this volume).

Since the colonial period, tradition and modernity have been framed as binaries, inversely related states of being for Pacific Islanders and other non-European societies. Lachy Paterson (2018, 234) emphasizes that "Indigenous spaces are sometimes conceptualized in opposition to colonized spaces." This was particularly true in Fiji, where early governors instituted a system to maintain Indigenous culture and political structures, at least as they perceived them, through indirect rule. This long-standing understanding of indigeneity has situated iTaukei in the city as out of place. Urban residence was a temporary state, with permanent home and cultural identity tied to land and communities elsewhere. Subsequent colonial and postcolonial governments have focused their policies and policing of iTaukei around these assumptions. As John Connell writes of twenty-first-century Suva, "Ironically, practice has turned full circle towards colonial order and the idea of a virtuous hard-working nation where the ideology of rurality that was fostered in colonial times remains in place" (2003, 251). These practices include restrictions upon and attempts to remove the urban poor, especially those working in the informal sector such as shoeshine "boys," souvenir sellers or sword sellers, and prostitutes, or those living in informal settlements.

By contrast, Samoan scholar Albert Wendt (1976, 52) asks, "Is the differentiation we usually make between the culture(s) of our urban areas (meaning *foreign*) and those of our rural areas (meaning *traditional*) a valid one?" What if we resituate the city as an Indigenous space, and take seriously Wendt's suggestion? Examining the Indigenous heritage and continuous presence in the city—and the land on which the city is built—shows that the problems associated with recent urban expansion in fact reflect a long history of the denial of Indigenous presence and rights in city. The frequent perceived need to police Indigenous life in Suva speaks to the varied ways in which iTaukei (along with other communities) maintained their culture and existence in urban spaces in the face of such erasure.

This chapter examines the tensions between perceptions of in/authentic indigeneity and the reality of multigenerational life layered on the urban landscape of Suva. I argue that Indigenous Islanders have varied and long-standing urban "roots and routes" in Fiji, to take a significant concept from Pacific Studies scholarship (Diaz and Kehaulani Kauanui 2001; DeLoughrey 2007). I focus on two significant forms of urban indigeneity: iTaukei roots in the city despite a legacy of dispossession in Suva, and iTaukei routes to the city as part of a broader history of mobility across the ocean and islands (Banivanua Mar 2016, 24–25). To do so, I employ and expand Bronwen Douglas's (2009) method of analyzing "indigenous countersigns," where the agency of Indigenous and non-European individuals surfaces through government records, court cases, and press. Douglas (2006, 1n2) explains that countersigns are "inadvertent textual traces of the imprint of local actions and demeanor on the perceptions, reactions and representations of visiting outsiders." While certain outsider ideas about the Pacific and its peoples solidified into stereotypes, underlying these (mis)representations were interactions and experiences where Indigenous communities strategically navigated their relationships with newcomers. Though obscured by the prejudices of the authors, such countersigns permeate colonial writing. Similarly, though sources on Suva's development were often authored by colonial and postcolonial officials and elites, their concerns with Indigenous presence and behavior in the city reveal the mobilities and choices of residents beyond the boundaries of state and chiefly control.

While Jolly (1992) uses this method to understand cross-cultural encounters during early European voyaging in the region, this approach also enables the chapter to examine more recent histories and to draw from archives accessible during the border restrictions of the COVID-19 pandemic, which have delayed planned research, interviews, cultural observances (such as *isevusevu*), and community engagement in Suva. This chapter therefore draws on published sources and some previous archival research as the basis for a broader project working on diverse histories of Suva working with colleagues and students at the University of the South Pacific. Jolly's approach is valuable for indicating, if not recovering, some of the diverse Indigenous histories from these colonial and archival sources. It can also be expanded to read the urban landscape for countersigns of Indigenous presence and histories among the façades of colonial concrete. As Margaret Purser demonstrates for Levuka, the urban space should be examined as a "series of superimposed layers of historical landscapes of which each preceding pattern of land-use helped to shape and define what came next."[4] Urban spaces can thus be read as palimpsests that reveal longer histories of Indigenous occupation—disrupted but not fully erased by colonial occupancy and postcolonial urban growth. Indeed, "in the deep-time scheme of things, even concrete breaks down," as Greg Dvorak (2018, 27) reminds us, providing a useful metaphor for looking beyond the apparent solidity and permanence of colonial and state histories to deeper, relational, and Indigenous histories of place. In unpacking the limits and impacts of colonial binaries on perceptions of urban life, I also emphasize the need for more Indigenous histories of Suva, especially led by community members and using Fijian language sources.[5]

The following sections first contextualize Suva in the broader scholarship on the urbanity in the Pacific and in the history of Fiji's colonial, economic, and demographic development. I then turn to the roots and routes shaping indigeneity in Suva in the face of colonial erasures.

Scholarship on Urbanity and Indigeneity in Oceania

Urban sites have been largely neglected by Pacific scholars, who have often focused on the village, the plantation, and the beach as sites of "traditional" life or cultural encounter (Dening 1980; Lal, Munro and Beechert 1993; see also Howe 2000). Existing historical scholarship of Pacific towns and cities often centers on the moment of early settlement, examining harbors and ports as the "first indigenous spaces to be disciplined by imperial . . . power" (Salesa 2008, 119). The emergence of urban space in the Pacific was closely linked to nineteenth-century colonization. Today's Pacific cities typically began as trading ports and administrative centers, connecting Indigenous communities with arriving traders, planters, and settlers, as well as the wider global economy. While most Pacific communities lived in smaller settlements, the political and economic opportunities associated with newcomers meant chiefs often moved to port locations to maximize their status and influence over rivals, as Kamehameha did in Hawai'i (Ralston 1977). Many of these settlements evolved into the political and demographic capitals of their respective island groups, such as Honolulu, Papeete, and Apia, though others like Levuka (Fiji) and Kororareka (New Zealand) were superseded by planned colonial settlements.

Yet little scholarship charts the development of urban life beyond these foundational moments. There is a gap between studies of nineteenth-century port-town foundations and studies of contemporary urban issues in the region since the 1960s and 1970s, when increasingly rapid urbanization generated renewed political and academic attention.[6] Recent scholarship, predominantly by social scientists and policy makers, explores the social and environmental challenges associated with urbanized island spaces, but generally situates these problems as relatively new phenomena.[7] Moreover, the predominant narrative in development studies positions urbanization in the Pacific as a challenge, rather than an opportunity, something to be mitigated and managed and even ideally reversed. The underlying assumption that animates these works reiterates the view that Indigenous life is most authentic and fulfilling outside the city, and that Islanders have a village home to which they can easily return. Other scholarship focuses on external migration to Pacific Rim nations such as Australia, New Zealand, and the United States, all home to significant and often urban Pacific diasporas. These accounts often draw on the idea that island states and their cities are constricted by MIRAB economies: dependent on migration, remittances, aid, and bureaucracy (Bertram and Watters 1985; see also Bertram 2006). Though thoroughly challenged by a more expansive view of oceanic connectivity, this deficit framing of contemporary Pacific nations permeates developmental approaches and can limit our vision of Oceanic cities (notably following Hau'ofa 1994).

Surprisingly, Suva has largely been absent from both older and recent examinations of the emerging Pacific city.[8] Earlier works focused on Levuka as the town at the center of early trade and cross-cultural exchange, and the site is currently the nation's only UNESCO World Heritage site. One of the larger Pacific cities, Suva has a distinct and multicultural history, drawing in not only colonial officials and Indigenous Fijians but also former indentured laborers from India and across the Pacific Islands, as well as migrants and visitors. Indigenous Fijians, or iTaukei, refer to the original inhabitants of the islands and make up about 57 percent of Fiji's population (Fiji Bureau of Statistics 2008). This includes the Indo-Fijian community, descendants of colonial-sponsored indentured migrants, who were the majority population in Fiji prior to outward migrations following four coups between 1987 and 2000.[9] Alongside these groups are various communities of Islanders, drawn to Suva through long-standing connections with Fiji (such as Rotumans, Tongans, and Samoans), through the Pacific indentured labor trade (especially ni-Vanuatu and Solomon Islanders), or through regional institutions or education opportunities (such as the Central Medical School or University of the South Pacific). In this context, indigeneity and ethnicity has seemingly underpinned ethno-nationalist conflict since independence. However, as Jacqueline Leckie (2002) argues, these tensions also reflect debates over tradition, chiefly authority, land, and class within iTaukei society. Here it is valuable to note that though the term *Fijian* was used historically to refer to iTaukei or Indigenous Fijians specifically, in contemporary state usage, *Fijian* encompasses all ethnicities and refers to citizenship of the nation-state.[10] This chapter focuses particularly on iTaukei relationship to Suva, though within the broader context of ethnic diversity and division largely created through colonial rule.

Creating Racial and Spatial Divisions in Fiji and Suva

Austronesian voyagers settled Fiji around three thousand years ago, as part of a long history of Oceanic migrations.[11] Over subsequent generations, Indigenous Fijian society and politics evolved in the island landscape, though transoceanic ties with neighboring Tonga remained strong, especially in eastern Fiji. Communities lived in small settlements, both coastal and in the mountainous interior, with a hierarchical chiefly system of authority familiar in much of Polynesia. The interrelationship between peoples, and between people and place is encompassed by *vanua* (land): "The Fijian term 'Vanua' has physical cultural and social dimension that are interrelated. It does not only mean land area one is identified with, and vegetation, animals and other objects on it, but it also includes the social and cultural system—the people, their tradition and custom, beliefs and values, and various other institutions established for the sake of achieving harmony, stability, and prosperity within a particular social context" (Ravuvu 1983, 76; Nabobo-Baba 2006). Though vanua provides an underpinning framework for Indigenous identity and relationship to place, rootedness is complemented by routes, by mobility. Communities and hierarchies were fluid, and displacement and migrations were a feature of shifting alliances and enmities between different kin-based groups.

By the time of European voyaging in the Pacific in the eighteenth and nineteenth centuries, Fiji society was in "a state of flux due to an ongoing transition from a weakly hierarchical and diffusely connected chiefly system to larger and more complex lineage aristocracies based on geographical suzerainty rather than purely kinship ties" (Bayliss-Smith et al. 1988, 47).[12] The subsequent emergence of towns and cities followed a pattern of cross-cultural entanglement familiar across the Pacific region: European voyagers were followed by waves of missionaries, traders (seeking bêche-de-mer, whales, copra, and labor), and by planters and settlers. Islanders made the most of the opportunities for trade and travel, though misunderstandings and violence also accompanied new relationships across languages and cultures. In Fiji, the anchorage and growing trade centered around Levuka, on the island of Ovalau, and helped the ascendency of Bauan chief Ratu Seru Epenisa Cakobau.

Increasing conflict eventually drew the British government—somewhat reluctantly—into colonization, with Fiji annexed in 1874. In particular, unrest increased between ambitious but indebted Cakobau and rival chiefs from surrounding areas, as well as between traders, settlers, and Indigenous Fijians. These disputes centered on land sales and debts, resource use and labor, dispossession and questions of legitimate authority over different regions surrounding Bau, Levuka, and Lau (Legge 1958; France 1969, chaps. 5 and 6; Scarr 1968, 7–8). Cakobau's European-style government, backed by local Europeans who served as ministers, deteriorated within three years of its establishment in 1871, with settlers petitioning the Colonial Office for protection (Nicole 2010, 23–25). The problem of law and order had thus become sufficiently detrimental to British interests and reputation to overcome the Colonial Office's reluctance for formal intervention.

The official strategy for the new colony had to balance contrasting emphases on the Colonial Office's expectation of financial self-sufficiency and a paternalistic humanitarian impulse led by the first career governor Arthur Gordon. Gordon aimed to preserve Indigenous culture and communities from the perceived deleterious impact of the capitalist economy, which he had observed across the imperial world during his previous tenures in New Brunswick, Trinidad, and Mauritius (Kelly 2003; Brown 2006; Newbury 2010; Chapman 1964).[13] His early colonial policies sought to preserve Indigenous Fijians on their land, and thus separate from the colonial economy, in an attempt to prevent the dispossession and degradation experienced by Indigenous peoples in other British colonies. His paternalistic views reflected a wider British impulse toward "imperial benevolence" in the Pacific during the mid-nineteenth century, in which "primitive" Islanders needed imperial protection from unscrupulous European newcomers and the opportunity to gradually "civilize" (Samson 1998). In Fiji, Gordon was also allied with, and to some degree dependent on, his relationship with the Fijian chiefs, and these relationships influenced his understanding of local society and land tenure (Newbury 2011).

Working with chiefly allies, Gordon established indirect rule—frugally co-opting Indigenous leaders and "traditional" customs—as the founding principle of "native policy," and complemented this political strategy with an economic one of large-scale government-sponsored Indian indentured labor migration from 1879.[14] The resultant colonial policies helped shaped a particular legal and administrative definition of indigeneity in Fiji, as well as the spatial and economic structure of the colony and then nation upon independence in 1970. Though the Fijian chiefly system predated colonization, Governor Gordon's administration institutionalized chiefly power. Colonial understanding of iTaukei society was partial, and these policies reified male, chiefly authority as orthodoxy and erased diversity and fluidity in practice across the islands. Indirect rule supported an outsider interpretation of Fijian society weighted toward elite and Bauan views, while "ordinary Fijians . . . sometimes had to be told by white men what their customs were" (Thomas 1994, 108).

Following the Deed of Cession, the administration divided the islands into twelve districts headed by Roko Tui (leading chiefs), and subdivided them into smaller areas presided over by Buli (minor chiefs). The Native Affairs Ordinance of 1876 established the Native Regulation Board and courts that operated under the authority of the Roko and colonial officials.[15] Native Stipendiary Magistrates assisted in enforcing chiefly jurisdiction and the associated Native regulations over the villages. A chief Native commissioner oversaw this hierarchy. The colonial chiefly elite, which was based largely on aristocratic lineage, exercised considerable influence through the Bose Vakaturaga (or Council of Chiefs), a forum that drew together the Roko, Buli, and Native magistrates from across the islands to debate and advise on Indigenous affairs from 1876 (Newbury 2006).[16] In the opening decade of colonial rule, the views of this group were crucial in shaping Native regulations, justice, and punishments, particularly regarding obedience toward chiefs, labor recruitment, marriage, divorce and adultery, communal services, and taxation.[17]

The colonial administration, supported by chiefly elite, enacted policies to ensure that the vast majority of land in the islands remained under Indigenous communal title and that Indigenous communities remained on their land and in their villages. Though subsequent administrations were more open to individualism and market forces, Gordon's legislation and policy orientation remained important structures, creating divisions on racial, spatial, and economic lines and enshrining the assumption that "true" indigeneity was life in village and rural areas—not the growing urban settlements. The link between rural, village life and the reification of chiefly authority and tradition was thus particularly strong in Fiji. Fijians were encouraged to maintain a "traditional" lifestyle and largely nonmonetary economy in villages. For example, Native Regulation No. 5 (1878) restricted Fijians' movements, requiring chiefly permission to leave the village or to take up paid labor (Fiji Government 1883, 38–39). Though restrictions on entering paid labor were relaxed somewhat in 1912, the importance of village life and obedience to chiefs remained the idealized norm. Today, over 80 percent of land in Fiji remains as iTaukei land (Ward 1969; Lal 1992, 134–35). This land cannot be sold, transferred, or mortgaged but may be leased with the iTaukei Land Trust Board, established from 1940 to manage leases (iTaukei Land Trust Board 2018). The continuation of Indigenous tenure and the high level of customary land is similar to many other Pacific nations, including Samoa, the Solomon Islands, and Vanuatu.[18] Indeed, land tenure is frequently framed as one of the major issues limiting Pacific Islands' economic development, though the area remaining as iTaukei land is considerably less around Suva than elsewhere in Fiji, as explained below.[19]

The protectionist policy toward Indigenous Fijians required importation of labor to support the plantation economy based on sugar and satisfy settler demands for manual workers to support the industry. Indentured labor migration from India offered a cheap and seemingly abundant workforce, simultaneously solving the issues of labor shortages and preserving "benign" administration of Indigenous affairs (Gillion 1962, 69–70).[20] From 1879 to 1916, over sixty thousand *girmitiyas*, or Indian indentured laborers, arrived to work the sugar plantations on five-year contracts. Laborers who reindentured for a further five years earned their return passage to India. Most remained in Fiji after their first harsh and violent experience of indenture, set up communities on the outskirts of the plantations, and established agricultural and trading businesses on leased land.[21] Many former laborers and their descendants also subsequently moved to Suva and other urban settlements, either from necessity as leases ended or to pursue opportunity in businesses and education. The administration thus created a colonial society fractured along racial, spatial, and economic lines. This meant to "each race . . . its allotted sphere": Fijians in the villages, Indians and Islander laborers on the plantations, colonial officials in towns.[22]

At the time these policies were established, European settlement was concentrated at Levuka, a strategic port town with anchorage in the realm of Cakobau. Prior to the 1880s, Levuka was the heart of European settlement and administration in Fiji. Gordon based his administration at Levuka and frequently hosted chiefs as he sought to incorporate Indigenous custom into British governance of the islands. It was quickly apparent, however, that the surrounding environment was insufficient for a growing administration and trading center. The steep hills rising behind Levuka limited the space for expansion, and the settlement has grown "in a haphazard manner" with little suitable land available for the colonial government (Derrick 1953, 206; see also Donnison 1880). From the late 1870s, officials sought a port location more suited for the growing administration and commerce—one where a more orderly town could be established under the guidance of planners. This would be a "fresh start" from the disorderly and dissolute Levuka, in the words of Colonel W. T. Smythe.[23] Officials considered Savusavu Bay, Suva, Galoa Harbor, Nadi, or another location on Ovalau. Suva's harbor and surrounding fertile land, as well as settlers' offer of land discussed below, won out, and from 1876 engineer Colonel Pratt and his team relocated to Suva to establish roading and town plans (Derrick 1953, 206–7). In contrast to Levuka, Suva as the new capital was thus imagined as part of a paternalistic narrative of bringing order and stability to the islands. However, realizing this vision involved removing the existing village from the peninsula.

In the early twentieth century, Colman Wall collected oral histories of the migration, settlement, and history of Suva, located to the southeast of Viti Levu, the largest island in the group. Tabanimanakoveve, a chiefly descendent of Degei (a supreme Fijian deity) and a princess of the *veli* (dwarf race), led the migration across Viti Levu, past Waimanu River to Suva Peninsula.

The main settlements around the peninsula were initially *koronivalu* (hill forts) such as Uluvatu. In the early nineteenth century, led by Tabukaucoro, communities migrated downhill to the site of the present city. The main settlement was built at the heart of the contemporary Botanic Gardens and government house, known as Naqasiqasi (Wall 1996, 36–37). It was "a prosperous place and its chiefs were high standing."[24] However, allied with Bau through marriage, the Suva residents were rivalries of Rewa, and Suva was the site of a particularly fiercely fought battle in 1843 during a period of tribal warfare. Both the settlement and population were weakened as a result.

In 1868, the Melbourne-based Polynesian Company purchased the Suva Peninsula from Ratu Seru Cakobau of Bau. Cakobau was a preeminent chief, or Vunivalu, and had claims to authority over Suva through familial ties to local chiefs. In debt to U.S. traders due to damage to property prior to annexation, Cakobau sold the land on the basis of his kinship to Suva chiefs on the agreement that the Polynesian Company paid off the U.S. debts of over $40,000. The deed of cession covered over twenty thousand acres of land on the peninsula (Derrick 1953, 303). The company divided much of the peninsula for sale to settlers from Australia, some of whom established themselves in the area in the early 1870s, while three hundred acres was set aside as a "Native Reserve." The newcomers tried both sugar and cotton crops, but their plantations floundered on the shallow soils. James McEwan and Company bought up much of the Polynesian Company's Suva interests (Derrick 1953, 204). Their manager subsequently negotiated with the colonial government, offering alternate blocks of land as an inducement to relocate the administration to Suva. After five years of engineering and planning, the second governor, William Des Voeux, moved to Suva in mid-1882.

From Naqasiqasi to a Koro Vavalagi: Displacing Indigeneity from Town

The story of relocation as one of colonial progress from disorder elides the existing occupation of the area. Suva, according to Derryck Scarr (2001, 162), became "a recognized koro vavalagi or foreign village." Yet the very heart of government overlay an iTaukei village. Suva—the administrative heart of a colony based on paternalistic governance—was founded upon Indigenous dispossession and European settlement in a pattern more familiar in settler colonial states. As Jane M. Jacobs (2012, 145) describes in Australia, such displacement from the city was not just a historical event but "an *ongoing* process of settlement/unsettlement," albeit an uneven and contested one.

With the Polynesian Company purchase, the traditional landowners were provided a "Native Reserve" in present-day Suva. However, the reserve did not form part of plans for the new city. Moreover, in contrast to practice elsewhere in the group, the colonial government kept the land in Suva as crown land (rather than return it) when it investigated various preannexation European land claims and found them lacking. The iTaukei inhabitants of Old Suva, or Naqasiqasi (referring specifically to the reserve area around the government house and botanic gardens), were removed from the peninsula in 1882 to clear the land for government and commerce. These residents were transplanted across the harbor to Narikoso, becoming Suvavou (literally, New Suva; Miyazaki 2004, 33–36 and 33n13; Ward 1953) In an ambiguous form of compensation, the community was to be paid £200 a year in perpetuity for the three hundred acres surrounding the government house (Chambers 2008). From the late nineteenth century, the Suvavou community have contested their land rights and the annual payment's purpose and adequacy, which they argued was insufficient in the face of population growth, the city's expansion, and inflation. Working with the Suvavou community, anthropologist Hirokazu Miyazaki highlighted that the unsympathetic official response was particularly significant given the colonial government's ostensible policy toward protecting Indigenous lands (Miyazaki 2004, 37).

Most recently, in 1999 the Tui Suva Ratu Epeli Kanakana and ten others took a case to the High Court, arguing that Native title to Suva had never been extinguished and seeking compensation for the loss of the whole peninsula. The case was only concluded in 2010, after Kanakana's passing. Judge Sosefo Inoke found against the Suvavou claimants. His approach to navigating the evidence revealed the difficulties for iTaukei trying to challenge the continued influence of colonial narratives and evidence:

> How do I decide what took place 136 years ago? I think the proper approach is to give more weight to the evidence recorded in the documentation held in the State archives than to the evidence of the witnesses, including the expert evidence, for three reasons. Firstly, the archive documents are contemporaneous or written soon thereafter. Secondly, the expert evidence is the expert's interpretation of what is in those documents, a task which this Court, with the greatest of respect,

> can do equally just as well. Thirdly, a more complete picture is painted by these documents.[25]

Lodging an appeal, the claimants contested this dismissal of oral accounts.[26] Nevertheless, the case reaffirms Miyazaki's finding that Suvavou claimants were consistently positioned as unsophisticated and unable to understand legal arrangements of the land sales (Miyazaki 2004, chap. 2).

Through the colonial and postindependence period, condescending views also continued outside the court: sympathy toward the displaced as an exemplification of problems inherited from colonialism collides with the perception that Suvavou people are no longer "authentic" iTaukei due to their proximity and interaction with the city and city life. These contests over the definitions of authentic indigeneity—as the editors to this volume note—date from the start of urbanization and continue into the postcolonial period in Fiji, especially for the Suvavou community. Their experiences parallel some of the ongoing struggles over identity and recognition negotiated by the Mapuche in Santiago and by Indigenous Lowland South Americans in Madre de Dios, discussed by Sandra del Valle Casals and Daniel Peluso (chaps. 7 and 6, respectively) in this volume.

With the increase in cruise ship tourism to Suva during the interwar years, Suvavou residents developed innovative economic strategies, such as coming to town to sell Fijian artifacts. So-called swordselling—informal approaches to tourists to sell engraved wooden swords or masks—has been the subject of periodic government restriction since the 1930s (Halter 2020; Hirokazu 2005, 284–86). The goods sold were generally considered cheap and inauthentic, and the behavior of the sellers disruptive and unwelcoming, even inauthentic like their curios. In the mid-1930s, the secretary for Native Affairs argued, "It is only a certain type of Fijian who live in Suva and who look on the tourist as fair prey; a class of person quite apart from residents. The tourists leave a fair amount of money with Fijian sellers of beads, coral &c." (quoted in Halter 2020, 44).

The Suvavou sellers (as well as those from elsewhere in the islands) have been a continued presence in the urban landscape, a countersign disrupting official narratives of a model colony or an idyllic tourist paradise. In a 1995 report, tourism official and researcher Samisoni Sawailau drew attention to Indigenous persistence in Suva as a symptom of their erasure from Suva's economic life:

> Swordselling is a mean[s] of their survival after the inherited order of being pushed away from their original landsite by the early whites. . . . It is an issue embodied with "control" of Fijian communities within the legal boundaries of municipalities where those with economic powers control. This has unfortunately led to the suppression and manipulation of the Indigenous population in suburbs like Suvavou in Suva. (Quoted in Miyazaki 2005)

Yet Suvavou chiefs retain important symbolic and spiritual authority over the vanua on which the city is built. In this context, their connection to the environment from which they were displaced is considered salient when a blessing or apology is required, but otherwise their indigeneity is questioned due to close and long association with the city. For example, when three workers died while working on a reclamation project at Walu Bay, the main port in Suva, the city council ascribed the fatalities to the fact that the council hadn't sought the appropriate permissions from the Tui Suva before commencing the works in the early 1990s (Miyazaki 2005, 152n39).[27] In early 1991, the Suva City Council ran into difficulties while building a bridge over Nubukalou Creek and approached the Tui Suva Ratu Epeli Kanakana for aid. Rather than accept the belated request by the council, the Tui Suva initially refused to meet with council officials, then stated that they needed to perform an offering (*bulibuli*) first and consult before the bridge project rather than after. Only then did he seek the gods' approval through a *vakasobuduru* ceremony at the site: "Some may think this is black magic but this ceremony is performed to show the visitors that land has owners."[28] This event highlighted the continuity of Suva as an Indigenous space, and of the chief's connection to place, in a very public way.

Similarly, in 2019 the current Tui Suva, Ratu Sanaila Mudunavosa, protested against government plans to gift some of the land beside Thurston Gardens to the Indian government for a new high commission. The Indian government had gifted the Fijian government a substantive piece of land in Delhi in 2014, and the proposed land would return the favor. However, while the Suvavou community accepted the botanic gardens, museum, and president's house on the site of their former village, the Tui Suva opposed any further development on this land. Rejecting the government's plan, Mudunavosa highlighted the ongoing significance of Suva people's traditional and moral authority over the area:

Na kena vakabaitaki tu ena bai ni kovana na kena nanuma ni na maroroya tiko na matanitu na iyau bula ni yavutu ni vanua o Suva, ena gauna keimami toki mai kina. Ia ena gauna saraga e dai ni sa tukuna tiko na cakacaka baleti iratou, ena noqu itutu ni veiqaravi, ena noqu itutu vaka Roko Tui Suva, au sa sega saraga ni duavata kina, me baleta na kena nanuma me caka kina na cakacaka.

(We had faith in the government to protect our old village site, now they are saying that work can continue, in my position as chief of my people and Roko Tui Suva, I will never accept it.)

Kevaka sa mani toso na cakacaka e dua na ka me ratou nanuma vinaka tiko ni vanua oya e vanua taukeni, ni dua na ka ena yaco vei iratou me ratou kua ni nanuma me ra qai mai e na koro, me mai caka e dua na ka ni veivakameautaki.

(Should they proceed with work, they must remember there are the real owners of the land. Should something happen to them, we will not be in a position to accept their traditional request of apology.)

Au sa tukuna talega vei ira na gone ni mataqali, dou kua ni ciqoma na cakacaka ni veivakameautaki, kevaka e dua na vakacala e yaco ena tiki ni vanua oya.

(I have also told members of my clan not accept anyone who want to seek the blessing of the vanua), added the Roko Tui Suva who is the head of the mataqali and yavusa Vatuwaqa.

Na vanua oya e tawa tu, ni dua na ka na yaco kina mera kakua ni tovolea mera rai mai e na koro, baleta ni sa kece na neitou itukutuku me kakua ni vakayagataki na tiki ni qele oya. Na vanua saraga oya era tauyavu mai kina na qase ni bera nira toki mai ke. Na kena mositi keimami tu, neimami nanuma ni na maroroya na matanitu na veika me baleti Suva.

(They should not think of turning to us if something happens to them, it hurts us because this is our old village site, this is our beginning where our forefathers once lived before we were told to move.)[29]

Many in Suvavou supported this view, with over a thousand people signing a petition against the proposed rezoning and gifting of the land, though two *mataqali* (landholding kin group / clan) supported the government's plans (Susu 2019); (Danford 2019).

Though their village was physically removed in the nineteenth century, Suvavou people have since remained a consistent presence in the city in multiple and contested ways. Consequently, they appear liminal, considered neither Indigenous nor modern by the state and by some other Fijians. Their continued navigation between seeking appropriate recognition of their authority and identity, along with adaptability to new—if limited—economic opportunities, suggests an alternative understanding of urban Indigenous identity that is deeply rooted in the vanua.

Nubukalou to All Nations Street: Controlling Indigeneity in Town

The city was envisaged as a European settlement. Following the original dispossession of Indigenous occupants from their lands, various regulations policed non-European presence in the city. As Nicholas Thomas and Robert Nicole explore, the regulations limited physical and economic mobility for men and women, and paid particular attention to the private and intimate lives of villagers (Thomas 1994, 108–12; Nicole 2010). Alongside the limits on working outside the village, ordinances imposed a curfew on all non-Europeans in Suva, limited access to alcohol, prevented *meke* (dances) without a permit, and restricted the types of residences constructed in the town (Fiji Government 1914; McHugh 1943). Jacqueline Leckie (2020, 37–38) notes that urban vagrancy contributed to the institutionalization of Indigenous Fijians, as well as Indo-Fijians, at St. Giles Asylum, further highlighting the ways in which non-European presence in Suva was problematized and controlled.

Despite government attempts to restrict Indigenous presence in the city from its foundation, continued inward migrations of iTaukei, as well as indentured Indian laborers and their descendants, from villages and plantations across Fiji transformed this European administrative center to a social and economic hub from its earliest years. By 1921 nearly two thousand Indigenous Fijians lived permanently in Suva out of the town's population nearing thirteen thousand, with others visiting for varied reasons and lengths of time (Scarr 1984, 137; Whitelaw 1966, 53). Their numbers roughly equaled the European and part-European population of the town at the time, with Indians in the majority. More broadly at the time of this census, the iTaukei / Indigenous Fijian population living away from their village was just 5 percent, but it grew rapidly in subsequent decades to 17.5 percent in 1936 and 22 percent by 1946 (Overton 1989, 25–26).[30]

Suva was thus cosmopolitan within a generation of its foundation. Alongside internal migration of iTaukei and Indo-Fijians, Suva was also a city of Indigenous people from across the region, reflecting both the historical processes of unfree labor migrations in the Pacific and the routes that long connected Oceanic peoples. Indentured labor schemes brought diverse Pacific Islanders to Fiji from the mid-nineteenth century. While intended to form the backbone of the plantation labor force alongside the Indian migrants, many of these individuals spent time in the towns and cities. Some only transited through the ports, though others served as domestic workers, wharfies, waiters, or laundresses for varied periods, and some built lives and communities across generations in the city. In 1921 there were over 1,400 Polynesian, Chinese, or Other residents in Suva and suburbs out of a total population of around 13,000 (Whitelaw 1966, 53).

The demographic shift highlights another contested indigeneity in Suva: a continuous growth of iTaukei and other non-European residents, though they were presumed to be temporary and problematic visitors. This diversity contributed to the general view of colonial cities as "disordered" spaces (Gulliver 2014). Notwithstanding its colonial foundations, when an unelected, European-dominated Suva Town Board was constituted in 1936, Suva's population was just 14 percent European, indicating that its growth was driven by Fijian, Indian, and other newcomers (Whitelaw 1966, 59). As Coll Thrush (2017) argues, such figures challenge the common perception of colonial cities as white, not Indigenous, spaces. Suva thus became simultaneously the site of ongoing displacements and incoming migrations that reconfigured the place of indigeneity in the city, even if not recognized at the time. As the Suvavou community lived at the margins of the city literally and symbolically, iTaukei from across the Fiji Islands—alongside other Indo-Fijian, Islanders, Chinese, and Europeans—created homes and communities in Suva. Those following varied routes to the city dominated urban demography and discourse over those with roots in the local vanua. These migrations and transformations, and the anxieties surrounding them, suggest the continued struggle over belonging and rights in Fiji's urban space. These tensions were particularly evident through the 1920s and 1930s, following the end of

Indian indenture contracts and the start of iTaukei population recovery after decades of decline resulting from contact, colonization, and various deadly epidemics.

By the early twentieth century, diverse residents and visitors transformed the area around Nubukalou Creek into a "Quartier Indigène" (quoted in Steel 2011, 183). Nubukalou itself had a longer history as a place of exchange, serving as a trading area prior to European settlement, its banks convenient for moving goods by creek or harbor (Ward 1953, 216). The area on the south of the creek was the site of the first European shipping and trade, including the rough Suva Hotel. The streets around the north of Nubukalou, however, really developed from the start of the twentieth century. By the early 1920s, Cumming Street in particular was "the principal business portion of the town for the natives."[31] Among Suva residents, it was known as All Nations Street: a gathering place for diverse communities in the city. The street combined Indian-run general stores with eating houses, *yaqona* (kava) saloons, gambling, and opium dens, with accommodation on the second floors above the commercial spaces at street level (Whitelaw 1966, 116). During this period over sixty Indigenous Fijian women worked in the saloons, much to the concern of officials, missionaries, and chiefs (Scarr 1984, 137). This commercial and social area, alongside the nearby market, served as a visible symbol of the failure of chiefs and officials to implement racial, economic, and physical segregation. This was a space of mixing and opportunity: iTaukei in and near Suva brought in produce to sell; wage earners in town completed their shopping; and food, *yaqona*, alcohol, and opium were all available to lubricate the social life of the town. The market was thus the most visible, long-standing, cosmopolitan challenge to the view of allotted spheres.

Official concerns over this area specifically, and the presence and behavior of iTaukei in the town generally, points to the varied ways that iTaukei men and women adopted and adapted to new urban opportunities despite attempts to crystallize a village-based alternative. Through chiefly influence on the Native Regulations, customs were codified in ways that did not necessarily reflect the fluidity and flexibility of social practices.[32] The mobility between village and city could thus be a continuation of existing practices. However, departure from village for work and social opportunities elsewhere—on plantations or urban centers—could also be an act of resistance against the constraints on mobility and labor enacted by the alliance of colonial and chiefly power (Nicole 2010).

Departure from the village temporarily or permanently was a means to avoid communal labor service, seek new relationships and experiences, or earn money and status through paid work. Most individuals did not leave archival records, but countersigns of their choices to move exist in the discussions of the Bose Vakaturaga, court cases, and newspaper articles. Chiefs expressed concern about the loosening of their authority over their communities. These concerns were gendered: men who left the village for paid labor elsewhere reduced the labor that chiefs expected. As one Buli (district chief) stated, "They shirk all communal obligations and leave their villages to go to Suva to earn a little money with which they buy collars and neckties and coats! and save 2 [shillings] for a fine when they return home. Let them be whipped, then they will listen and take heed of us. If we attempt to assert our position and authority as Chiefs they go to Suva and say we are oppressing them: they lie and scheme and are becoming quite demoralized."[33]

By contrast, chiefs were particularly concerned over the numbers of women who left for relationships with non-Fijian men in towns or plantations. At the first gathering of the Bose Vakaturaga in 1875, Native Stipendiary Magistrate Mafi stated, "The white man's style of simply cohabiting with a woman is the rule now at Bau, and the land has become filthy through it, and we have been much pained and annoyed. The elders of the people have cried out 'what is to be done in this matter?' We have tried to prevent it but are met by 'All are now British subjects and it is Vakapiritania and all please themselves.'"[34]

Every year, anxieties over relationships between Fijian women and European men were revisited by the Bose Vakaturaga, indicating the frequency of such relationships and the level of disquiet they generated. Of particular concern were the cases of Fijian women who ran away from their husbands and received protection from European men.[35] The negative impact of contact with non-Europeans on iTaukei men and women was a recurrent issue, though the chiefs felt they had little ability to control non-iTaukei and hoped the governor would oversee the behavior of other communities.

Court records and newspaper accounts highlight official and European settler concerns over the negative impact of racial mixing in the town, while providing countersigns of the varied experiences of Suva life. In one Supreme Court case, a Fijian man was charged with the rape of a Tokelauan woman, both of whom were living with the victim's husband, a Solomon Islander, and a Chinese man in Suva.[36] Such cases hint at the diversity of living arrangements and economic participation in the capital. More generally, the *Fiji Times* reported on police cases and varied "disturbances" from the Cumming Street area regularly, with liquor consumption, theft, and occasional violence often linked to the problematic influence of urban temptation and racial mixing on individuals deemed less educated or civilized.[37] Though the desire to preserve iTaukei from the perceived deleterious impacts of urban life and racial mixing reflect a specific genealogy of paternalistic imperialism in Fiji, concerns around cultural and genetic hybridization were (and are) common globally as part of a discourse serving to delegitimize or erase Indigenous modernities (see introduction, this volume; and Smith 1999, 72–74).

On the night of Saturday, February 10, 1923, the largely timber buildings lining Cumming Street's southern side caught fire. The blaze fire spread rapidly along the street as residents fled with what they could carry. The south side and much of the north was destroyed, as the fire brigade's water supply and hose failed. The concrete buildings of Morris Hedstrom store and a shift in the wind stopped the fire from moving farther into the town, and the event led to the development of the fire service and greater building regulation.[38] In a pattern of colonial commentary, newspaper reports on urban disasters such as the 1923 fire situated such events as a positive, if unfortunate, means by which unsavory elements of the city might be cleansed and reconstructed in a new, and more orderly, manner.[39] The fact that an environmental disaster was gratefully received as a potential remedy to the perceived challenges of urban cosmopolitanism speaks to the limits and frustrations of officials and European settlers attempting to assert their authority over Suva's residents and development.

Nevertheless, the street was quickly revived as a key trading street and a shopping and sightseeing destination for curious tourists (Whitelaw 1966, 120). While officials and chiefs agonized over the degradations of urban life and the deleterious impact of cross-cultural contact on Indigenous Fijians in Suva, All Nations Street contributed to Suva's growing reputation as a cosmopolitan port, unique in the region for bringing together the Pacific and Asia. The *Otago Daily Times* special correspondent painted the scene, in a style replicated by varied visitors:

> The first thing to be seen next day was, of course, the part of Suva that all tourists remember—All Nations street. It is no wonder the tourists remember it, for no stranger cross between the Pacific and the East

could be imagined. In stalls opening on to the street Indians are selling tobacco, made up in rope about half an inch thick, and coiled up like a ball of brinder-twine. Next door is a fish market, then an open-fronted shed where oranges, bananas, taro, yams and a dozen other kinds of fruit and vegetables are for sale. A young Indian man and an old Indian woman are selling to customers, and apparently buying the produce they sell from the Fijians, who bring it in canoes, poling them along the tidal creek that runs at the back of the street.

A Chinese shop is opposite, and close by the headquarters of the Kuo Min Tang. A notice in a nearby window tells of the approach of the All-Fiji Sanatanist Conference. This street is something new in cosmopolitanism. Ramadar Singh has his jewelry shop next door to the premises of Yong Lin Tan, where ginger and silk are sold. These are not real names; they sound well, and I lost the paper on which I copied out some of the actual ones. Tall, muscular, mop-headed Fijians swagger along, meeting weedy Hindus. A white man is buying crabs in an open section, probably for an hotel [*sic*].[40]

The area lay on the route through town for most tourists arriving by ship. The street's reputation was further enhanced following the influx of servicemen in World War II, creating a greater market for curios that continued to flourish in the postwar period (Schutz 1978).

The growing number of tourists and military engaged with the urban space and diverse urban residents with greater freedom, in ways that the government couldn't control, and thus challenged existing hierarchies of race and class (Halter 2020; Leckie and Durutalo 2016, 183–201). The street further developed as a duty-free shopping street, with general stores and tailors sidelined by the fluorescent adverts for global electronic brands (Tarte 2014, 112; Whitelaw 1966, 132). By the late 1970s, Albert Schutz described the Cumming Street area as "one of the most picturesque parts of the city," suggesting that the perceived problematic reputation of the area had been reevaluated partly in light of the visitor gaze (Schutz 1978, 20). Today, the market, the Cumming Street shops, and the largest department store in the city sit together in a cluster to the north of Nubukalou Creek. The area speaks to the evolving intersections of different lifeways and prosperity for Suva's residents and visitors, as well as the continuation of existing patterns of exchange and interaction in the area.

Conclusion: Acknowledging Urban Indigeneity

In this postwar era, Suva officially moved from a town to a city, its boundaries formally extended to encompass the whole of the peninsula in 1952.[41] At a similar time, restrictions on Indigenous mobility in the city were loosened, and the durability of Indigenous life in Suva first acknowledged. As an Indigenous anthropologist, Rusiate Nayacakalou provided one of the first examinations of iTaukei urban life based on his fieldwork in the early 1960s. He argued that "there is little doubt that the great majority of the Fijians living in Suva are destined to be fairly permanently settled there. . . . The fact that they are, on the whole, permanently settled in Suva has not always been recognized in the past. . . . And the assumption that Fijians will return to their village in old age is very largely unfounded" (Nayacakalou 1963; see also Nayacakalou 1985). Though Nayacakalou emphasized the connections that "every Fijian" maintained with his village, and with others from the village in the city, he also noted new forms of social ties emerging in Suva that enabled Indigenous residents to continue to uphold and participate in social obligations, such as gifting of mats and *tabua* (whales' teeth). His research, alongside Oscar Spate's government-sponsored 1959 report on the economic future of Fiji for which Nayacakalou served as a research assistant, represented the start of new debates and research on urbanization in Fiji. Though Nayacakalou highlighted the permanence of urban indigeneity, concern over the perceived incompatibility between urbanity and indigeneity continue to permeate conversations about Suva.

However, as the examples discussed in this chapter emphasize, Suva has always been an Indigenous space, a historical reality obscured by colonial discourse that places Indigenous people in villages. This is not to deny the enduring significance of vanua and village, but to highlight how urban indigeneity has long coexisted and adapted alongside, rather than in opposition to, them. Indigeneity has taken two main forms in Suva: firstly, indigeneity uprooted and displaced outward in the early 1880s but has been persistently present in the city since, physically in the peri-urban area, as workers and as swordsellers and as insistent voices in government records asserting their relationship to the vanua, but also as the ceremonial and spiritual authority, a role recognized most visibly where permission or forgiveness are required to further develop the urban landscape. The persistence of the Suvavou community in Suva highlights the "intricacy of identity reconfiguration, which is deeply spiritually linked to the ancestral territory, and the new interactions in plural-heterogeneous settings circumscribed by always-evolving cities" (Brablec and Canessa, introduction, this volume).

Secondly, alongside Indigenous rootedness, iTaukei migration inward to the city has been continual since Suva's foundation. Despite legislation to limit Indigenous presence in the city and place Indigenous Fijians instead in an "authentic" village setting, iTaukei found in Suva new opportunities and identities that incorporated the urban. To some chiefs, these individuals may have been "at back of, or beyond, the law," but they were foundational to the cosmopolitanism of Suva from its early years.[42] Though Pacific cities did not predate colonialism, they have consistently evolved in ways that the colonial (and indeed postcolonial) state struggled to control, as exhibited by the constant anxiety surrounding the residents of All Nations Street living, trading, and socializing in Suva since its foundation. Indigenous Fijians thus have deep roots in the city and longstanding routes to the city: urban indigeneity has been part of Indigenous identity and experience negotiated from the nineteenth century, if only recognized by scholars and policymakers in the late twentieth century. The roots in and routes to Suva suggest the need for deeper histories that incorporate the continuation of Indigenous worldviews, identities, and experiences in urban spaces.

Acknowledgments

Vinaka vakalevu to the team at the National Archives of Fiji, Dr. Apo Aporosa and Dr. Nic Halter for insightful feedback, the writing zui and book reviewers for helpful suggestions, and to the editors for their support in the research and writing of this chapter despite pandemic delays. The research was supported by the Marsden Fund (contract UOW2012).

Notes

1. On this binary more generally, see Peters and Andersen (2013), especially the introduction; Porter and Yiftachel (2017); Gagné and Trépied (2016); Jolly and Thomas (1992); and Jolly (1992).
2. On British imperialism, city building, and legacies, see Home (2013); and Jacobs (1996). For other British colonial towns and cities in Oceania, see Moore (2019); Ralston (1977); Rodman (2001); Goddard (2010); and Spoehr (1963). On

comparative experiences of French Pacific colonial cities, see also Dussy (2012); and Dussy and Wittersheim (2013).

3. UN Habitat (2012); and Phillips and Keen (2016); Fiji Bureau of Statistics (2018).
4. Purser, quoted in UNESCO World Heritage Nomination for Levuka, https://whc.unesco.org/uploads/nominations/1399.pdf.
5. As Damon Salesa (2014) notes, history as an academic discipline has not been a welcoming space for Indigenous historians despite significant historical knowledge and practices.
6. For a genealogy of anthropological interest in urban Melanesia since the 1960s, see Lindstrom and Jourdan (2017).
7. For example, see Spoehr (1963); Bakker and Davis (1986); Chandra (1996); and Connell and Lea (2002). On similar erasure in Pacific Rim settler colonies, see Edmonds (2010), especially the introduction; and Thrush (2009).
8. Other cities have recieved more attention, for example: Dussy (2012); Goddard (2005); Moore (2019); and Williams (2015).
9. On the coups and ethnic relationships more generally, see Lal and Pretes (2008). See also Dunham and Kaplan (2001); and Norton (1977).
10. The Fijian Affairs (Amendment) Decree 2010 replaced references to *Native* or *Fijian* (when referring to Indigenous Fijians) with *iTaukei* in all legislation, while under the 2013 Constitution, the term *Fijian* encompasses all citizens.
11. For a general history of Fiji, see Scarr (1984); and Lal (1992).
12. On social hierarchy and organization in the region more generally, see the classic text by Marshall D. Sahlins (1963), alongside a critique of its limits by Bronwen Douglas (1979).
13. Gordon also published various papers and correspondence on his time in Fiji, which he felt was his most interesting post (Lord Stanmore 1897–1912).
14. For general histories covering this period and its legacy, see Legge (1958); France (1969); Bain (1988); and Nicole (2010).
15. Native Affairs Ordinance (No. 35 of 1876), Fiji Certified Copies of Acts 1875–80, CO 84/1, NAK; and Native Regulations No. 1 of 1877 (for the better administration of provincial affairs) and No. 2 of 1877 (respecting courts), Fiji Government (1883), 3–15; Section IV–Native Affairs, Fiji Colonial Report No. 848 (Report for 1914), Fiji Colonial Reports 1905–1920, National Archives of Fiji (NAF), provides an overview of the administrative and judicial organization created by this ordinance.
16. Copies of the discussions and resolutions of the Bose Vakaturaga annual meetings are held in the National Archives of Fiji (NAF).
17. See especially "Proceedings of the Native Council or Council of Chiefs," September 1875, NAF.
18. See Australian Agency for International Development (2008, 4) for a comparative of land tenure systems in the Pacific Islands. By contrast, Indigenous peoples in other parts of the region, such as Aotearoa New Zealand and Hawai'i,

experienced settler colonialism, with the extensive and rapid dispossession of land that more closely parallels colonial processes in the Americas.

19. Australian Agency for International Development (2008); see map of land tenure in Greater Suva in Phillips and Keen (2016, 5).
20. On Islanders in the labor trade, see for example, Shlomowitz (1986).
21. See Brij Lal, particularly (2000), which compiles his various essays on plantation life; Gillion (1962), especially chap. six; Ali ([1979] 2004); and Naidu (2004).
22. J. W. B. Money, quoted in Kelly (2003, 88). As noted, the colonial era migrations and divisions have flowed into contemporary politics, including multiple coups since 1987, a recent history not covered in the chapter; see work by Brij Lal.
23. Quoted in Schutz (1978, 8). Smythe suggested this as early as 1861. See also Gorrie (1882–83).
24. John Mitchell (2020), quoting 1959 article by Colman Wall.
25. Judge Sosefo Inoke, in Kanakana and Others v. State [2010] FJHC 563; HBC116.1999S (December 22, 2010), http://www.paclii.org/cgi-bin/sinodisp/fj/cases/FJHC/2010/563.html.
26. Kanakana v. Attorney General [2012] FJCA 24; Misc15.2011 (March 30, 2012), http://www.paclii.org/fj/cases/FJCA/2012/24.html.
27. It is unclear if these are unrelated or the same incidents.
28. "Tui Suva Performs Bridge Ceremony," *Fiji Times*, March 19, 1991.
29. Quoted in Sikeli Qounadovu (2019a); see also Qounadovu (2019b). Translations from the original, which include the Fijian and English as quoted.
30. The impact of measles and flu epidemics on different communities likely also affected the shifting demographics over the late nineteenth and early twentieth centuries.
31. "Fire at Suva," *Sydney Morning Herald*, February 12, 1923, 9.
32. As Nicholas Thomas (1994, 108) states, "What the authorities understood of customary arrangements tended, predictably, to be inflected by the interests of whomever happened to be their informants": the appointed village, district, and provincial chiefs, especially of Bau and the east coast of Viti Levu.
33. Buli Buresaga, Rewa Provincial Council Minutes, 1908, quoted in Steel (2011, 180).
34. Mafi (Native Magistrate), September 29, 1875, "Proceedings of the Native Council or Council of Chiefs," Draiba, Ovalau, September 1875, NAF.
35. December 5 and 9, 1876, "Proceedings of the Native Council or Council of Chiefs," Waikava, Vanua Levu, November–December 1876, NAF.
36. Supreme Court Criminal Sittings Case 15/1884, NAF; Stevens 2022.
37. For example, in one month: "Local and General News," *Fiji Times*, January 8, 1924; "Police Court," *Fiji Times* January 14, 1924; "Larceny: Fijian Takes Bicycle," *Fiji Times*, January 17, 1924.
38. "Suva Ablaze," *Sun* (Sydney), February 11, 1923, 2; "The Blaze in Suva: Additional Details," *Brisbane Courier*, Friday, February 23, 1923, 7.

39. Jack Staff [pseud.], "All Nations Street: Suva's Old Landmark Gone." *Daily Telegraph* (Sydney), March 3, 1923, 14.
40. "Visit to Suva," *Otago Daily Times*, May 11, 1935, 22.
41. Albert Lee, "Historical Notes on the City of Suva with Particular Reference to the Central Business District," 1974, NAF.
42. Roko Tui Ba and Yasawa, September 22, 1875, "Proceedings of the Native Council or Council of Chiefs," Draiba, Ovalau, September 1875, NAF.

References

Newspapers

Brisbane Courier.
Daily Telegraph.
Fiji Times.
Otago Daily Times.
Sun (Sydney).
Sydney Morning Herald.

National Archives of Fiji (NAF)

Colonial Reports.
Proceedings of the Native Council.
Supreme Court Criminal Sittings.

National Archives, Kew London (NAK)

CO 84/1 Fiji Certified Copies of Acts, 1875–1880.

Published Sources

Ali, Ahmed. (1979) 2004. *Girmit: Indian Indenture Experience in Fiji*. Suva: Fiji Museum.

Australian Agency for International Development. 2008. *Making Land Work*. Vol. 1, *Reconciling Customary Land and Development*. Canberra: AusAID.

Bain, 'Atu. 1988. "A Protective Labour Policy? An Alternative Interpretation of Early Colonial Labour Policy in Fiji." *Journal of Pacific History* 23 (2): 119–13.

Bakker, Solrun, and Michael M. Davis. 1986. *Fijians in Town*. Suva: USP.

Banivanua Mar, Tracey. 2016. *Decolonisation and the Pacific: Indigenous Globalisation and the Ends of Empire*. Cambridge: Cambridge University Press.

Bayliss-Smith, Tim, Richard Bedford, Harold Brookfield, and Marc Latham. 1988. *Islands, Islanders and the World: The Colonial and Post-Colonial Experience of Eastern Fiji*. Cambridge: Cambridge University Press.

Bertram, Geoff. 2006. "Introduction: The MIRAB Model in the Twenty-First Century." *Asia Pacific Viewpoint* 47 (1): 1–13.

Bertram, I. G., and R. F. Watters. 1985. "The MIRAB Economy in South Pacific Microstates." *Pacific Viewpoint* 26 (2): 497–519.

Brown, Laurence. 2006. "Inter-Colonial Migration and the Refashioning of Indentured Labour: Arthur Gordon in Trinidad, Mauritius and Fiji." In *Colonial Lives across the British Empire: Imperial Careering in the Long Nineteenth Century*, edited by David Lambert and Alan Lester, 204–27. Cambridge: Cambridge University Press.

Chambers, Kenneth. 2008. "*Ratu Epeli Kanakana v A-G for Fiji* (The Suvavou Case): Blending Equitable Relief with Judicial Review." *Journal of South Pacific Law* 12 (1): 111.

Chandra, Rajesh. 1996. "Urbanisation in Fiji, 1976–1986: A Preliminary Analysis." *Journal of Pacific Studies* 19 (1): 23–45.

Chapman, J. K. 1964. *The Career of Arthur Hamilton Gordon*. Toronto: University of Toronto Press.

Connell, John. 2003. "Regulation of Space in the Contemporary Postcolonial Pacific City." *Asia Pacific Viewpoint* 44 (3): 243–57.

Connell, John, and John P. Lea. 2002. *Urbanisation in the Island Pacific: Towards Sustainable Development*. London: Routledge.

Danford, Iva. 2019. "Two mataqali of Suvavou Village Supports Govt in Construction of Indian Embassy at Botanical Garden." *Fijivillage*, February 26, 2019. https://fijivillage.com/news/Two-mataqali-of-Suvavou-Village-supports-govt-in-construction-of-Indian-Embassy-at-Botanical-Garden-59ks2r.

DeLoughrey, Elizabeth. 2007. *Routes and Roots: Navigating Caribbean and Pacific Island Literatures*. Honolulu: University of Hawai'i Press.

Dening, Greg. 1980. *Islands and Beaches: Discourse on a Silent Land: Marquesas, 1774–1880*. Carlton, Australia: Melbourne University Press.

Derrick, R. A. 1953. "The Removal of the Capital to Suva (Read 19 July 1943)." *Transactions and Proceedings of the Fiji Society of Science and Industry* 2 (1): 203–9. Suva: Fiji Society of Science and Industry.

Diaz, Vicente M., and J. Kehaulani Kauanui. 2001. "Native Pacific Cultural Studies on the Edge." *Contemporary Pacific* 13 (2): 315–42.

Donnison, Henry. 1880. *Fiji: The Suva Land Quest, by One of the Party*. Melbourne: Stilwell. http://nla.gov.au/nla.obj-52759807.

Douglas, Bronwen. 1979. "Rank, Power, Authority: A Reassessment of Traditional Leadership in South Pacific Societies." *Journal of Pacific History* 14 (1): 2–27.

———. 2006. "Slippery Word, Ambiguous Praxis: 'Race' and Late-18th-Century Voyagers in Oceania." *Journal of Pacific History* 41 (1): 1–29.

———. 2009. "In the Event: Indigenous Countersigns and the Ethnohistory of Voyaging." In *Oceanic Encounters: Exchange, Desire, Violence*, edited by Margaret Jolly, Serge Tcherkézoff, and Darrell Tryon, 175–98. Canberra: Australian National University Press.

Dunham, John, and Martha Kaplan. 2001. *Represented Communities: Fiji and World Decolonization*. Chicago: University of Chicago Press.

Dussy, Dorothée. 2012 *Nouméa: ville océanienne? S'appropier la ville*. Paris: Karthala.

Dussy, Dorothée, and Eric Wittersheim, eds. 2013. *Villes invisibles: anthropologie urbaine du Pacifique*. Paris: L'Harmattan.

Dvorak, Greg. 2018. *Coral and Concrete: Remembering Kwajalein Atoll between Japan, America, and the Marshall Islands*. Honolulu: University of Hawai'i Press.

Edmonds, Penny. 2010. *Urbanizing Frontiers: Indigenous Peoples and Settlers in 19th-Century Pacific Rim Cities*. Vancouver: University of British Columbia Press.

Fiji Bureau of Statistics. 2008. "Census 2007 Results: Population Size, Growth, Structure and Distribution." *Statistical News*, no. 45.

———. 2018. "2017 Population and Housing Census." *Fiji Bureau of Statistics Release No. 1*, January 5, 2018.

Fiji Government. 1883. *Regulations of the Native Regulation Board: 1877–1882*. London: Harrison and Sons.

———. 1914. *Ordinances of the Colony of Fiji*. Suva: Fiji Government Printer.

France, Peter. 1969. *The Charter of the Land: Custom and Colonisation in Fiji*. Melbourne and London: Oxford University Press.

Gagné, Natacha, and Benoît Trépied. 2016. "Introduction to Special Issue Colonialism, Law, and the City: The Politics of Urban Indigeneity." *City & Society* 28 (1): 8–22.

Gillion, K. L. 1962. *Fiji's Indian Migrants: A History to the End of Indenture in 1920*. Melbourne: Oxford University Press.

Goddard, Michael. 2005. *Unseen City: Anthropological Perspectives on Port Moresby, Papua New Guinea*. Honolulu: University of Hawai'i Press.

———, ed. 2010. *Villagers and the City: Melanesian Experiences of Port Moresby, Papua New Guinea*. Oxford: Sean Kingston.

Gorrie, John. 1882–83. "Fiji as It Is." *Proceedings of the Royal Colonial Institute*, no. 14, 160–85.

Gulliver, Katrina. 2014. "City as the Site of the Other: The (Dis)Ordered Colonial City." In *Cityscapes in History: Creating the Urban Experience*, edited by Katrina Gulliver and Heléna Tóth, 101–14. New York: Routledge.

Halter, Nicholas. 2020. "Tourists Fraternising in 1930s Fiji." *Journal of Tourism History* 12 (1): 27–47.

Hau'ofa, Epeli. 1994. "Our Sea of Islands." *Contemporary Pacific* 6 (1): 148–61.

Home, Robert. 2013. *Of Planting and Planning: The Making of British Colonial Cities*. 2nd ed. New York: Routledge.

Howe, Kerry. 2000. *Nature, Culture, and History: The "Knowing" of Oceania*. Honolulu: University of Hawai'i Press.

iTaukei Land Trust Board. 2018. "The Creation of TLTB." https://www.tltb.com.fj/About-Us/Back-In-Time.

Jacobs, Jane M. 1996. *Edge of Empire: Postcolonialism and the City*. London: Routledge.

———. 2012. "Commentary: Property and Propriety: (Re)Making the Space of Indigeneity in Australian Cities." *Postcolonial Studies* 15 (2): 145.

Jolly, Margaret. 1992. "Specters of Inauthenticity." *Contemporary Pacific* 4 (1): 49–72.

Jolly, Margaret, and Nicholas Thomas. 1992. "The Politics of Tradition in the Pacific." *Oceania*, no. 62, 241–48.

Kelly, John D. 2003. "Gordon Was No Amateur: Imperial Legal Strategies in the Colonisation of Fiji." In *Law and Empire in the Pacific: Fiji and Hawaii*, edited by Sally Engle Merry and Donald Brenneis, 61–100. Santa Fe: School of American Research Press.

Kiddle, Rebecca. 2021. "Aotearoa's Towns and Cities Have Always Been Indigenous Places." In *Kia Whakanuia te Whenua*, edited by Carolyn Hill. Pukekohe, New Zealand: Mary Egan Publishing.

Lal, Brij. 1992. *Broken Waves: A History of the Fiji Islands in the Twentieth Century*. Honolulu: University of Hawai'i Press.

———. 2000. *Chalo Jahaji: On a Journey through Indenture in Fiji*. Canberra and Suva: Australian National University and Fiji Museum.

Lal, Brij, Doug Munro, and Edward Beechert. 1993. *Plantation Workers: Resistance and Accommodation*. Honolulu: University of Hawai'i Press.

Lal, Brij, and Michael Pretes, eds. 2008. *Coup: Reflection on the Political Crisis in Fiji*. Canberra: Australian National University E-Press.

Leckie, Jacqueline. 2002. "Return to Nukulau: The Troubled Waters of Ethno-Nationalism in Fiji." In *Politics of Indigeneity in the South Pacific: Recent Problems of Identity in Oceania*, edited by E. Kolig and H. Mückler, 119–42. Hamburg, Germany: LIT Verlag.

———. 2020. *Colonizing Madness: Asylum and Community in Fiji*. Honolulu: University of Hawai'i Press.

Leckie, Jacqueline, and Alumita Durutalo. 2016. "Kai Merika! Fijian Children of American Servicemen." In *Mothers' Darlings of the South Pacific: The Children of Indigenous Women and U.S. Servicemen, World War II*, edited by Judith A. Bennett and Angela Wanhalla, 183–201. Honolulu: University of Hawai'i Press.

Legge, J. D. 1958. *Britain in Fiji, 1858–1880*. London: Macmillan.

Lindstrom, Lamont, and Christine Jourdan. 2017. "Urban Melanesia." *Journal de la Société des Océanistes*, nos. 144–145, 5–22.

McHugh, Mrs. J. J. 1943. "Recollections of Early Suva." *Fiji Society of Science and Industry*, July 19, 1943, 210–14.

Mitchell, John. 2020. "150th anniversary: The Long Line of Suva Chiefsk." *Fiji Times*, June 8, 2020.

Miyazaki, Hirokazu. 2004. *The Method of Hope, Anthropology, Philosophy, and Fijian Knowledge*. Stanford: Stanford University Press.

———. 2005. "From Sugar Cane to 'Swords': Hope and the Extensibility of the Gift in Fiji." *Journal of the Royal Anthropological Institute* 11 (2): 284–86.

Moore, Clive. 2019. *Tulagi: Pacific Outpost of British Empire*. Canberra: Australian National University Press.

Nabobo-Baba, Unaisi. 2006. *Knowing & Learning: An Indigenous Fijian Approach.* Suva: University of the South Pacific.

Naidu, Vijay. 2004. *The Violence of Indenture in Fiji.* Lautoka: Fiji Institute of Applied Studies.

Nayacakalou, R. R. 1963. "The Urban Fijians of Suva." In Spoehr 1963, 33–41.

———. 1985. *Leadership in Fiji.* Suva and Melbourne: Institute of Pacific Studies at University of the South Pacific in association with Oxford University Press.

Newbury, Colin. 2006. "*Bose Vakauraga*: Fiji's Great Council of Chiefs, 1875–2000." *Pacific Studies* 29 (1/2): 82–127.

———. 2010. *Patronage and Politics in the Victorian Empire: The Personal Governance of Sir Arthur Hamilton Gordon.* Amherst, N.Y.: Cambria Books.

———. 2011. "Biography and Patronage in Crown Colony Governorships: Sir Arthur Hamilton Gordon and 'Personal Administration.'" *Journal of Historical Biography,* no. 9, 1–36.

Nicole, Robert. 2010. *Disturbing History: Resistance in Early Colonial Fiji.* Honolulu: University of Hawai'i Press.

Norton, Robert. 1977. *Race & Politics in Fiji.* New York: St. Martin's Press.

Overton, John. 1989 *Land and Differentiation in Rural Fiji.* Canberra: National Centre for Development Studies, Australian National University.

Paterson, Lachy. 2018. "Pāora Tūhaere's Voyage to Rarotonga." In *Indigenous Mobilities: Across and Beyond the Antipodes,* edited by Rachel Standfield, 233–54. Canberra: Australia National University E-Press.

Peters, Evelyn Joy, and Chris Andersen, eds. 2013. *Indigenous in the City: Contemporary Identities and Cultural Innovation.* Vancouver: University of British Columbia Press.

Phillips, T., and M. Keen. 2016. *Sharing the City: Urban Growth and Governance in Suva, Fiji.* State, Society & Governance in Melanesia Discussion Paper 6. Canberra: Australian National University.

Porter, Libby, and Oren Yiftachel. 2017. "Urbanizing Settler-Colonial Studies: Introduction to the Special Issue." *Settler Colonial Studies* 9 (2): 177–86.

Qounadovu, Sikeli. 2019a. "Tui Suva Not in Favour." *Fiji Times,* February 11, 2019.

———. 2019b. "The 'Idle Land'—Revisiting Suva, Part 1." *Fiji Times,* March 3, 2019.

Ralston, Caroline. 1977. *Grass Huts and Warehouses: Pacific Beach Communities of the Nineteenth Century.* Canberra: Australian National University Press.

Ravuvu, Asesela. 1983. *Vaka i Taukei: The Fijian Way of Life.* Suva: Institute of Pacific Studies at University of the South Pacific.

Rodman, Margaret. 2001. *Houses Far from Home: British Colonial Space in the New Hebrides.* Honolulu: University of Hawai'i Press.

Sahlins, Marshall D. 1963. "Poor Man, Rich Man, Big-Man, Chief: Political Types in Melanesia and Polynesia." *Comparative Studies in Society and History* 5 (3): 285–303.

Salesa, Damon. 2008. "Contested Oceans" in "Review Forum: *The People of the Sea*," *Journal of Pacific History* 43 (1): 111–124.

———. 2014. "The Pacific in Indigenous Times." In *Pacific Histories: Ocean, Land, People*, edited by David Armitage and Allison Bashford, 31–52. London: Palgrave Macmillan.

Samson, Jane. 1998. *Imperial Benevolence: Making British Authority in the Pacific Islands*. Honolulu: University of Hawai'i Press.

Scarr, Deryck. 1968. *Fragments of Empire: A History of Western Pacific High Commission, 1877–1914*. Canberra: Australian National University.

———. 1984. *Fiji, a Short History*. Sydney: George Allen & Unwin.

———. 2001. *A History of the Pacific Islands: Passages through Tropical Time*. Abingdon: Routledge.

Schutz, Albert. 1978. *Suva: A History and Guide*. Sydney: Pacific Publications.

Shlomowitz, Ralph. 1986. "The Fiji Labor Trade in Comparative Perspective, 1864–1914." *Pacific Studies* 9 (3): 108–52.

Smith, Linda Tuhiwai. 1999. *Decolonizing Methodologies*. Dunedin: University of Otago Press.

Spate, O. H. K. 1959. *The Fijian People: Economic Problems and Prospects: A Report*. Suva: Government Press.

Spoehr, Alexander, ed. 1963. *Pacific Port Towns and Cities*. Honolulu: Bishop Museum Press.

Stanmore, Lord. 1897–1912. *Fiji: Records of Private and Public Life, 1875–1880*. 4 vols. Edinburgh: R. and R. Clark.

Steel, Frances. 2011. *Oceania under Steam: Sea Transport and the Cultures of Colonialism, c. 1870–1914*. Manchester: Manchester University Press.

Stevens, Kate. 2022. "Supreme Court Stories: Narrating Violence in Suva Streets and Homes." In *Suva Stories: A History of the Capital of Fiji*, edited by Nicholas Halter, 229–46. Canberra: Australian National University Press.

Susu, Aqela. 2019. "Suvavou Villagers Intend to Meet Government to Reconsider Plans." *Fiji Times*, February 25, 2019.

Tarte, Daryl. 2014. *Fiji: A Place Called Home*. Canberra: Australian National University Press.

Thomas, Nicholas. 1994. *Colonialism's Culture: Anthropology, Travel and Government*. Princeton: Princeton University Press.

Thrush, Coll. 2009. *Native Seattle: Histories from the Crossing-Over Place*. Seattle: University of Washington Press.

———. 2017. "Placing the City: Crafting Urban Indigenous Histories." In *Sources and Methods in Indigenous Studies*, edited by Chris Andersen and Jean M. O'Brien, 110–17. New York: Routledge.

UN Habitat. 2012. "Fiji: Greater Suva Urban Profile." http://www.fukuoka.unhabitat.org/projects/fiji/pdf/Fiji_Greater_Suva_Urban_Profile.pdf.

Wall, Colman. 1996. "Historical Notes on Suva." *Domodomo* 10 (2): 28–39.

Ward, Albert E. 1953. "Old Land Marks of Suva (Read on 19 July 1943)." *Transactions and Proceedings of the Fiji Society of Science and Industry* 2 (1): 215–17. Suva: Fiji Society of Science and Industry.

Ward, R. Gerard. 1969. "Land Use and Land Alienation in Fiji to 1885." *Journal of Pacific History* 4 (1): 3–25.

Wendt, Albert. 1976. "Towards a New Oceania." *Mana Review* 1 (1): 49–60.

Whitelaw, James. 1966. "People, Land and Government in Suva, Fiji." PhD thesis, Australian National University.

Williams, Melissa Matutina. 2015. *Panguru and the City: Kāinga Tahi, Kāinga Rua.* Wellington: Bridget Williams Books.

CHAPTER THREE

Making Money and Ends Meet

Racialization, Work, and Gender among Bolivian Market Vendors

AIKO IKEMURA AMARAL

Doña Saturnina sells sweets and refreshments from a small stand nested in a sea of car accessories and sound systems that dominates this part of La 16, a street market in El Alto, Bolivia. Saturnina's was one of the over ten thousand stands that popped up on Thursdays and Sundays, drawing in thousands more visitors. Business was yet to pick up on that particular morning and I was the only person around. But Doña Saturnina did not stop for a second, tidying up her products before more promising customers arrived. We chatted about the market and her activities, and I asked her about what she felt was the importance of her work for herself and her family. Unexpectedly, to me, her answer was, "I don't work." It was not her duty to do so, she added, noting that "a man provides for the household while a woman takes care of the house." Seeing how busy she was, I asked her if she did not think she was also "providing for the household" with her business at the market. She stopped for a bit. "Well . . . my father handed this stand over to me, so I have to carry on with it. Everyone needs to help with what they've got."

Doña Saturnina was one of the many market women I met during my research at three Bolivian urban street markets—Kantuta and Coimbra, located in São Paulo, Brazil, and La 16, in El Alto, Bolivia. Like her, many of these women could be considered Indians by others—most were born in the rural areas of Bolivia and could speak an Indigenous language—although none of them presented themselves as Indigenous. Having migrated from rural areas toward a city in Bolivia or abroad, they found a place in the popular economy where they all acknowledged they worked hard. Yet Doña Saturnina was not the only one who presented her activities at the market as nonwork. How does migration to an urban milieu—and the racialized, gendered, and classed hierarchies that operate in these spaces—affect these women's relationship to the activities they perform in the markets? Answering this question, this chapter explores the gendered effects of the urbanization of indigeneity on how labor and its outcomes are understood by these women.

Introduction: Ambiguous Intersections

Until the late twentieth century, Bolivia was largely a rural country. In the 1980s, however, the combined pressures of climate change over subsistence agriculture and the effects of neoliberal reforms over the role of the state and markets unleashed dramatic changes to the temporalities and directions of migration, both domestically and internationally. These processes drove a rapid urbanization in Bolivia, while increasing longer-term, urban-directed international migratory flows, especially to neighboring countries. Once in the cities, the popular economy offered a leeway to make money and ends meet when faced with increasingly precarious urban labor markets. This trend continued during the governments of Evo Morales (2005–2019), despite the economic boom of the Pink Tide, changing the face not only of cities but also of the practices and identities hitherto largely associated with rurality, including indigeneity.

Throughout the Andes, both historically and presently, popular markets—as well as domestic work—have served as crucial spaces for the incorporation of Indigenous women in the material and symbolic spaces of the city. Yet this form of urban incorporation has come with specific caveats for women joining the labor market. On the one hand, mobility to urban centers imparted a certain rupture with Indigenous communities, identities, and practices, and was seen as leading to a process of acculturation of Indigenous migrant women. On the other hand, however, that both market vending and domestic work have been activities racialized as nonwhite from the outset also contributed to racialization of the women who perform these chores, making them more Indian than other urban dwellers. In being urban, Indigenous market women were thus said to be somewhere in between the poles of the superposing dualities that constitute the imagery of the Andes: Indigenous/non-Indigenous, rural/urban, traditional/modern (Seligmann 1989; see also Albro 2010; Buechler and Buechler 1996; Peredo 2001; Weismantel 2001).

This in-betweenness is also reflected by the stereotypical representation of market women as cholas. Much like the term *indio* (Indian), *cholo* emerged as a colonial category employed to classify the population in the Americas and was used to refer to individuals of "mixed-blood" deemed closer to indios than mestizos, also a mixed-race category for those who were closer to Europeans and their descendants. Processes of miscegenation—or *mestizaje*—however, were not just products of sexual intercourse but also the result of cultural exchanges and imposition, as well as migration (Radcliffe 1990; Rivera Cusicanqui 1996; 2010b). In many Latin American contexts, *mestizaje* has been deployed as a mechanism of elimination via the assimilation of Indigenous peoples; although, as Poets (2021, 278) argued, miscegenation also served as a site "of indigenous resurgence, where knowledge and ways of being were recovered and (re-)invented" against hegemonic state practice and discourse. In Bolivia, *mestizaje* and migration have from colonial times served emancipatory purposes and served as a survival strategy for Indigenous women, as Rivera Cusicanqui (2010b) has shown. As a result, rather than being effaced by processes of social and spatial mobility, indigeneity persists through—transforming and being transformed by—urbanization and miscegenation.

As such, migration to urban spaces made cholas out of Indigenous women both to enable their inclusion into the urban centers and as a means of distinguishing them from their rural counterparts. This is also represented by what became cholas' distinctive garment—the voluminous, multilayered *polleras* (skirts), in particular. Initially used only by women of European descent, the polleras have been almost exclusively associated with cholas since the nineteenth century, and they were rarely seen in the countryside until at least the mid-twentieth century (Barragán 1990; Canessa 2012, 47). Although polleras and the distinctive derby hat used by cholas have since been adopted both as costumes in national celebratory festivities and by rural Indigenous women—both of which emphasize the garment's representation as an indicator of Indigenous "tradition"—they were originally urban, working-class markers. Nowadays the quality and make of the garment (the type and meterage of fabric and the number of layers) and accessories (such as the material used for the shawls, the type and brand of the hats, and the exuberance of the jewelry) continue to be important markers of distinction between urban cholas and rural Indigenous women (see figs. 3.1, 3.2, 3.3).

FIGURE 3.1 Dancers wearing the full chola costume (multilayered polleras, shawls, and derby hats) in the celebrations of the 16 de Julio, which is organized and performed by traders at the eponymous El Alto market. Photograph by the author, 2016.

FIGURE 3.2 Polleras are also everyday, working-class garments, currently used by both rural and urban Indigenous women. Here, low-cost, simple polleras are being sold at La 16. Photograph by the author, 2016.

FIGURE 3.3 Derby hats, gold and silver jewelery, and alpaca shawls signal the wealth of a well-faring urban chola. These were all secondhand items sold at more accessible prices at La 16. Photograph by the author, 2016.

If their sartorial distinctiveness currently makes them stand out among an otherwise dressed urban crowd and makes them look more "traditional," the intermediary position between the idealized Western(ized) city and the Indigenous rural community is also reflected in the myriad descriptions of the chola in the literature: "urban indigenous" (Bigenho 2006), "Indian mestizas" (de la Cadena 2002), "neither 'indio' nor 'mestizo'" (Albro 2010), "at once Indian and white" (Weismantel 2001), and even "hybrids" (Tassi 2010). In fact, cholas could be best described by Silvia Rivera Cusicanqui's (2010a, 70) notion of *ch'ixi*, or the "parallel coexistence of multiple cultural differences that do not merge into another completely [*no se funden*] but instead antagonize and complement each other." The *ch'ixi* then refers both to the very ambivalence embedded in processes of miscegenation that, as noted, have emerged as spaces for claiming urban indigeneity and to reinstating Indigenous identity in the city, while also working as a hegemonic practice and discourse of acculturation and elimination of indigeneity through urbanization. Rather than hybrids—where the encounter of opposing poles gives rise to a new, third homogenous subjectivity—cholas and, I would argue to a certain extent, all the market women I met in my research are characterized by this ambiguity. That is to say, market women's subjectivity simultaneously embodies and rejects the dualities inaugurated by the colonial encounter and reproduced by processes of Indigenous urbanization today.

This ambiguity is also reflected in how the literature has addressed the underlying structures that characterize market women's subaltern incorporation into the urban labor market. On the one hand, inequalities faced by these women have been described as a product of the continuation of traditional gender roles from rural Indigenous communities into the city—where "progress" toward a modern economy would eventually catapult women into more equal positions simply as laborers. On the other hand, the issue has been seen as one of the capitalist economy; Indigenous communities, in which gender relations were based in principles of complementarity, were less patriarchal than the urban, capitalist sexual division of labor, which often presents women's work as nonwork.[1] Between the different diagnostics of needing to decolonize or modernize how women's work in urban contexts is understood, the overarching devaluation of market vending seems to rely on the gendered nature of the activity.

Gender, however, must be understood in relation to other forms of exclusion that reenact colonial hierarchies through contemporary inequalities in the labor market. Work and its outcomes are structured by these intersectional vectors of power (Collins 2000)—gender, race, and class—creating complex and mutually reinforcing forms of segregation. These hierarchies are also fundamentally spatial, specifically as regards the rural/urban duality that is central to dominant notions of indigeneity. In this vein, internal colonialism continues to inform the (re)configuration of these hierarchies long after formal colonialism is gone (Rivera Cusicanqui 2010b). This is true not only in relation to broader structures of power but also through the intimate spaces of everyday life. As will be discussed below, as colonial hierarchies are internalized, they are also expressed in how market women assess their own labor and their outcomes in very ambivalent ways.

In this chapter, I employ an intersectional perspective to explore the ambiguities that underpin market vendors' understandings of their activities at the market as work or, conversely, nonwork. Previous research on gender has highlighted both the racialized and the racializing dimensions of market women's positions, but the articulation between these two dimensions still deserves further attention. Market vending has been described as contributing to make "women more Indian" (de la Cadena 1995). And as Bolivians migrate abroad, they also become "more Indian," as they are incorporated into a precarious labor market of feminized and racialized occupations like garment manufacture (Ikemura Amaral 2022). But market women's own relation with indigeneity is much less clear-cut. Urban markets operate as venues for economic ascent, which can be described as cemented on practices and networks from the rural Indigenous communities, or *provincias*, from which produce is procured and so on. Urban markets can also be seen, however, as enabling one's break with these very communities, as women vendors adopt and are put into complex, intersectional positions that are often considered distant from indigeneity. Socio-spatial mobility—rural-urban migration, international migration, and higher socioeconomic status—and work itself thus constantly change these women's position, thereby transforming their relation to indigeneity.

I draw on Silvia Rivera Cusicanqui's (2013) notion of *ch'ixi* to describe this "meat-grinding" process (2013) enacted by migration and by the products of these women's success (or lack thereof) as traders in the markets. Market women's work is often marginalized, but hardly ever marginal for themselves, their families, and their broader communities, providing new life prospects but also subjecting them to new forms of prejudice. This ambiguity is furthermore reflected in how they assess both their activities at the markets and the outcomes (what is work and what does it do to people?) in ways that, informed by urban practices, are simultaneously gendered, classed, and racialized—but also, and mutually, gendering, classing, and racializing.

The ethnographic vignettes used here draw on research carried out between 2015 and 2016 at the three Bolivian street markets mentioned earlier—although, to safeguard the identity of my interlocutors in the much smaller markets in Brazil, I do not specify the locations where they held business. Following this introduction, I meet market neighbors Rocío, Carmen, and Ramona at La 16, in the second section of this chapter. While none of them present market vending as work, they admire Rocío's labor as a *campesina*—even if this means she lacks the proper urban accolades of a "real" market vendor. While market vending drove them apart from definitions of work based on agricultural labor, the third section dialogues with the notion that "women are more Indian" (de la Cadena 1995), to highlight that the labor performed by market women is devalued (including by themselves) not only because it is feminized but also because of how it is racialized. Returning to Saturnina, I highlight how the work of women racialized as nonwhite is often unaccounted for in idealized representations of womanhood, making market women also "less of a woman." In section four, I meet Margarita, whose constant travels equipped her multiple business ventures in Brazil, building on her ties to her *provincia* back in Bolivia. Contrastingly, in section five, Barbara, whom I also met in São Paulo, underscores how her economic success made her a very different person than those she left behind in the *provincia*.

By referring to my interlocutors as *market women*, I do not mean to imply that they constitute a homogenous group of people or that market vending is a defining feature of their identity for them. In fact, these women had myriad other identities and used a variety of terms to refer to themselves and others around them. For instance, not all self-identified as cholas—in fact, none in Brazil described themselves as such. While a discussion on all the categories employed by market women to describe themselves and others is beyond the scope of this chapter, it is important to underscore that all terms referred to intersectional identities these women held. Some terms were clearly racialized, whereas others were less obviously so. For instance, *campesina* literally means peasant but is mainly used to refer to Indigenous women in ways that highlight how rural origins, class, and race are deeply enmeshed. Others refer to the clothes worn; *mujer de pollera*, or "woman in a pollera," usually refers to chola women, whereas those wearing a dress (*de vestido*) or trousers (*de pantalón*) might refer to mestiza or white women. *Mestiza* itself is a term that combines urban origins with notions of miscegenation, as well as (real or aspired) middle-class status and a claim to nationhood (Canessa 2012; Rivera Cusicanqui 2010b). In this chapter, the terms *Indian* and *india* are also used, although these were not employed by the women I met; rather, I use it here to emphasize its coloniality, where indigeneity emerges as a racialized, often ruralized, identity, which is seen as out of place in the modern urban economy.

Conducting a multisited research also meant that my positionality changed from one context to another. As a non-Indigenous Brazilian woman doing her PhD in the United Kingdom, my experiences of womanhood, my migratory background, and my occasional encounters with discrimination were different from those of these women, and bridging these differences to create some form of rapport was not always straightforward. Doing research was also considered nonwork by my interlocutors, and my privileges as an academic often made me whiter to them than I see myself. Differences notwithstanding, it was possible to forge strong—and sometimes lasting—ties with these women, some of whose stories are discussed below.

Labor Is What Makes a Person

Twice a week, sitting on the back of a packed minibus from La Paz to El Alto, I witnessed the first market stands, with their orange and blue canvasses, emerge as we reached the high point on the highway. From here, it is hard to imagine the full extent of the Feria del 16 Julio. Once inside it, it is even harder to conceive how these stands are assembled here on Thursdays and Sundays only. At points, the extension of La 16, as it is commonly called, meets the horizon. Like many other markets in the Andes, most of the traders are women, the majority of whom are *de* pollera—even if many other traders are wearing trousers, men included. The commodities sold in this market range from the mundane to the extraordinary: from secondhand clothes, foodstuff, and cars to llama fetuses for ritual purposes.

Although I heard multiple stories about the origins of La 16, they are all enmeshed with those of the city around it, El Alto. Located at the intersection of multiple highways connecting La Paz to the rural areas of the country, or *provincias*, El Alto's growth was fueled by processes that contributed to the emptying out of some Indigenous communities. Indigenous peoples were pushed out by climate change, which served to increase the pressure over subsistence agriculture already made less resilient after centuries of land encroachment and territorial reconfiguration in the Andes, and by the dismantling of state mines, which left many unemployed and cash poor in an increasingly monetized economy, but they were also attracted by promises of waged labor in the city. Initially described as a satellite or a dormitory city to the then much bigger La Paz, El Alto's recent migratory background gave this city its distinctive Indigenous face, while its residents built a city of economic and political importance in its own right.[2] Even today, the close relation, and continuous movement, between the *provincia* and El Alto remains a constitutive element of the everyday of La 16.

Most of my visits to this market began with a stop for a long chat with three neighbors–Doña Ramona and Doña Carmen, who sold fleece garments from their two small stands, and Doña Rocío, who sold citruses from a canvas spread on the floor. Our conversation, in Spanish, was peppered with words in Aymara—which I do not speak, and which Ramona rightfully noted as a crucial skill to navigate the market. Ramona and Carmen balanced small derby hats on their heads, while Rocío, otherwise in similar dress as her neighbors, did not. Rocío—the two fleece traders never missed an opportunity to remind me—was a *campesina* and not a bona fide trader and a chola, like themselves. As indicated in the introduction, the make of the hat and the quality of the pollera were key markers of difference, complemented in Rocío's case by the embodied features—such as calluses—of a woman who worked the land.

When Doña Rocío would not show up in La 16, the others commented that she lacked the cultural and economic fluency, as well as the urban skills, required fully to grasp the importance of the role of a "real market vendor." While she commuted to El Alto exclusively on market days, Rocío's main occupation was tending to a small plot of land she owned with her husband, where they produced just about enough for their own subsistence. The vending of citruses—bought from a wholesaler before heading to the market—and her husband's odd jobs provided a small but welcomed additional cash flow. If her lack of urban credentials subjected her to criticism from her colleagues, Doña Rocío, however, was always admired on the basis that she *did work*.

Throughout the Andes, agricultural work plays a central role in the exchanges between Indigenous communities and the animate landscape, through which "humans feed the mountain through agricultural labor and ritual, and the land feeds them crop" (Bold 2017, 120). This is "connected to Andean notions of fertility of work, community and social person in rural areas," where fertility is "seen as created and maintained through a logic of reciprocity, circulation and exchange" (Ødegaard 2008, 255, 242). To "make the earth bear fruit"—borrowing the words of Harris (2000)—is a responsibility shared by men and women, who are required to participate in seeding, harvesting, and husbandry. Complementarity, not equality, dictates a gendered division of labor (Rivera Cusicanqui 2010b) and the overarching principles of social life. This is also reflected by the centrality of the conjugal pairing, or *chacha-warmi*—a composition between the Aymara words *chacha* (man or husband) and *warmi* (woman or wife)—as one of the essential thresholds for achieving full personhood (*jaqi*; Canessa 2012; Maclean 2014, 80). Agricultural labor, therefore, defines a proper person (*jaqi*), while the specific tasks performed are what makes this person a man or a woman (Canessa 2006, 107).

If (agricultural) labor is an essential part of what makes one a *jaqi*, the exploitation of this labor is, by opposition, what defines their Other: the *q'ara*. The word *q'ara*—used in reference to the non-Indigenous, urban-dwelling populations—literally means "bare" or "peeled," effectively portraying white people as stripped of both moral and cultural content (Canessa 2012, 250). The use of this term also emphasizes *q'ara*'s parasitism, feeding on the fruits of Indigenous labor (Iamamoto 2015). The construction of the *q'ara* as the *jaqi*'s alterity bears an important message in terms of both what defines labor and who performs it. "*Q'aras* are despicable," writes Iamamoto (2015, 89), "because they were unable to produce food and, therefore, were dependent on peasant workforce for all their activities." Similarly, the *pishtaco* (or *kharisiri/kharikhari* in Aymara), discussed in detail by Weismantel (2001) and described as the white, male stranger who robs Indigenous peoples of their fat, presents the relation between *q'ara* and *jaqi* as one's arrogation of another's life forces. Reproducing this colonial duality, the *kharikhari* is a representation not only of the colonial exploitation of Indigenous labor—at the fields, in the mines, and in the homes—but also of the expropriation of Indigenous lands and, ultimately, their vitality.

"*Kharikharis* act in the minibuses that connect El Alto to the *provincias*!" I was repeatedly warned. This also served as a reminder that colonial dualities continue to cast a shadow over the continuous movement of people and goods between these rural and urban spaces. El Alto, however, is a *ch'ixi* space, in the sense that it draws on antagonistic and complementary dimensions of indigeneity that coexist in this urbanity. As such, it is constituted simultaneously on the subaltern inclusion of Indigenous peoples in the urban labor market and on Indigenous successes in the very economy that marginalizes them. Reciprocity, circulation, and exchange in kinship relations, as well as gender complementarity, shape the popular economy of El Alto (see also McNelly 2022; Yampara, Mamani, and Calancha 2007). But so do profit-seeking, individualistic entrepreneurial logics and transnational economic connections that tie the city and La 16 to ports in Chile and manufactures in China (Tassi 2017). In order to succeed, market vendors need to be well versed in these different grammars (see also Buechler and Buechler 1996; Seligmann 1989). Rocío's implied inability to become a "proper" market vendor in the eyes of her neighbors highlights the coexistence of these opposing economic rationales, which are enabled by processes of Indigenous urbanization—or, in fact, their *ch'ixi* economic form. Which is to say, the *ch'ixi* character of Indigenous urbanization implies that it can only occur when it simultaneously draws upon rural Indigenous practices and leverages them in ways that, at face value, would deny their indigeneity, holding these elements in tension in the urban context.

But these coexisting contradictions are also reflected by how these women define what is or is not work. In my conversations with Ramona, Rocío, and Carmen, market vending was never described as work. It was, however, a very different activity from others labeled by them as nonwork—my research included—all of which could be seen as *q'ara*, middle-class, and urbanite. Yet none of the market vendors I met could ever be considered *q'ara*. All but a few—whether cholas, like Carmen and Ramona, or not, like Saturnina and the women I met in Brazil—were first-generation rural-urban migrants, and some of them, like Doña Rocío, split their times between the city and the countryside. Market vending, after all, is not a *q'ara* activity—even if it was seen to take these women further away from what makes one a *jaqi*. Urbanization brought them closer to other forms of laboring and understanding labor.

More Indian, Less of a Woman

In her famous essay about a peasant community near Cusco, de la Cadena (1995) presented a critical gender perspective on the racialized effects of the work performed by rural Andean men and women. Land tenure, family structures, and a sexual division of labor were presented as central to distinguishing what was or was not labor. Strenuous agricultural work (using the plough, in particular), was the unquestionable marker of work in the rural context, while in the city, work was defined in terms of enabling the acquisition of mestizo skills—which could yield both economic and political gains. The common denominator between the two activities was that they were performed by men. Women, by contradistinction, were prevented from using the plough in the rural community, while their activities in the city—mostly market vending, but also domestic work—were seen as both derivative of men's agricultural work (as in the produce being traded) and reliant on domestic abilities they already possessed. As such, these activities provided little of the urban skills and economic gains of men's activities, particularly because the money made through vending was most likely immediately reinvested into the fulfillment of primary needs.

Questioning the previous emphasis on gender complementarity in the literature about the Andes, de la Cadena concluded that women were perceived as inferior and infantile—in fact, as "more Indian"—than men. There are important considerations I would like to highlight in her argument. First, it frames the analysis of the work of women in terms of a sexual division of labor between productive and reproductive labor assigned, respectively, to men and women. As market relations radiated from the city toward rural Indigenous communities, and as rural populations migrated to the city and entered the market in a subaltern position, the capacity to translate labor into economic (and political) accolades favored men. This contributed to render the labor performed by women invisible—as it was chronically un- (or under-) paid, it was only seen as subsidiary to and dependent upon men's waged labor (Federici 2014, 75; Gago 2017, 89–90). When Doña Saturnina argued that it was not her (but her husband's) duty to provide for the family, she too drew on a discourse that sustains a similar duality between the housewife and the breadwinner. Dominant gender norms in capitalist societies—as in patriarchal definitions of the family, household, and heterosexual relations—are structuring of the "work women are allowed to perform" but can also exclude women from the category of workers (Mohanty 2003, 142). In this sense, for Saturnina, she was not working when laboring at the market.

This does not mean that Doña Saturnina was not aware of—or not overwhelmed by—the gendered imbalances that informed this division of labor. When I returned to Bolivia for a second round of fieldwork, I reencountered

Saturnina in her stand, where she told me to sit on the small bench she had for her customers. She was puffing—she had arrived late—and decided to join me on the bench for a quick rest. She was tired, she said, tired of having so much to do on her own. She said she was feeling overwhelmed with her responsibilities at home and that her husband was never around. He was always at his carpentry workshop, even if he had little to do there. She, on the other hand, had to take the grandchildren to day care, keep the house tidy, do the laundry, cook, and, as though that were not enough, she also had the market. That and, of course, the shop she kept on the ground floor of her house—something she had never mentioned before when she said she did not work. She wanted to sell her post at La 16 so she could spend more time with her children and grandchildren, but they could not afford to lose the income it provided. Even though she did not consider that to be work, she knew, after all, that she worked hard.

The overlapping and continuity between domestic work and market vending have been underscored in the literature (see, for instance, Peredo 2001; Sikkink 2001). This literature highlights that market vending, more than just an extension of reproductive chores, also involves activities that, even if not too distant from domestic tasks, would be considered strictly productive, effectively adding value to the products that are sold (see Babb 1989; 2018). As was the case for Doña Saturnina, market women are involved in different activities, applying skills and knowledges that are not necessarily an extension of those required within the household (see also Maclean 2013; Ødegaard 2010; Müller 2017). Moreover, the importance of their economic contribution to the household extends beyond immediate investment in subsistence items; both Saturnina and her husband were self-employed and had to make do with the variability of their income. Effectively, the fact that she could not abandon her post at La 16 highlighted that Doña Saturnina's sales made her an important provider in her family, regardless of her identifying herself as not having that responsibility in our earlier interaction.

Simplified representations of gendered roles have systematically failed to account for the labor performed by nonwhite women. This takes me to the second point in de la Cadena's argument: that the work performed by rural Indigenous women in the city fails to enact their passage from indias to mestizas. In de la Cadena's work, the urban appears as a masculine sphere, while the community becomes feminized. On a different level, Canessa (2012, 222, emphasis added) argues that Indigenous men's time in the army rendered them whiter and more masculine, but also made "*Indians more female*." In both cases, the relational character of mobility is emphasized in the sense that both its causes and its effects are simultaneously gendered, sexualized, and racialized. While men's mobility allows them a relative if subaltern inclusion into the dominant mestizo paradigm of the nation, women's relative immobility reinforces the stigma that Indigenous peoples are backward, as well as spatially and culturally incarcerated. This stigma, however, is not embodied only by the women who stay; mobility to urban spaces works through, and not necessarily against, these interlocking dimensions of inequality.

If within the rural sphere women are seen as more Indian because of the reasons discussed above, mobility also racializes them in the urban context—although, I argue, for reasons other than those discussed by de la Cadena. As previously mentioned, domestic services and street trade share an important continuity with Indigenous women's historical occupations in the Andean urban contexts since colonial times (see also Barragán 1990; Gill 1993; Radcliffe 1990). These patterns of migration and insertion into the urban, monetized economy share little resemblance to the ones that brought men closer to the ideal of citizenship symbolized by the army (see also Gill 1997). Moreover, they also differ considerably from the activities performed by women who are *q'ara*. In fact, domestic services and street trade have been not only gendered but also racialized from the start. As Rivera Cusicanqui (1996; 2010b) underscores, mobility—as in migration or as a product of achieving a new social position—is both a driver and a product of *mestizaje*, creating opportunities for women to gain personal autonomy, to seek better lives for themselves and their children, and to claim rights. At the same time, however, it also subjects them to other forms of exploitation and prejudices. All the time, as women move through space and social ranks, they contribute to the motley, *ch'ixi* configurations that characterize urban Andean subjectivities. In so doing, they also reveal the inherent tensions and contradictions in the various categories and dimensions of social hierarchies. Mobility, rather than permanence, presents market vendors with ambiguous prospects. It frames the possibility for claiming and realizing new forms of autonomy while also subjecting them to exploitation at home and outside it.

Practices of differentiation that define who does what and what is labor are at the heart of capitalist processes of exploitation and expropriation (Bhattacharyya 2018). Labor performed by Indians and women are similarly devalued and seen outside of the "modern" urban economy (Gago 2017, 93–94).

And the articulation of these gendered and racial categories with a working-class position produces conflicting representations. Since the 1980s, black feminists in the United States have underscored how the categories of *woman* and *black* build on normative assumptions that systematically exclude the experience of black women (Crenshaw 1989; Collins 2000). Similarly located at these intersections, market women fail to satisfy the conditions of idealized womanhood as one who has exclusively to take care of the family and the household (see Stephenson 1999). While market vending is seen as making one less *jaqi*, it also makes one more Indian when compared to other urban dwellers or to their male counterparts back in the rural community, precisely because it is a job for Othered, racialized women. At the same time, working on their own and out in the open in the masculine urban sphere, market women also contest representations of women as both domestic and domesticated. As a result, their inclusion in this racialized activity not only renders market women "more Indian," but also makes them "less of a woman."

Transnational Connections

When I first met Doña Margarita, she told me she was one of the first people to hold business in the market held and named after Padre Bento Square, in a neighborhood not far from Kantuta in Canindé and Coimbra in Brás. She arrived in this city in 1989, along with her children and her husband, who joined her at the market every Sunday. Like many other Bolivian migrants here, Doña Margarita and her family began their lives in São Paulo working in garment manufacturing. After three years, she had already made enough money to run her own *oficina*—as garment workshops are known. The Brazilian economy was faring badly in the early 1990s, however, and many Bolivians decided to go to Argentina, where prospects were more promising. She followed suit, working for the garment industry in Buenos Aires instead, where she remained until the end of the decade, when she returned to São Paulo.

Like many others I met in Brazil, Doña Margarita picked up market vending later in life. For her, it all began after she returned from Buenos Aires when she and other Bolivians saw an unexplored market opportunity in the weekend gatherings of fellow nationals in areas surrounding *oficinas* in the neighborhood of Pari. "I'd seen how successful the Bolivian street markets were in Buenos Aires. I wanted to do the same thing here in São Paulo. I am a pioneer," she concluded proudly. She began by selling Bolivian snacks, only later incorporating food imported from Bolivia—her main trade to this day—to her portfolio as the market at Padre Bento Square grew in size. Attracting a big crowd, the gathering also brought complaints from neighbors, who demanded public authorities remove the market from the square altogether (Freitas 2014, 94–95). The vendors organized to find a new spot, reestablishing the market at its present location—a formerly derelict and unnamed cul-de-sac located between low-income residential towers and a dumping ground for the city's landscaping department. They named the area Kantuta Square—after the Andean flower that bears the three colors of the Bolivian flag—and claimed a bit of São Paulo for themselves. Every Sunday, from eleven in the morning until late in the evening, Kantuta is the market at the heart of the Bolivian migrant community here.

Not far from Kantuta, Coimbra takes place in an eponymous road in a popular commercial area. There you can find a variety of established Bolivian shops and restaurants as well as a growing number of services targeting the increasingly multicultural migrant community that holds businesses in Brás. Initially, Coimbra, too, followed the rattle of the sewing machines from the workshops that have historically existed in the area, although trade, rather than production, provides a more faithful characterization of the neighborhood today. Taking place on Saturdays and Sundays, Coimbra is much less of a tourist attraction for Brazilians but offers a more varied choice of products.

Although these markets are much smaller than La 16, they still attract thousands of visitors every weekend. At the time of my fieldwork research, it was estimated that around 250,000 Bolivian migrants were living this city,[3] where many are employed in garment manufacturing. Those seeking a new job might come to Kantuta and Coimbra later in the day, when contracts are negotiated on the spot. But during most of the day and the early evenings, visitors enjoy the opportunity to relax—to have a family lunch or a haircut, to meet old friends and future lovers, and to rekindle their ties with Bolivia through food, music, and cultural celebrations.

In order to fulfil her customers' demands, Doña Margarita made constant trips to the rural areas in the Bolivian altiplano where she was born. There she would purchase her products—freeze-dried potatoes, preserved fruits, maize, herbs—from a variety of suppliers before packing them in voluminous bags and bringing them back to Brazil by coach. If lucky, she could avoid detection from border checks, which could either tax or, worse, dispose of her products altogether. Even if her age made it more difficult for her to carry out all of these tasks by herself, Doña Margarita continued to do so, taking the opportunity to attend to celebrations in the *provincia* whenever possible. Doña Margarita presented herself as a true entrepreneur, with a good eye for new profitable opportunities. She had had different business ventures—the *oficina*, the market stand, and a now-defunct Bolivian restaurant. Importantly, her diversified portfolio had enabled her to make enough money to allow her daughters to lead a life away from the rattle of the sewing machines. The youngest had continued with her mother's trade at the market, but the other two were "professional workers"—a secretary and a dentist—Doña Margarita proudly added. She and her family had not stopped moving, even if that meant going back constantly to keep both her business in Brazil and her networks in Bolivia in check.

Doña Margarita's navigation of international borders to create profitable trade opportunities is an example of how members of the urban popular economy are increasingly able to reach commodities and to mobilize networks beyond locally established trade routes, with a larger promise of profits (Gago 2017; Maclean 2013; Müller 2017; Ødegaard 2017). Tassi's (2017) ethnography of La Paz and El Alto, for example, describes the successes of Aymara entrepreneurs who thrive in commercial niches left aside by "traditional" business elites in Bolivia. These successful traders (in Tassi's book, mostly men) establish transnational networks sustained through Indigenous social strategies, such as extended fictive kin. This case of "globalization from below" (Lins Ribeiro 2010) illustrates how marginalized groups might prosper without having to compromise their cultural backbone. Quite on the contrary, these Indigenous practices emerge as constitutive of a material fabric that enables their economic success (see Gago 2017).

Individual narratives of entrepreneurial success should be problematized against the question of how this inclusion into global flows of capital allows for individuals' actual empowerment (Nagar et al. 2002). This success does not trickle down to all or most of those involved in the popular economy and might, in fact, elude poor, Indigenous women in their struggle to make ends meet. The promotion of self-sustaining forms of economy, where the "petty entrepreneur" is able to keep a livelihood on their own terms (however much deprivation that might actually entail), is often hailed as a developmental path by neoliberal theorists and international agencies alike. Simultaneously, however, they show the unevenness of the processes of development and the precarity in which many of these people live and work (Antrosio and Colloredo-Mansfeld 2015, 23).

Discussing the case of La Salada—the very market that inspired Doña Margarita to trade in Brazil—Gago (2017, 35) presents this reliance on Indigenous networks and practices as ambiguous, "capable of functioning as a means of self-management, mobilization, and insubordination but also as a means of servitude, submission, and exploitation." For Gago, these *ch'ixi* contradictions challenge the very notion of progress itself. Among the women I met in the markets, it was generally the case that the income they obtained with sales was not translated into further investments to expand their business. Not all market women were just getting by, but it was frequently the case that they had to juggle between aspirations of social mobility and a tenuous income/expense balance. Financial gains were often translated into paying back debts and to guaranteeing that the next generation would not have to continue in the same trade as themselves. As such, women did not directly question the notion of progress itself, even if they warped it in ways that made it much less linear than is usually understood.

Refining Oneself

The outcomes of this increased transnational mobility are not necessarily empowering. Global patterns of international migration have been characterized by the growth in undocumented and feminized migratory flows, marked by an international context of market liberalization with increased mobility of capital and labor. Bolivians arriving in the 1980s in the United States, Argentina, and Brazil; in the 1990s in Chile; and since the 2000s in Spain often had to face precarious working conditions while enduring prejudice and racism (see also Gago 2017; Grimson 2005). Many live without documents and work for low wages, lacking access to health and social security services, as well as to labor and other basic citizenship rights (for the cases of Argentina, Spain, and Chile, see, respectively, Bastia 2019; Parella 2013; Ryburn 2018). In Brazil, Bolivian workers have been often described in public discourse as "slaves" and "Indians." Their exploitation in garment manufacturing is presented as anachronic (rather than chronic) in a modern capitalist economy, but also as implicitly enabled by Indigenous peoples' supposedly inherent backwardness (Ikemura Amaral 2022). As Gago (2017, 149) has indicated, presenting Bolivian migrants as Indians infantilizes them and diminishes their agency over their processes of mobility and work. These processes of racialization, I have argued, bind together indigeneity and labor exploitation, contributing to the devaluation of the work performed by Bolivian migrants while also reinforcing the idea that they are refractive to modernity and progress (Ikemura Amaral 2022). In this sense, the representation of migrants' work as slave labor parallels the marginalization of women's labor, also subsumed as inferior to that of (male) free, waged labor.

Doña Barbara retired from garment manufacturing after decades working for the sector. Nowadays she busies herself solely with market vending, and at the market she sells traditional clothes and souvenirs. Doña Barbara first came to Brazil with expectations of a new start in life for herself and her three children—two of whom remained in Bolivia with relatives. She arrived with the promise of a job and boarding at her sister's *oficina*. But arriving there, she was not properly paid or fed and had to work for hours on end in order to pay back the debts incurred by her travel, meals, and accommodation—while carrying her baby on her back. This harsh start was contrasted with her current situation. She was able to bring her other children to São Paulo with the help of a brother, and worked her way out of her sister's *oficina* into more dignifying jobs in other workshops. She eventually met her second husband, with whom she had other children and a happy life. Now a widow, Barbara sustains her established social standing with the earnings she makes at the market and with the financial help from her daughters—one of whom chose to join her mother at the market, not without some resistance from Doña Barbara. But Barbara also sustains her upward social mobility by establishing a clear threshold between where she came from and her current self.

Barbara was born in a small village around Lake Titicaca, and our interactions were full of fantastic stories about her childhood years. From otherworldly lights in the evening sky to incursions into caves packed with Inca figurines, the village was an unmissable stop for a visitor in Bolivia, she said, adding that I should go there whenever I had the opportunity to do so. Two of her sisters still lived there, she told me. They are "proper" market vendors, she said, who "*still* wore polleras and all." I asked her if she too wore polleras before coming to Brazil. Lowering her voice and hiding her lips behind a fan she was using to dissipate the hot summer heat, she said, "I have refined myself."

"Refinement," according to Peredo (2001, 31), is a common trope used to emphasize the process of distancing oneself from the discriminatory connotations associated with being Indigenous or chola. While Doña Barbara did not use the word *progress*, she similarly referred to an idea of moving forward, which, as Cecilie Ødegaard (2010, 16) highlights, "often involves an attempt to redefine [a person's] position in society, of re-conceptualizing self and identity in the attempt to become somebody different from who they were before." As Rivera Cusicanqui (2010a) has argued, this sums up to an internal reproduction of colonialism, inherently marred by conflicts between self-affirmation and self-denial. If the notion of *ch'ixi* later sustains a more positive reading of this motley coexistence of difference, the strife for liberating oneself from what oppresses also has ambiguous results. In consonance with what W. E. B. Du Bois (2007) has described as a "double consciousness," this internally colonized subjectivity attempts to avoid prejudice by bringing oneself closer to the position of the oppressor, thus relying on the same hierarchies that subjected them in the first place (see also Peredo 2001, 106).

Like cholas who first adopted the pollera, or the distinction drawn by Carmen and Ramona between themselves and Rocío, the garment is also emphasized by Barbara to highlight how she has moved on from other features and practices that could racialize her as an india, urban or not. Regardless of the real or aspired social mobility experienced by Doña Barbara, however, refining herself does not necessarily make her less india to others. But presenting herself as refined allows her to reinstate a sense of difference in relation to those considered still to be more india than herself.

Notions of progress are intimately tied to processes of socio-spatial mobility to the mestizo and the urban (Canessa 2012; Ødegaard 2010). But even if framed by racialized ideas and ideals of modernity that essentially involve a departure from a rural Indigenous background, progress might be impossible without one's ties to and fluency in the latter. As Ødegaard (2010, 60) has also found, notions of progress and mobility not only transform but also are transformed by local meanings and identities in ambiguous ways. This is illustrated by the parallels we can see in the stories of Doña Barbara and Doña Margarita, both of whom present narratives of spatial mobility as engendering processes of social mobility that spill over to the next generations. Yet while Barbara was anxious about establishing a much sharper cut between her past and current selves, Doña Margarita moves across the borders nonchalantly, presenting them as mutually reinforcing elements of her trajectory. If, for Barbara, distancing herself from these networks was part and parcel of her narrative of success, for Margarita, her networks in rural Bolivia were the backbone of her successful business strategies.

Conclusion: Making Money and Ends Meet

The market women I met at La 16, Coimbra and Kantuta, constitute a heterogeneous group of socially and spatially mobile women. They all acknowledged they worked hard, even if market vending was excluded from what constituted labor for them. In this chapter, I have analyzed how these understandings are built on mutually reinforcing conceptions of what labor is and does to people in ways that are racialized as they are racializing, gendered as they are gendering, and that are organized around the rural/urban duality. I have argued that social and spatial mobility has variegated effects over one's relation to indigeneity in ways that are necessarily ambiguous. These *ch'ixi* articulations, furthermore, are expressed in how these women assessed their work—at times in reference to Indigenous understandings of labor as constitutive of a person, at times in reference to capitalist definitions of labor that present work performed by women and people racialized as nonwhite as nonwork. Spatial mobility and the quest for social mobility also extend indigeneity beyond the rural communities, spreading toward cities in Bolivia and abroad, which in itself creates new articulations, tensions, and possibilities for change. In some cases, these are built on the very practices that are constitutive to the life in the *provincias*. In others, they entail a rupture with what makes one more Indian in the eyes of others and themselves. Rather than different phenomena, the point is that these are related products of the ambiguity brought by mobilities, whereby a marginalized incorporation into the urban economy or economic success are separated by the flip of a coin.

The urbanization of indigeneity provides women who are racialized as Indians with ambiguous prospects. It is not possible to argue if Doña Saturnina's understanding of market vending as nonwork relies exclusively on normative assumptions of labor from an Indigenous or non-Indigenous perspective. Neither gender complementarity nor a sexual division of labor can individually account for how she rationalizes her position as a wife, mother, and caregiver, as well as a trader and a provider. As these women move from the *provincia* to the city, and from Bolivia abroad, they are furthermore faced with processes of racialization that further undermine and downplay the importance of their labor in the social mobility they experience. If women become market vendors for myriad reasons, the outcomes of that labor are likewise not univocal. The means for personal and economic autonomy, which many women are at such pains to achieve through their labor, might also be reinvested in the perpetuation of practices that are not advantageous to them.

Even so, the ambiguity embedded in processes of urbanization also provides spaces for reclaiming and resignifying indigeneity. (Urban) Indigenous groups have organized and contested hegemonic discourses and processes that have sought to eliminate indigeneity through dispossession, exploitation, and miscegenation. While there continue to be systematic efforts to undermine these endeavors, the notion of *ch'ixi* also points to the possibility of moving beyond the colonialism that characterizes our societies. Ambiguity, rather than a cause for distancing oneself from indigeneity, emerges as a form through which indigeneity can thrive alongside—and not despite—the forms of being and seeing that presently seek to eliminate it. It entails, moreover, the possibility of challenging gendered and racialized forms of exploitation and exclusion. This holds promise even for those who, like the women I met at the markets, are not part of organized Indigenous movements, but who are equally creating the *ch'ixi* fabric of urban indigeneity. To make money and ends meet and to aspire to a more consolidated social standing are both equally important in determining these women's relation to their labor—and, ultimately, are what it means to be perceived as Indigenous in these urban contexts.

Notes

1. For an excellent description of this debate, see Babb (2018).
2. Whereas the most recent censuses in Bolivia indicated that between 18 and 34 percent of the population in urban centers self-identified as Indigenous, in El Alto this percentage was substantially higher (ca. 81 and 49 percent, in 2001 and 2012, respectively).
3. Most recent official data indicate there are eighty thousand Bolivians residing in the city of São Paulo (Observatório das Migrações em São Paulo 2018), which is believed to be an underestimation that does not account for undocumented migrants.

References

Albro, Robert. 2010. "Neoliberal Cultural Heritage and Bolivia's New Indigenous Public." In *Ethnographies of Neoliberalism*, edited by Carol J. Greenhouse, 146–61. Philadelphia: University of Pennsylvania Press.

Antrosio, Jason, and Rudi Colloredo-Mansfeld. 2015. *Fast, Easy, and In Cash: Artisan Hardship and Hope in the Global Economy*. Chicago and London: University of Chicago Press.

Babb, Florence E. 1989. *Between Field and Cooking Pot: The Political Economy of Marketwomen in Peru*. Austin: University of Texas Press.

———. 2018. *Women's Place in the Andes: Engaging Decolonial Feminist Anthropology*. Oakland: University of California Press.

Barragán, Rossana. 1990. *Espacio urbano y dinámica étnica: La Paz en el siglo XIX*. La Paz: Hisbol.

Bastia, Tanja. 2019. *Gender, Migration and Social Transformation: Intersectionality in Bolivian Itinerant Migrations*. London: Routledge.

Bhattacharyya, Gargi. 2018. *Rethinking Racial Capitalism: Questions of Reproduction and Survival*. London: Rowman and Littlefield.

Bigenho, Michelle. 2006. "Embodied Matters: Bolivian Fantasy and *indigenismo*." *Journal of Latin American Anthropology* 11 (2): 267–95.

Bold, Rosalyn. 2017. "*Vivir Bien*: A Study in Alterity." *Latin American and Caribbean Ethnic Studies* 12 (2): 113–32.

Buechler, Hans, and Judith-Maria Buechler. 1996. *The World of Sofía Velasquez: The Autobiography of a Bolivian Market Vendor*. New York: Columbia University Press.

Canessa, Andrew. 2006. *Minas, mote y muñecas: identidades e indigeneidades en Larecaja*. La Paz: Mama Huaco.

———. 2012. *Intimate Indigeneities: Race, Sex, and History in the Small Spaces of Andean Life*. Durham: Duke University Press.

Collins, Patricia Hill. 2000. *Black Feminist Thought: Knowledge, Consciousness and the Politics of Empowerment*. New York and London: Routledge.

Crenshaw, Kimberlé. 1989. "Demarginalizing the Intersection of Race and Sex: A Black Feminist Critique of Antidiscrimination Doctrine, Feminist Theory and Antiracist Politics." *University of Chicago Legal Forum*, no. 140, 139–67.

de la Cadena, Marisol. 1995. "'Women are More Indian': Ethnicity and Gender in a Community near Cuzco." In *Ethnicity, Markets, and Migration in the Andes: At the Crossroads of History and Anthropology*, edited by Brooke Larson, Olivia Harris, and Enrique Tandeter, 329–48. Durham and London: Duke University Press.

———. 2002. "The Racial-Moral Politics of Race: Mestizas and Intellectuals in Turn-of-the-Century Peru." In *Gender's Place: Feminist anthropologies of Latin America*, edited by R. Montoya, L. J. Frazier, and J. Hurtig, 155–75. New York: Palgrave.

Du Bois, W. E. B. 2007. *The Souls of Black Folk*. Edited and with an introduction and notes by Brent Hayes Edward. Oxford: Oxford University Press.

Federici, Silvia. 2014. *Caliban and the Witch: Women, the Body and Primitive Accumulation*. New York: Autonomedia.

Freitas, Patrícia Tavares. 2014. *Projeto Costura: percursos sociais de trabalhadores migrantes, entre a Bolívia e a indústria de confecção das cidades de destino*. PhD dissertation, Universidade Estadual de Campinas.

Gago, Veronica. 2017. *Neoliberalism from Below: Popular Pragmatics & Baroque Economies*. Durham: Duke University Press.

Gill, Lesley. 1993. "'Proper women' and city Pleasures: Gender, Class and Contested Meanings in La Paz." *American Ethnologist* 20 (1): 72–88.

———. 1997. "Creating Citizens, Making Men: The Military and Masculinity in Bolivia." *Cultural Anthropology* 12 (4): 527–50.

Grimson, Alejandro. 2005. "Ethnic (In)Visibility in Neoliberal Argentina." *NACLA Report on the Americas* 38 (4): 25–29.

Harris, Olivia. 2000. *To Make the Earth Bear Fruit: Fertility, Work and Gender in Highland Bolivia*. London: University of London, Institute of Latin American Studies.

Iamamoto, Sue A. S. 2015. *Collective Memories and Social Struggle in Contemporary Bolivia: A Study of Narratives of the Past during the "Gas War" in La Paz (2003) and the Civic Strike in Potosi (2010)*. PhD dissertation, Queen Mary University of London.

Ikemura Amaral, Aiko. 2022. "Neither Natives nor Nationals in Brazil: The 'Indianization' of Bolivian Migrants in the city of São Paulo." *Bulletin of Latin American Research* 41 (1): 53–68.

Lins Ribeiro, Gustavo. 2010. "A globalização popular e o sistema mundial não-hegemônico." *Revista Brasileira de Ciências Sociais* 25 (74): 21–38.

Maclean, Kate. 2013. "Evo's Jumper: Identity and the Used Clothes Trade in 'Post-Neoliberal' and 'Pluricultural' Bolivia." *Gender, Place & Culture* 21 (8): 963–78.

———. 2014. "*Chachawarmi*: Rhetorics and Lived Realities." *Bulletin of Latin American Research* 33 (1): 76–90.

McNelly, Angus. 2022. "Baroque Modernity in Latin America: Situating Indigeneity, Urban Economy and the Popular Economy." *Bulletin of Latin American Research* 41(1): 6–20.

Mohanty, Chandra Talpade. 2003. *Feminism Without Borders: Decolonizing Theory, Practicing Solidarity*. Durham: Duke University Press.

Müller, Juliane. 2017. "Place-Based (In)Formalization: A Bolivian Marketplace for Consumer Electronics and Global Brands." *Latin American Research Review* 52 (3): 393–404.

Nagar, Richa, Victoria Lawson, Linda McDowell, and Susan Hanson. 2002. "Locating Globalization: Feminist (Re)Readings of the Subjects and Spaces of Globalization." *Economic Geography* 78 (3): 257–84.

Observatório Das Migrações Em São Paulo. 2018. *Banco Interativo Observatório das Migrações em São Paulo*.

Ødegaard, Cecilie Vindal. 2008. "Informal Trade, Contrabando and Prosperous Socialities in Arequipa, Peru." *Ethnos* 73 (2): 241–66.

———. 2010. *Mobility, Markets and Indigenous Socialities: Contemporary Migration in the Peruvian Andes*. Farnham and Burlington: Ashgate.

———. 2017. "'Made in China': Contraband, Labor and the Gendered Effects of 'Free-Trade', China-Peru." *Journal of Development Studies* 53 (3): 346–60.

Parella, Sònia. 2013. "Bolivian Migrants in Spain: Transnational Families from a Gender Perspective." In *The International Handbook on Gender, Migration and Transnationalism: Global and Development Perspectives*, edited by Laura Oso and Natalia Ribas-Mateos, 312–34. Cheltenham and Northampton: Edward Elgar.

Peredo, Elizabeth. 2001. *Recoveras de los Andes: una aproximación a la identidad de la chola del mercado*. La Paz: Fundación Solón.

Poets, Desiree. 2021. "Settler Colonialism and/in (Urban) Brazil: Black and Indigenous Resistances to the Logic of Elimination." *Settler Colonial Studies* 11 (3): 271–91.

Radcliffe, Sarah. 1990. "Ethnicity, Patriarchy, and Incorporation into the Nation: Female Migrants as Domestic Servants in Peru." *Environment and Planning D: Society and Space*, no. 8, 379–93.

Rivera Cusicanqui, Silvia. 1996. "Trabajo de mujeres: explotación capitalista y opresión colonial entre las migrantes aymaras de La Paz y El Alto, Bolivia." In *Ser mujer indígena, chola o birchola en la Bolivia postcolonial de los años 90*, edited by Silvia Rivera Cusicanqui, 163–300. La Paz: Ministerio de Desarrollo Humano, Secretaría Nacional de Asuntos Étnicos, de Género y Generacionales, Subsecretaría de Asuntos de Género.

———. 2010a. *Ch'ixinakax utxiwa: Una reflexión sobre prácticas y discursos descolonizadores*. Buenos Aires: Tinta Limón.

———. 2010b. *Violencias (re)encubiertas en Bolivia*. La Paz: La Mirada Salvaje.

———. 2013. "Prólogo." In *Los senderos de Fausto Reinaga*, Gustavo Cruz, 15–28. La Paz: CIDES-UMSA.

Ryburn, Megan. 2018. "Uncertain Citizenship: Everyday Practices of Bolivian Migrants in Chile." Oakland: University of California Press.

Seligmann, Linda J. 1989. "To Be in Between: The Cholas as Market Women." *Comparative Studies in Society and History* 31 (4): 694–721.

Sikkink, Lynn. 2001. "Home Sweet Market Stand: Work, Gender, and Getting Ahead among Bolivian Tradition Medicine Vendors." *Anthropology of Work Review* 22 (3): 1–6.

Stephenson, Marcia. 1999. *Gender and Modernity in Andean Bolivia*. Austin: University of Texas Press.

Tassi, Nico. 2010. "The 'Postulate of Abundance': Cholo Market and Religion in La Paz, Bolivia." *Social Anthropology/Anthropologie Sociale* 18 (2): 191–209.

———. 2017. *The Native World-System: An Ethnography of Bolivian Aymara Traders in the Global Economy*. New York and Oxford: Oxford University Press.

Wade, Peter. 2009. *Race and Sex in Latin America*. 2nd ed. New York: Pluto Press.

Weismantel, Mary. 2001. *Cholas and Pishtacos: Stories of Race and Sex in the Andes*. Chicago: University of Chicago Press.

Yampara, Simón, Saúl Mamani, and Norah Calancha. 2007. *La cosmovisión y lógica en la dinámica socioeconómica del qhatu/feira 16 de Julio*. La Paz: Fundación PIEB; UPEA; CEBIAE; Centro de Promoción de la Mujer Gregoria Apaza; Red Habitat; Wayna Tambo; CISTEM.

CHAPTER FOUR

From *nanas* to *presidentas*

Leadership Trajectories of Mapuche Women within Indigenous Associations in Santiago de Chile

DANA BRABLEC

Recently, different sources around the world have informed us about the successful performance of Indigenous women in high-profile political events: Deb Haaland, Sharice Davids, and Yvette Herrell, all Native Americans, were elected as representatives to the U.S. House of Representatives in the November 2020 elections (Aratani 2020). In turn, Nanaia Mahuta was the first female Māori to be appointed as minister of foreign affairs in New Zealand (Hollingsworth 2020). Although these events still represent exceptions, they are slowly setting a precedent for the opening of political spaces for Indigenous women in their respective countries. From a high-profile political viewpoint, the Chilean Mapuche case has been rather discreet. In 2021, after being elected as one of the Mapuche representatives for the first Constitutional Convention of Chile, Elisa Loncón became the person in charge of leading this body that has the mission of writing the constitution that will replace the current one inherited from the Pinochet era. Dressed in traditional Mapuche clothing, speaking in Spanish and Mapuzungun (the Mapuche language), and openly supporting the social demands of her people, Loncón assumed her role in the building that once housed the National Congress located in the heart of Santiago. Loncón, who once ventured into domestic work to cover her education expenses (El Mostrador 2021), is now one of the most prominent Mapuche linguists, activists, and academics. However, the case of Loncón remains an exception in the national political scene. At present, the leadership role of Mapuche women has been based almost entirely on the community-based work articulated through Indigenous associations.

This chapter joins a growing body of literature on the Mapuche diaspora in Santiago de Chile by placing colonial reformulations, racial/class/gender articulations, and the increasing urbanization experienced by Indigenous peoples at the center of the debate. This chapter analyzes how mobility is creating translocal Indigenous organizational worlds and ways of exercising community-based leadership by exploring how socio-spatial relationships are being reorganized regarding indigeneity, gender, and rural-to-urban migration. Based on ethnographic data, this chapter examines how female Mapuche leaders who once were—or still are—*nanas* (domestic workers), navigate their role and produce new relational engagements from the interstices of the white-mestizo (mixed race) city. In doing this, the chapter illustrates how Mapuche women navigate different social roles by occupying leadership positions in the growing number of ethnic associations that have been directing the re-creation of Indigenous identity in Santiago de Chile. The chapter suggests the (re)emergence of new forms of sociopolitical relational interactions that presage pluriversal futures for those *presidentas* (female presidents of Indigenous associations), thus overcoming the patriarchalism of leadership roles that have relegated them to the background of the urban organizational scene.

The arrival of the Spanish colonizers in the sixteenth century, the invasion of Indigenous lands, and the subsequent "pacification" of the territory south of the Biobío River by the Chilean nation-state in the nineteenth century, which resulted in a loss of nearly 90 percent of the former Mapuche territory (Rain, Llombart, and Mora 2020), had a disastrous effect on Mapuche women: ongoing dispossession, disempowerment, and the onset of a forced displacement to cities. As a result, the life of Mapuche women and gender relations in rural communities suffered a dramatic change. The new system deprived women of land ownership and personal autonomy and restricted the economic, political, social, and spiritual domains that had existed prior to the advancement of the Chilean nation-state into the Wallmapu, or ancestral territory, since the late nineteenth century. It also involved the implementation of dominant patriarchal systems that have shaped the relationship not only within communities but also with those who define themselves as the non-Indigenous white-mestizo Other.

Attracted by a sense of economic opportunity denied to them in their rural territory of origin, the Mapuche are increasingly settling in Santiago, where now 35 percent of the Mapuche live, mostly on the city's peripheries. As a result of their rapid inclusion into the urban labor market due to the demand for domestic work, Mapuche women, in comparison to their male counterparts, were particularly prone to migrate to cities in search of better economic possibilities to support their homes (Bello 2002). Accordingly, Mapuche men started to be cut off from certain traditional economic roles, with Mapuche women able to independently generate their own means of subsistence and create their own support networks in the city. Nearly 95 percent of the Indigenous population in Santiago (metropolitan region) are Mapuche, of whom 50.8 percent are women. The participation of Indigenous women in the labor market reaches 48.7 percent, similar rates as those of non-Indigenous women (48.9 percent). Poverty rates are considerably higher, as 10.9 percent of the urban Indigenous population is classified as "poor by income," versus 7.1 percent of the non-Indigenous population (CASEN 2017).

Throughout the twentieth century, employment arrangements ranged from live-in domestic schemes to casual weekly work for a few hours. However, newly arrived rural-to-urban female Mapuche migrants were drawn to the domestic service sector to work as live-in nanas as it offered the option of housing (Alvarado-Lincopi 2016). Employing a live-in Mapuche domestic worker was, in turn, a manifestation of economic power linked to a social whitening process of the urban society. This evidences the fluidity of racial classifications and their intricacy concerning class and gender understandings. Inscribed in a colonial continuity framework marked by territorial dispossession and agency denial to subvert to the dominant white-mestizo patriarchal order, Mapuche women found themselves immersed in a rigid urban class system, poorly paid, and with labor dynamics marked by physical and psychological exploitation: long working hours, a wage not proportional to their work, and in many cases, victims of sexual harassment and abuse (De Casanova 2013). That is to say, domestic service was, in many cases, equated with the availability of Indigenous women's bodies, both as cheap labor and for sexual utilization by the houses' men. Therefore, as Antileo (2015) maintains, domestic work as "racialized work" is based on colonial historical structures that consolidate current racial, gender, and class hierarchical articulations.

The home, as a sometimes contradictory milieu, has traditionally been considered a gendered feminine space. The permeable boundaries that define how the domestic sphere is experienced, especially concerning the figure of the white-mestizo mistress (*la señora*), have been differently interpreted; some see it as the site of women's oppression while others of their autonomy or even authority (Haskins and Jacobs 2007). Nevertheless, the urban household experience for the subjugated Indigenous Others, as a contested sociocultural space that reifies the workings of colonial dynamics, has been characteristic not only of Mapuche but also of female Latin American Indigenous domestic workers in general (Stoler 2001). For example, Gill (1994) already pointed out more than twenty-five years ago that the labor relations between internal migrant Aymara women and their employers were based on a race/class subordination resulting from inherited colonial constructions that placed the Indigenous in an inferior category. Following a similar approach, and based on the case of Ecuadorian domestic workers in Guayaquil, De Casanova (2013) argues that domestic workers' bodies are resources that can be used by alleged racial/class superior Others to profit from their cheap labor, while, at the same time, these bodies are understood according to intersectional hierarchies that position them in subaltern categories of the urban social landscape. Thus, as Ryburn (2018) maintains, Indigenous women in Latin America have been understood by those in a position of power as a "natural fit" for domestic work, given their alleged submissive and hard-working natural qualities and their lower social standing based on gender, race, and class differentiations. Hence, relationships based on exploitation and, consequently, the privilege of those employers who benefit from (post)colonial hierarchies are maintained in contemporary Latin American societies.

In Santiago, labor exploitation and discrimination have coexisted with material subsistence and cultural resistance (Rain, Llombart, and Mora 2020). While migration often occurs under economic desperation, new predicaments in the diaspora population may be conducive to a positive renegotiation of gender relations based on the new opportunities opened to Mapuche women. Since the 1980s, associational processes have flourished in Santiago. However, it was not until the 1990s, hand in hand with the enactment of the Indigenous Law and the creation of the Indigenous Development Corporation (CONADI), that Santiago experienced a multiplication of Mapuche associations (Brablec 2019). One of the unexpected outcomes of the Mapuche rural-to-urban migration—in a context of uprooting, deterritorialization, and displacement that presaged the ethnocide and assimilation of Indigenous identities into the dominant white-mestizo urban society—has been the considerable number of Mapuche women leading Indigenous associations as presidentas, whose principal role is cultural recovery and maintenance. The accumulated historical experience of racism, gender violence, and economic inequality, characteristic of the domestic service sector, has been challenged from the ethnic organizational arena by Mapuche women who lead the processes of Indigenous cultural implementation in the city. This work has been fundamental for the Mapuche to resist attempts to render the urban Indigenous experience invisible in cities, and thus claim a Mapuche identity that is not fixed in a romanticized past, but is instead shaped by multiple interactions with different people, artifacts, and situations that occur in the individual's life (Brablec 2021). However, despite their crucial role in cities, female Mapuche leaders have only recently been made visible in the academic literature. As maintained by Spivak (1988), subalternation as an active, violent process of agency removal, implied in the Latin American domestic service domain, has been coupled with sociopolitical invisibility. In the case of Chile, domestic service has been feminized and racialized as exclusive to Indigenous women (and, more recently, female Latin American immigrants), and thus has been constructed as virtually incompatible with any kind of leadership role beyond the purely domestic arena (Fitzgerald 2006). The complexities of the leadership trajectories of Mapuche women in Santiago de Chile, who once were or still are nanas, are discussed in the next sections.

On Colonialism, Urbanization, and the Subalternation of Urban Indigenous Women: Looking Toward a Critical Urban Indigeneities Framework

The growing Mapuche population in Santiago raises the question of the role of Indigenous women in (post)colonial socioeconomic structures and in the rearticulation of a sense of people when living outside the territory of origin. Indigenous mobility, community organizing, and place making are reorganizing the production of socio-spatial relations in Santiago (Brablec 2020). In conversation with, primarily, female scholars looking at decolonial gender studies (Oyěwùmí 1997; Paredes 2017), critical indigenous studies (Tuhiwai Smith 2005), and critical Latinx indigeneities (Blackwell 2017), this chapter advances a critical urban indigeneities framework by bringing the urban component to the fore to navigate the intricacies of the leadership trajectories of Mapuche women in Santiago and develop a critical analysis around it. In this way, the necessary theoretical basis can be provided to understand migratory (and diasporic) labor, organizational, and sociopolitical leadership trajectories by virtue of the interactions and experiences delimited not only by ancestral territories but also in cities that currently house a growing proportion of Indigenous peoples in Chile and the world. In cities, new and old forms of Indigenous relationality emerge and are forged, including gendered systems of power, impacting the lives of Indigenous women in their multiple exchanges, including Indigenous intraorganizational leadership (de/re)constructions. In this way, critical urban indigeneities allow an understanding of the ways in which Indigenous women are racialized, marginalized, and sexualized differently in various urban situations. Thus, I place the leadership trajectories of Mapuche women in cities within this framework that positions Indigenous organizational happenings in conversation with gender, race, class, and urbanization. By highlighting the multiple urban Indigenous experiences, without leaving previous scholarly articulations behind, I seek to create a network of different Indigenous epistemological heterogeneities beyond possible geographic essentialisms.

This conversation between and extension of theoretical approaches thus enables a holistic understanding closer to Indigenous world views that, differently than Western perspectives, are concerned with the whole and not with compartmentalized comprehensions. A clear example of these universal knowledges is the Mapuche conceptualization of gender relations. In traditional Mapuche society, both men and women are necessary components of a collective whole, and both are part of the *meli newen* (four strengths) represented by the old man (*fücha*), old woman (*kude*), young man (*weche*), and young woman (*ülcha*). Therefore, all people are part of a complementary collective identity, which entails respect and reciprocity with nature, and survival as a people depends on the responsibility of the group to value each person for their abilities, strengths, and attributes. As Bacigalupo (2003) argues, according to the Mapuche traditional worldview, genders are fluid, moving away from understandings that classify them as fixed, binary categories.

In fact, this Western categorical understanding of gender and gender relations has also been questioned by postcolonial feminists outside the Latin American region. For instance, Nigerian sociologist Oyèrónkẹ́ Oyěwùmí (1997), in her acclaimed book *The Invention of Women*, discusses modern

Yoruba patriarchal structures and gender stratification as a Western colonial construct. According to Oyěwùmí's (1997) thought, gender was a social construction introduced by the West as a tool of domination. Women, then, were defined in relation to men, as being those who did not have power and were not allowed to participate in the public arena. Similarly, the Mapuche experience shows that the subordination of women to men (both white and Mapuche) and their placement as actors not eligible for leadership roles was an adoption that came with colonization. One of the main impacts on Indigenous (post)colonial social structures was the transformation of power into male power, achieved partly by the exclusion of women from political systems. Consequently, colonization imposed not only racial regimes of power and domination but also systems of gender subordination based on a Western patriarchal order. Therefore, for Indigenous women, the (post) colonial social order implied a twofold process of racial inferiorization and gender subordination to the present day (Oyěwùmí 1997; Lugones 2016).

According to Loncón (2020), the tendency of Western epistemologies to categorize gender identities as binary, opposed, and hierarchical has led many Mapuche women to be reluctant to accept traditional Western feminist frameworks, considering them both predisposed to white colonizing principles and also insufficient to understanding the complexity of their social relationships. In fact, Lugones (2016, 13) maintains that the white feminist struggle "became one against the positions, roles, stereotypes, traits, desires imposed on white bourgeois women's subordination." As a result, traditional Western feminism did not focus on colonialism and did not appreciate either the differential construction of gender along racial lines or labor as both racialized and gendered.

Mapuche men have also tended to be critical of Western feminism. As Painemal (2013) attests, some groups have adduced that this alien colonizing philosophy only contributes to dividing the Mapuche movement and thus obstructs their struggle to recover their land. In this sense, Catrileo (2019) points out that a nonwhite, non-Western approach has to dialogue both with community forms of Indigenous resistance and with the appreciation of the multiplicity of feminisms that value each reality beyond constructed categories of class and race. With an equally critical appreciation of traditional Eurocentric feminism, Millaleo (2016) points out that both Indigenous men and women occupy subordinate positions compared to non-Indigenous men and women. However, Oyěwùmí (1997), with a more critical stance, recognizes that the colonial imposition of a racial regime brought the inferiorization of women, which tended to be accepted by Indigenous and tribal men by colluding with white men in this process. As a result, women were excluded from leadership roles and lost power over land and other important economic domains. Similarly, the Native American poet Paula Gunn Allen (1992) maintains that the inferiorization of Indigenous women, with the collaboration of Indigenous men, is intimately linked to the domination and transformation of (post)colonial Indigenous community social life.

The urban experience brings its own complexities, as cities have been historically understood as exclusive spaces of white-mestizo domination. As Libby Porter and Oren Yiftachel (2019) maintain, this is because invasion receives organizational form through urbanization processes. Thus, cities' foundations and development are regarded as manifestations of progress by the colonial power, constituting "a distinct activity literally building the settler-colonial nation" (Porter and Yiftachel 2019, 177). Urbanization continues to be a mechanism that operationalizes Indigenous peoples' spatial and economic dispossession (Porter and Yiftachel 2019). The processes of colonial urbanization have penetrated the social imagination to the present day, turning the urban into a place alien to Indigenous identities without considering that many of these same cities settle in violently dispossessed Indigenous territories (Brablec 2022). Building on an understanding of critical urban indigeneities, Indigenous feminism should thus not be cultivated only within the ancestral territories, as the subalternation of Indigenous women has been inextricably linked to the corporality of their racialized bodies. As Linda Tuhiwai Smith (2005) maintains, the pervasive effect of colonialism on Indigenous women positioned them in roles that were primarily domestic. This historical condition of imposed gender/racial domination reaches even clearer borders by restricting Indigenous female urban belonging to a limited space of entrapped labor subordination.

As a response to this scenario, the Aymara activist Julieta Paredes (2017) introduces the term "*feminismocomunitario*" (community feminism) which is, according to her, the feminism of peoples. In this sense, both Paredes (2017) and Millaleo (2020) call for feminism to be reappropriated from an Indigenous perspective in such a way as to accommodate the experiences, past and present, of women in rural and urban areas. In other words, as the feminist sociologist Silvia Rivera Cusicanqui (2010) points out, decolonization must be not only a discourse but also an affirmative practice. This Indigenous community feminist approach has been developed from the Mayan and Aymara worlds, which, according to Mapuche activist Ange Valderrama (2019), originates from the resistance of a patriarchy incorporated during colonization as well as an ancestral patriarchy that merged with the patriarchy that the conquerors brought to the "New World."

Similarly to Oyěwùmí (1997) and Gunn Allen (1992), Paredes (2017) says that the hegemonic system of discrimination and oppression that has been imposed over women's bodies is today replicated by Indigenous men because of internalized colonialism. In cities, one of the clearest manifestations of this colonialism is the invisibility of the identities and experiences of those Indigenous women who have had to make the urban milieu their home. One of the main spaces of urban sociopolitical subordination is the labor market, which has been complicit in the reification of the multiple colonialities that have positioned the bodies of Indigenous women in categories of domestic servitude. Promoting a critical Latinx indigeneities framework to understand the trajectories of the Mexican Indigenous diaspora in Los Angeles, Blackwell (2017) argues that the anti-Indigenous prejudice onto which Mexican racial hierarchies are configured facilitates labor segmentation and hyperexploitation of (female) Indigenous migrants in increasingly globalized economies. Therefore, Indigenous women not only navigate the geography of a new city but also deal with the racialized and gendered geographies of labor and care work as domestic workers. In addition, their cultural and political organizing and translocal community making are producing new spatial relationships and geographies of indigeneity in the cities of the world.

As Millaleo (2020) points out, and intertwining her view with a critical urban indigeneities perspective, an Indigenous feminism in the city, active and of resistance, implies the recovery of spaces denied by the dominant non-Indigenous society. In this sense, from a socio-community, and not from the highest political leagues as reflected in the electoral victory of Loncón introduced in the first paragraphs of this chapter, the work of Mapuche presidentas can be understood as, while not restricting itself to, *feminismocomunitario*. As will be examined in the next sections, through the revindication of urban Indigenous community leadership spaces, presidentas have slowly left behind roles of domestic subordination, appropriating the cultural revival of their people.

Methods

The following analysis is drawn from a broader research project on Mapuche identity re-creation practices within Indigenous associations in Santiago de Chile. This chapter intends to produce situated and context-specific understanding, grounded in detailed ontologies and lifeworlds. The chapter focuses on the narratives, knowledges, and experiences shared by Mapuche women who once were—or still are—nanas while also performing the role of Indigenous community-based leaders, or, in local jargon, presidentas.

This chapter draws on over five years of collaborative ethnographic research and more than forty in-depth semistructured interviews, both in situ and online, with Mapuche members of eleven Indigenous associations around the city of Santiago. Seven interviewees were presidentas at the time of the interview, five of whom are or were nanas. The age of these women ranged from forty-two to sixty-five years old and included first-generation rural-to-urban migrants and their daughters. Moreover, the interviews also included women who, at some point of their lives, were presidentas and still performed an active role in their corresponding associations.

In addition to interviews, the methods included active participation and observation in the eleven associations under study. The fieldwork in Chile included attending dozens of events such as monthly business meetings, traditional ceremonies, and camaraderie activities. This approach favored engagement through long conversations with individuals and groups of members in the eleven associations, which allowed a deep understanding of their life trajectories as workers, leaders, and, in some cases, mothers. As Tuhiwai Smith (2005) maintains, each individual Indigenous story has a place in the collective story of their people, connecting different generations, the past with the future. Inevitably, this conversational process activated memories, some of them based on painful stories of abuse, poverty, and alienation. In most cases, this also triggered a parallel articulation of the healing and transformation processes through the recovery of their agency made possible by the women's active participation in the collective identity recovery, implementation, and maintenance channeled through urban organizational work.

As Loncón (2020) points out, in order to understand the trajectories of Mapuche women, it is necessary to identify the keys that guide their political actions in their roles as both nanas and presidentas. In this sense, it is important to know their own account of their experiences as urban Indigenous leaders. As such, this chapter's exploration of Mapuche women's leadership roles, within the framework of urban Indigenous associations in light of their participation in the domestic service arena, is rooted in these conversations. While the empirical information presented here favors the intervention of Mapuche women, it does not limit the contribution of Mapuche men who were also part of this study. From an ethnographic perspective, the next sections detail these experiences. All names used in this chapter are pseudonyms.

Traversing the City: From *nana* to *ñaña*

In a recent interview with Aura Cumes (2021, 19), the Guatemalan Maya-Kaqchikel researcher maintains that "European patriarchy was not built on ideas alone. The interiorization of women through sex made it possible for any power they had to be questioned. How could they have healing powers, the ability to support their families and leadership in their communities if they were weak and inferior?" Cumes's statement is particularly relevant to the case of Mapuche women in Santiago, whose leadership role in urban society has been diminished due to their invisibility within the domestic service sphere in their work as nanas. Although the word *nana* resembles that from English origin, *nanny*, there seems to be a degree of agreement in inferring its connection to that of Quechua origin *ñaña*, a term that designates an older sister or an older woman (Millaleo 2016). Mapuzungun incorporated the notion *ñaña* with a meaning similar to Quechua, nowadays widely used to refer to other Mapuche women. However, it is the term *nana* as a domestic worker that has effectively been given a transversal use in Chilean Spanish.

With the sustained rural-urban migration of Mapuche women to Santiago, an urban social imaginary developed to this day that linked gender and race with the work of nanas (Calfío 2016; Millaleo 2016). This condition was made evident when in 2014, during the performance in Santiago of the Chilean singer Ana Tijoux in Lollapalooza, groups in the audience yelled "nana face" as an insult because of her alleged Indigenous phenotype (Cooperativa 2014). In this way, the bodies of Indigenous women have been, in many instances, resignified as domestic service bodies (Millaleo 2016) and either entrapped by the frame of the rural ancestral territory or confined by the borders of the urban household.

Mapuche women in cities slowly adopted the responsibility of economically sustaining their communities of origin, challenging traditional expectations of gender division of labor. Nevertheless, Mapuche women were still defined as the keepers not of their own home but of others, caretakers for the children of white-mestizo women. That is to say, the boundaries of labor division of nanas have been and continue to be ambiguous despite recent improvements in their working conditions. The nana is the one who takes care of the children, not only being a babysitter but also dedicating herself to domestic tasks such as cooking, cleaning, and ironing. Without being legitimate members of the family, nor exclusively servants, they occupy subordinated positions that are sometimes blurred and often difficult to define. As Stoler (2001) maintains, these "tense and tender ties" were shaped by gender and race relations of superiority/subordination within the intimacy of the (post)colonial household, in which acts of kindness frequently disguised the violence of exploitation.

In this way, gender roles are complicated by emerging forms and changing dynamics of the division of labor, in which Mapuche women have engaged with the "feminization" of the service economy through domestic work. More recently, they have adopted a role of leadership within urban Indigenous associations mostly dedicated to the re-creation of their culture. In this way, the forced uprooting has gone hand in hand with the opening of new social roles, influenced by a variety of sociocultural factors in constant motion that question what norms of typical behavior are envisioned for an Indigenous woman. However, as discussed in the following paragraphs, the alleged deviation from traditional roles by Mapuche women in Santiago has been negatively sanctioned by those Mapuche who affirm that non-Indigenous values have pervasively influenced the Mapuche, thus threatening the basis on which their identity as a people is constituted.

About Domestic Work

The narratives of Mapuche women arriving in Santiago are marked by the experience of material scarcity resulting from land dispossession. As Enrique Antileo (2015) points out, the lack of land caused by the territorial reduction system imposed by the Chilean state during the twentieth century has been identified as the primary cause of rural community poverty resulting in urban Indigenous migratory waves. Mapuche women appear to have been particularly affected given that some rural communities implemented a patrilineal inheritance system of the few lands that remained in Mapuche hands. This situation was reflected in several interviews, as in the case of sixty-four-year-old Cristina, who has occupied several leadership positions within her Mapuche association. In Cristina's words:

> I was twelve when I arrived in Santiago, to work in domestic service. My sister arrived at eighteen. We came out of necessity, for not having food. An uncle took our land from us.

Soon after arriving in Santiago from her community of origin and while still a child, Cristina found a job in the domestic sector as a live-in nana. As reflected in the stories of many women who were employed as nanas in Santiago, in addition to the poor living conditions in which they lived in their rural communities, many were also displaced from their inheritances by male members of their families, truncating the possible development of their lives in the Wallmapu. With few options left, Mapuche women left their communities behind in search of ways of providing for them and their families. This is the case of Vanesa, who is forty-six. Vanesa is a first-generation Mapuche rural migrant in Santiago who has worked as a nana since arriving to the city thirty years ago. In the words of Vanesa:

> I left my house at seventeen to help my parents, to send something back, because you know that the poverty of those years in the south was stark. In addition, families are large, couples had no fewer than six children.

As Vanesa's experience reflects, journeys to Santiago were made, in many cases, to economically support families through remittances. The trip also implied an intense emotional dimension, especially the mourning for a world that was left behind to face a new unpredictable context. Similar to Vanesa, Rita is also an active member of her Mapuche association, holding different leadership roles within her association. As in the cases of Cristina and Vanesa, Rita's chronicle, when recalling her arrival in Santiago, reflects the emotional and psychological cost and the tacit violence implied in the uprooting of Mapuche girls in pursuit of salaried economic subsistence. In this regard, Rita, who is fifty-five, says that:

> *I came to Santiago to work. I was sixteen years old. I worked in domestic service. I had a hard time at first, I got sick. I almost died. It was a very abrupt change from the countryside to the city. The sorrow. . . .*

Migration from the countryside implied a high personal cost for Mapuche women who, for the first time, left the safety of their households behind. For many women like Rita, the first years in Santiago were lived in sadness, loneliness, and illness while their bodies were racialized and stigmatized through domestic service as nanas. As pointed out in one of our many conversations with Fernando, a forty-five-year-old Mapuche who actively participates with his family in a Mapuche association on the outskirts of the city, many Mapuche women did not have family networks to receive them in Santiago. In the absence of family, their future employers would wait for them at the exit of the central train station, eager for them to start with their work after the long journey. Subalternate domestic work, especially in the live-in sector, is an invisible space on a social and political level, within which the possibilities of various oppressions are frequent, even more so in an unknown city with different codes from that of a rural Indigenous community.

As Alvarado-Lincopi (2016) points out, live-in domestic work as a form of social relationship deepened the dependence and exploitation of nanas laboring in Santiago while also allowing them, paradoxically, to overcome the difficulties from which Mapuche women emigrated from the Wallmapu. The accounts of nanas of their first years in the capital are permeated with memories subject to pain. Together with the trauma of alienation, the abuse they suffered as subalternate Others resulted from racial hierarchies actively operating in this labor area consigned to Mapuche women. María, forty-five years old, is one of the most active presidentas in Santiago. Her trajectory in the city, however, started as many other Mapuche women who left their rural communities to support their families. When describing her arrival to Santiago, María said:

> My experience in Santiago was horrible at the beginning. I was psychologically abused, I was hungry, I was lonely. They treated me badly for coming from the countryside, for being poor. I had no choice but to work as a live-in nana.

The construction of their urban experience as female Indigenous servants confronted them with prejudices, stereotypes and racial, class, and gender discrimination. Coming from the countryside and being poor, as María stated, equaled being Mapuche; in other words, she was discriminated for being Indigenous. The bodies of Mapuche women were treated badly, as they suffered from psychological abuse and even hunger at the hands of those constructed as superior. In this sense, working as live-in nanas often implied immersing themselves in spaces where indigeneity was defined by its exploitability.

Cumes (2014) has comprehensively written about the situation of Indigenous domestic workers in Guatemala, emphasizing an analysis focused on colonialism, patriarchy, and racism in the sphere of Indigenous employment. In this sense, Cumes (2014) points out that domestic work constitutes a long-term institution of servitude that responds to patriarchal colonial structures based on violence and humiliation—that serves the interests of the colonizers and their descendants. The institution goes beyond a domestic sphere, controlling, in turn, the very life of Indigenous women. One of the main characteristics of the colonial violence executed over female Indigenous domestic workers was the invisibilization of their urban experience. In this respect, Marcela, a sixty-six-year-old former nana and current leader of a Mapuche association, says:

> Now I can have an opinion. Before I was discriminated against for being a nana. Now I can talk, because I am the head of the household at home and at work.

As Alvarado-Lincopi (2016) points out, obedience without protest was normalized by Chilean-mestizo employers, in which servants had to remain silent at all costs. The inferiorization of Mapuche nanas implied, for decades, the impossibility of articulating a fight against their invisibility within the domestic space that belonged to others. This is expressed in Marcela's words when she exemplifies the condition of subordination imposed by colonialism on Mapuche bodies: "Before I was discriminated against for being a nana. Now I can talk." The sentences "Now I can have an opinion" and "Now I can talk" refer to a time when Marcela, like many other Mapuche women, were silenced and their presence rendered invisible for being nanas. At the same time, these socio-racial hierarchies uncover silence as a micropolitical strategy to survive the violence exerted on Mapuche nanas within the urban households where they work.

The gradual independence conferred by economic improvement allowed Mapuche women to be able to gradually opt out of live-in domestic service.

Thus, they were able to aim for their own homes, combining their live-out nana work with other responsibilities often still associated with feminized tasks. As Gutiérrez-Rodríguez (2014) maintains, the employment of a woman to perform domestic and care duties represents a fundamental link in the re-creation of a patriarchal structure in which femininity is correlated with home and care. Although still framed in domestic tasks, as Marcela points out with the phrase "I am the head of the household at home and at work," leading their own homes gave Mapuche women a sense of security not only from a material viewpoint but also in terms of labor dynamics, allowing them to reveal their hidden voices: "Now I can talk." These newly recovered voices materialized in a quest to make their experience as Indigenous women in the city visible. Nanas, as Millaleo (2016) points out, were able to subvert their subordinated condition when their inner *ñañas* emerged, their Mapuche identity. It is in this same sense of Indigenous identity reencounter that the figure of the presidenta has begun to mold itself more clearly within the Mapuche associative margins in Santiago.

About Leadership

Economic independence and distance from rural community family structures, although challenging, have represented emancipatory opportunities to develop and strengthen the leadership position of nanas in the city. With the return to democracy in the early 1990s, the demands of the Mapuche people in Chile began to take a clearer shape. As Cuminao (2009) states, a discourse begins to develop from the outskirts of the city, which is differentiated by ethnic representations. The dimension of indigeneity has been the main component that brings together the Mapuche diaspora in Santiago. Mapuche women have positioned their leadership as part of the Mapuche struggle (Aguilera and Yon 2015). That is, gender identity is still mediated by their identification as Mapuche (Richards 2014; Vera 2014). Diva Millapán (2014), one of the most notorious Mapuche activists for the initiative of Mapuche women's leadership in Santiago, acknowledged that the creation of the Red de Mujeres Mapuche (Network of Mapuche Women) in 2012 served to present proposals to political parties raised as a Mapuche people more than exclusively based on gender-specific issues. As members of a subjugated people in Chile, and especially in the city, their ethnicity has usually been a more salient way to counteract invisibility-based discourses that equate authentic indigeneity with a rural dwelling. Despite the lack of gender-specific demands, Richards (2004) and Calfío (2009) recognize that, from the 1980s onward, women started to become more influential in the decision-making machineries within Mapuche associations. Challenging practices and customs that have relegated them to the background of recent history, Mapuche women have assumed leadership positions within urban Indigenous associations. Soledad, a fifty-one-year-old former nana and current presidenta of her Mapuche associations, explains this trend:

> Generally, women do everything at home and in the community. That is why today the greatest Mapuche leaders are women, and that is because they have the integrity, strength, responsibility, and love for our culture.

Presidentas have performed a broad range of duties, including the traditional role of cultural educators in areas such as language, health, and Indigenous crafts outside of the family and rural community—the expected milieu for these tasks (Brablec 2022). Indigenous migrant women in cities and their descendants have played roles that have been conceived as gender specific, related to the maintenance of tradition within their homes. At the same time, they are changing these same narratives of tradition by becoming leaders of community-based organizations in which their directive role extends beyond the educational area. Indigenous women in cities, as community leaders, play a key role in the creation of consciousness around indigeneity as a political stance, shared discourse, and international framework for rights. In many cases, indigeneity and its potential as a political tool is discussed, debated, and discovered within Indigenous associations. Many Indigenous migrants and their descendants start off describing their identity roots as Chilean or mestizo, but through their organizational participation, the framework of Indigenous rights gives them a language to name this experience as a Mapuche one. The growing Mapuche consciousness resulting from associational participation is making an impact in Santiago because Indigenous identity has not decreased. Some Mapuche women, such as María, recognize a feeling of loneliness and desire to connect with their Mapuche peers after years of confinement as a live-in nana as one of the motivations for creating and leading their Mapuche associations. In Maria's words:

> Mapuche women are very locked up because they work at home as nanas. At the beginning, we formed this association to have contact with our Mapuche people. Then I noticed that there were Mapuche who did not know anything about their culture but now they are learning with the help of the association. I work hard to recover and maintain my identity and the identity of my people here in the city.

The organizational leadership role as presidentas has been coupled with an identity reencounter for hundreds of Mapuche in Santiago. However, this unpaid, voluntary role has replicated social dynamics of excessive burden that often borders on abuse of their time and work—which are not atypical of community work—that add up to their poorly paid work as nanas and unpaid work as mothers and housewives. Their work has also expanded to other areas beyond the solely cultural, encompassing, in turn, political negotiation—especially at the municipality level—by virtue of generating greater and better spaces for the development of their associations. María continued:

> I am a leader, I am a housewife, I am a mother, I am a worker. I do not have the time and money. I spend the year too tired. But here I am. My challenge is to continue with the teaching of worldview, spirituality, and language in our association.

As maintained by Paredes (2017), Indigenous women have historically occupied a primary role in the teaching of their cultures, including, among other issues, Native languages and worldviews. In this way, they are possessors of a symbolic power in the recovery of Indigenous historical memories, on which to build emancipated futures that challenge cultural norms imposed by the dominant society. By using the legal framework provided by the state for the creation of Indigenous associations, Mapuche presidentas have been opening spaces of leadership, especially in associations that seek a cultural revival. Mapuche women have thus continued with a historical role of cultural transmission, being transformed into agents of cultural survival.

As stated by Fitzgerald (2006) for the New Zealand case, it is often wrongly assumed that Indigenous leadership positions, to date, are still unequivocally exercised by men, with women playing subordinate roles to male authority.

Mapuche presidentas who are or have been nanas have been actively working to re-create their identity, rebuilding their culture in the city in parallel with their role in domestic service. Through the reconnection and maintenance of ties with their Mapuche peers, presidentas have used urban Indigenous associations as sites for the collective expression of their ethnicity and resistance to racist oppression. The female Mapuche diaspora has been leaving behind social roles that relegate them to a domestic sphere, with cultural recovery and implementation gradually becoming their leadership strongholds in Santiago. Nevertheless, their work has not been immune to challenges, as described in the next section.

Challenges

Gender stereotypes have influenced traditional female occupations both within and outside Mapuche society, resulting in microaggressions toward those women who break acceptable, appropriate, or desirable gender roles. The role of nana, associated with the domestic sphere, and the role of presidenta, associated with leadership, would thus be intrinsically opposed by appealing to quasi-binary gender characteristics. In this way, those Mapuche women who position themselves in both roles, the domestic one as nanas and the leadership one as presidentas, intersecting the characteristics appreciated as feminine and masculine, have not been strangers to questionings about their supposed deviation from the expected social roles of a Mapuche woman. Valeria is a forty-seven-year-old Mapuche presidenta who was born in Santiago to Mapuche parents and worked as a part-time nana to be able to dedicate herself to raising her three children. Unlike other presidentas whose banner of struggle has been cultural recovery, Valeria has fought to create more participatory spaces for Mapuche women in Santiago. Regarding this role, Valeria comments:

> Other Mapuche have told me that I am not Mapuche because Mapuche women cannot lead groups. I have been fighting to create political spaces for women in Santiago. It is extremely important for society to begin to value us as Mapuche women for the work that we have been developing for years as leaders and not only for our work at the service of our and others' children.

The taught normativity of what supposedly are Indigenous ancestral gender roles, like any other social roles, are not static but their borders are constantly traversed by the attitudes, self-perceptions, and behaviors of migrant Indigenous women and their descendants in cities. However, from the urban Mapuche diaspora itself, voices against the socio-political role of presidentas have emerged with strength. Sergio is a fifty-three-year-old Mapuche *lonko*, or head of a rural community, who has lived in Santiago for more than twenty years. He is also one of the most influential leaders in Santiago in the area of Mapuche health. According to his words:

> The Mapuche culture clearly defines the roles and functions of each one. These new conceptions of leadership create a loss of the philosophical values and principles of our people. The sense that allows respect between genders is lost, the loss of spirituality.

Leaders like Sergio, holding views based on conceptions that supposedly respond to the ancestral Mapuche culture and claiming an intrusion of doctrines and fashions alien to Mapuche-ness into their traditional beliefs, have opposed the idea that presidentas can represent the urban Mapuche community vis-à-vis the state. Sharing her experience as a former nana and current presidenta who is trying to advocate for the rights of her association at the regional-metropolitan level, Valeria says:

> It is a struggle to be a leader and a woman. There is a patriarchal system within the Mapuche sociopolitical world. It is super complicated, because Mapuche women are subject to an exclusive domestic role. We are seen as not having the ability to be in a leadership position.

Like Valeria, several other presidentas in the interviews spoke of a marked patriarchal culture within the Mapuche sociopolitical world both at the intra- and the extra-associational levels. Despite these practices, the same presidentas are managing to create collaborations among themselves and demand changes in terms of the internal structure of urban Indigenous institutions in Santiago. As Bacigalupo (2003) maintains, in recent decades Indigenous women are slowly being recognized as thinking politically with particular ways of intervening in their historical situations. In this way, as Paredes (2017) and Tuhiwai Smith (2005) argue, the colonial categories understood in relation to the masculine/feminine binary must be deconstructed and relearned, either through *feminismocomunitario* or through the restoration of their "traditional roles, rights and responsibilities" in Indigenous societies (Tuhiwai Smith 2005, 152). Through their leadership role, Mapuche women are certainly moving in this direction.

Conclusion

By advancing a critical urban indigeneities framework that highlights an urban perspective in decolonial gender studies, critical indigenous studies, and critical Latinx indigeneities, this chapter ethnographically discussed how Mapuche women are counteracting the disempowerment of their labor positionality by reempowering themselves through their leadership role in ethnic associations in Santiago de Chile. Once rendered invisible by impositions and replications of a (post)colonial order that subalternized them to places of racial, economic, and gender inferiority, urban Mapuche nanas and presidentas have gradually formed a space of identity resistance through the leadership space offered by urban ethnic associations. When considering the pathways of migration, employment, and Indigenous leadership, it is imperative to understand how the categories of race and gender, as well as colonial hierarchies, have historically shaped the lives of Mapuche presidentas in Santiago. Although most associations in Santiago are led by presidentas, to date there are no specific policies that consider the challenges and that promote the rights of Indigenous women in cities (Gobierno Regional Metropolitano de Santiago 2017). Despite having lower employment rates than their male counterparts, currently no support programs allow a compatibility between the political-associational participation and other family and work roles of Indigenous women. Notwithstanding these difficulties, the future presents new opportunities for the daughters of those women who came to Santiago to work as live-in nanas. At present, the growing access to university education has gradually led Mapuche women to leave behind the role of domestic work, but not that of Indigenous associational leadership. Undoubtedly, this situation will lead to new associative and labor dynamics in which race, gender, and class should be analyzed by new academic studies in view of the urban trajectories of those nanas and presidentas who opened paths for the development of the younger generation of Mapuche women in Santiago.

References

Aguilera, Valentina, and Rocío Yon. 2015. "Trayectorias Dirigenciales de Mujeres Mapuche Urbanas Líderes de Base." Undergraduate thesis, Universidad Diego Portales.

Alvarado-Lincopi, Claudio. 2016. "Mapurbekistán, De Indios a Mapurbes En La Capital Del Reyno: Racismo, Segregación Urbana y Agencias Mapuche En Santiago de Chile." Master's thesis, Universidad Nacional de la Plata.

Antileo, Enrique. 2015. "Trabajo Racializado. Una Reflexión a Partir de Datos de Población Indígena y Testimonios de La Migración y Residencia Mapuche En Santiago de Chile." *Meridional. Revista Chilena de Estudios Latinoamericanos*, no. 4, 71–96.

Aratani, Lauren. 2020. "Record Number of Native American Women Elected to Congress." *The Guardian*, April 11, 2020. https://www.theguardian.com/us-news/2020/nov/04/native-american-women-elected-congress-record-number?CMP=fb_gu&utm_medium=Social&utm_source=Facebook&fbclid=IwAR235yObq1zbGzHzIIDfL7tAK4NRRm_c-TkajXuH-WpDsE2246__DxlLm10#Echobox=1604566185.

Bacigalupo, Ana. 2003. "Mapuche Shamanic Bodies and the Chilean State: Polemic Gendered Representations and Indigenous Responses." In *Violence and the Body: Race, Gender and the State*, edited by Arturo Aldama, 322–43. Bloomington: Indiana University Press.

Bello, Álvaro. 2002. "Migración, Identidad y Comunidad Mapuche En Chile: Entre Utopismos y Realidades." *Asuntos Indígenas IWGIA* 3–4 (2): 40–47.

Blackwell, Maylei. 2017. "Geographies of Indigeneity: Indigenous Migrant Women's Organizing and Translocal Politics of Place." *Latino Studies* 15 (2): 156–81. https://doi.org/10.1057/s41276-017-0060-4.

Brablec, Dana. 2019. "Relational Goods and Endurance of Voluntary Associational Participation: The Case of the Indigenous Mapuche in Santiago de Chile." *Bulletin of Latin American Research* 38 (2): 222–36. https://doi.org/10.1111/blar.12837.

———. 2020. "Indigenising the City Together: Ethnic Place Production in Santiago de Chile." *Journal of Ethnic and Migration Studies* 49 (3): 892–908. https://doi.org/10.1080/1369183X.2020.1814711.

———. 2021. "Who Counts as an Authentic Indigenous? Collective Identity Negotiations in the Chilean Urban Context." *Sociology* 55 (1): 129–45. https://doi.org/10.1177/0038038520915435.

———. 2022. "Indigenous Language Revitalisation: Mapuzungun Workshops in Santiago de Chile." *Bulletin of Latin American Research* 41 (1): 69–84. https://doi.org/DOI:10.1111/blar.13291.

Calfío, Margarita. 2009. "Mujeres Mapuche, Voces y Acciones En Momentos de La Historia." In *Participación y Políticas de Mujeres Indígenas En Contextos Latinoamericanos Recientes*, edited by Andrea Pequeño, 91–109. Quito, Ecuador: FLACSO.

———. 2016. "Cuerpos Marcados, Comunidades En Construcción." In *Mujeres y Pueblos Originarios: Luchas y Resistencias Hacia La Descolonización*, edited by Andrea Álvarez and Millaray Painemal, 33–38. Santiago de Chile: Pehuén.

CASEN. 2017. *Pueblos Indígenas: Síntesis de Resultados*. http://observatorio.ministeriodesarrollosocial.gob.cl/storage/docs/casen/2017/Casen_2017_Pueblos_Indigenas.pdf.

Catrileo, Daniela. 2019. "Daniela Catrileo, poeta mapuche: El feminismo no necesariamente está salvando a todas las mujeres." Interview by Camila Magnet. Radio Juan Gómez Millas. September 7, 2019. https://radiojgm.uchile.cl/daniela-catrileo-poeta-mapuche-el-feminismo-no-necesariamente-esta-salvando-a-todas-las-mujeres/.

Cooperativa. 2014. "Ana Tijoux: Todos En Chile Tenemos 'Cara de Nana' y No Hay Problema Con Eso." August 2014. https://www.cooperativa.cl/noticias/entretencion/musica/musica-chilena/ana-tijoux-todos-en-chile-tenemos-cara-de-nana-y-no-hay-problema-con-eso/2014-08-06/001202.html.

Cumes, Aura. 2014. "La 'India' Como 'Sirvienta.' Servidumbre Doméstica, Colonialismo y Patriarcado En Guatemala." PhD thesis, Centro de Investigaciones y Estudios Superiores en Antropología Social. http://repositorio.ciesas.edu.mx/bitstream/handle/123456789/283/D259.pdf?sequence=1&isAllowed=y.

———. 2021. "Entrevista con Aura Cumes: la dualidad complementaria y el Popol vuj: Patriarcado, capitalismo y despojo." Interview by Yásnaya A. Gil, Revista de la Universidad de México. https://www.revistadelauniversidad.mx/articles/8c6a441d-7b8a-4db5-a62f-98c71d32ae92/entrevista-con-aura-cumes-la-dualidad-complementaria-y-el-popol-vuj?fbclid=IwAR3cU50TiOvo872D6eKPcs2sVY5zaCcWQd_NtXvozaq56ke5dwj_5bD3JzE.

Cuminao, Clorinda. 2009. "Mujeres Mapuche: Voces y Escritura de Un Posible Feminismo Indígena." In *Participación y Políticas de Mujeres Indígenas En Contextos Latinoamericanos Recientes*, edited by Andrea Pequeño, 111–24. Ecuador: FLACSO.

De Casanova, Erynn Masi. 2013. "Embodied Inequality: The Experience of Domestic Work in Urban Ecuador." *Gender and Society* 27 (4): 561–85.

El Mostrador. 2021. "¿Quién Es Elisa Loncón? La Profesora Mapuche Elegida Presidenta de La Convención Constituyente de Chile." July 4, 2021. https://www.elmostrador.cl/nueva-constitucion/2021/07/04/quien-es-elisa-loncon-la-profesora-mapuche-elegida-presidenta-de-la-convencion-constituyente-de-chile/.

Fitzgerald, Tanya. 2006. "Walking between Two Worlds: Indigenous Women and Educational Leadership." *Educational Management Administration & Leadership* 34 (2): 201–13. https://doi.org/10.1177/1741143206062494.

Gill, Lesley. 1994. *Precarious Dependencies: Gender, Class, and Domestic Service in Bolivia*. New York: Columbia University Press.

Gobierno Regional Metropolitano de Santiago (GORE). 2017. "Política Regional Indígena Urbana." https://www.gobiernosantiago.cl/wp-content/uploads/2014/12/PRIU-2017-2025-RMS-final.pdf.

Gunn Allen, Paula. 1992. *The Sacred Hoop: Recovering the Feminine in American Indian Traditions*. Boston: Beacon Press.

Gutiérrez-Rodríguez, Encarnación. 2014. "The Precarity of Feminisation: On Domestic Work, Heteronormativity and the Coloniality of Labour." *International Journal of Politics, Culture, and Society* 27 (2): 191–202.

Haskins, Victoria, and Margaret D. Jacobs. 2007. "Introduction." *Frontiers: A Journal of Women Studies* 28 (1/2): ix–xvi.

Hollingsworth, Julia. 2020. "New Zealand's Jacinda Ardern Appoints Country's First Indigenous Female Foreign Minister." CNN. February 11, 2020. https://edition.cnn.com/2020/11/02/asia/new-zealand-foreign-minister-intl-hnk/index.html.

Loncón, Elisa. 2020. "Las Mujeres Mapuche y El Feminismo." *CIPER* (blog). March 13, 2020. https://www.ciperchile.cl/2020/03/13/las-mujeres-mapuche-y-el-feminismo/?fbclid=IwAR1lGpj3iVKmz3tYzfN4-evuq7yzodYbZw1yyOwspslrUyIxyCdABzckXaM.

Lugones, Maria. 2016. "The Coloniality of Gender." In *The Palgrave Handbook of Gender and Development: Critical Engagements in Feminist Theory and Practice*, edited by Wendy Harcourt, 13–33. London: Palgrave Macmillan U.K. https://doi.org/10.1007/978-1-137-38273-3_2.

Millaleo, Ana. 2016. "Ser Nana En Chile: Un Imaginario Cruzado Por Género e Identidad Étnica. Universidad de Chile." In *Mujeres y Pueblos Originarios: Luchas y Resistencias Hacia La Descolonización*, edited by Andrea Álvarez and Millaray Painemal, 39–50. Santiago de Chile: Pehuén Editores.

———. 2020. "Resistencia Desde El Fogón: Pensando Un Feminismo Mapuche." *Mapuexpress* (blog). September 7, 2020. https://www.mapuexpress.org/2020/09/07/resistencia-desde-el-fogon-pensando-un-feminismo-mapuche/.

Millapán, Diva. 2014. "Los Derechos de Las Mujeres Mapuche." In *¿Chile Indígena?*, edited by El Desconcierto, 186–96. Santiago de Chile: Publicaciones El Buen Aire S.A.

Oyěwùmí, Oyèrónkẹ́. 1997. *The Invention of Women*. New edition. Minneapolis: University of Minnesota Press. http://www.jstor.org/stable/10.5749/j.cttttovh.

Painemal, Millaray. 2013. "Mujeres Mapuche y El Aporte Del Feminismo En La Lucha Contra La Violencia de Género." *Observatorio Género y Equidad* (blog). December 5, 2013. http://oge.cl/mujeres-mapuche-y-el-aporte-del-feminismo-en-la-lucha-contra-la-violencia-de-genero/.

Paredes, Julieta. 2017. "El Feminismocomunitario: La Creación de Un Pensamiento Propio." *Corpus* 7 (1): 1–10. https://doi.org/10.4000/corpusarchivos.1835.

Porter, Libby, and Oren Yiftachel. 2019. "Urbanizing Settler-Colonial Studies: Introduction to the Special Issue." *Settler Colonial Studies* 9 (2): 177–86. https://doi.org/10.1080/2201473X.2017.1409394.

Rain, Alicia, Margot Llombart, and Enrico Mora. 2020. "Mujeres Mapuche En La Diáspora y El Retorno al Wallmapu: Entre Micro-Resistencias de Género y Despojos Coloniales." *Chungara (Arica)* 52 (2): 347–60.

Richards, Patricia. 2014. *Pobladoras, Indígenas, and the State: Conflicts over Women's Rights in Chile*. New Brunswick, N.J.: Rutgers University Press.

Rivera Cusicanqui, Silvia. 2010. *Ch'ixinakax Utxiwa: Una Reflexión Sobre Las Prácticas y Discursos Descolonizadores.* Buenos Aires: Tinta Limón.

Ryburn, Megan. 2018. *Uncertain Citizenship.* Oakland: University of California Press. http://www.jstor.org/stable/10.1525/j.ctv5cg9x0.

Spivak, C. G. 1988. "Can the Subaltern Speak?" In *Marxism and the Interpretation of Culture,* edited by Cary Nelson and Lawrence Grossberg, 271–313. Urbana: University of Illinois Press.

Stoler, Ann Laura. 2001. "Tense and Tender Ties: The Politics of Comparison in North American History and (Post) Colonial Studies." *Journal of American History* 88 (3): 829–65. https://doi.org/10.2307/2700385.

Tuhiwai Smith, Linda. 2005. *Decolonizing Methodologies: Research and Indigenous Peoples.* London: Zed Books.

Valderrama, Ange. 2019. "Feminismo Mapuche o Una Crónica Sobre Los Procesos Coloniales Hoy." *Rebelión* (blog). November 2, 2019. https://rebelion.org/feminismo-mapuche-o-una-cronica-sobre-los-procesos-coloniales-hoy/.

Vera, Antonieta. 2014. "Moral, Representación y 'Feminismo Mapuche': Elementos Para Formular Una Pregunta." *Polis,* no. 38, 1–18.

CHAPTER FIVE

Hidden Stories of Ainu in Tokyo

KANAKO UZAWA

Who are *ah inu*?

On March 12, 2021, the commentary by a Japanese comedian during a Nippon Television news program stirred up the public discourse on the Ainu when the Ainu were referred to as dogs, *ah inu* being the Japanese word for dog. The Nippon Television Network expressed deep regret for this inappropriate expression the following day, which was not carefully examined before the broadcast (Miyata and Ono 2021). The discriminatory expression of *ah inu* has been used for decades to slur the Indigenous[1] people of Japan, the Ainu. Such an incident triggers a bitter memory of Japanese colonial history in which the Ainu have been treated as inferior to the rest of society. This most recent news not only indicates a general lack of knowledge on the Ainu but also highlights the deeply rooted prejudice and discrimination toward the Ainu in Japanese society (see more in Uzawa and Gayman 2022).

The chapter explores my personal journey through my stories and encounters with Tokyo Ainu. I use autoethnography as a methodology to discuss the questions of who is entitled to be Indigenous and what does it mean to be Tokyo Ainu in the twenty-first century? I focus particularly on an Ainu restaurant, Rera Cise (house of wind), in Tokyo as a site of Ainu culture and identity. As I claim for myself a diaspora Ainu identity, I use a concept of Indigenous diaspora as an analytical tool to make a point that being part of the Ainu diaspora is not the end of my indigeneity but rather a new way to nurture her own Ainu-ness.

The word *Ainu* originally means human being,[2] which represents the Ainu world view of respecting coexistence with nature, animals, plants, and everything around human beings. The Ainu have traditionally lived in northern Japan, Hokkaido, and Russia with rich natural resources. The Ainu are known as people who hunt, fish, and forage wild plants and herbs, but also as people who engaged in trade. The Ainu have had contact, principally through trade, with ethnic Japanese, Wajin, all the way back to the fourteenth century (Siddle 2003, 451). Due to its geographical location, Hokkaido (Ainu Mosir in the Ainu), the main traditional land of the Ainu, was considered important with respect to relations with Russia and in the context of an expanding Japanese state. Hokkaido became part of the Japanese colonization strategy when the government redrew the northern national border in 1869 for defensive purposes from the West. Hokkaido, which currently comprises 20 percent of Japan's national territory, was renamed in 1869. The concept of *empty land*[3] (terra nullius in Latin) was used to justify the claiming of territory by transforming Hokkaido into a Japanese colony (Siddle 1999, 71–72). Oguma states that the purpose of the colonization strategies was to possess the land of Hokkaido for a defensive purpose rather than reforming the Ainu by sending large numbers of Wajin to Hokkaido. (For more discussion on this topic, see Oguma 1998, 53–55; and Uzawa 2020b, 12–14.)

Political Landscape of the Ainu

A year after the Meiji Restoration in 1868, Hokkaido became part of the Japanese state. From this moment onward, the Ainu were forcibly incorporated into Japanese legal and political structures. In 1899, the assimilation law, the Hokkaido Former Aborigines Protection Act (HFAPA), came into force, depriving the Ainu of their traditional livelihood of fishing and hunting and pushing them to engage with agriculture. This resulted in many Ainu suffering severe economic, social, and cultural hardship (see more in Osakada 2020; Uzawa 2020b). A segregated education system was imposed on the Ainu to transform them into Japanese under the HFAPA and the Kyūdojin Jidō Kyōiku Kitei in 1901 (Regulations for the Education of Former Native Children; Siddle 1996, 71). As of 2022 it is believed that there are no Native speakers of the Ainu language remaining in Japan. In 1997, ninety-eight years later after the enactment of the HFAPA, it was finally replaced by the Ainu Cultural Promotion Act (ACPA), or in full, the Law for the Promotion of the

Ainu Culture and for the Dissemination and Advocacy for the Traditions of the Ainu and the Ainu Culture (Siddle 2002; Sonohara 1997). However, the enactment of the ACPA brought much dissatisfaction to the Ainu community as it failed to make a binding resolution to recognize the Ainu as Indigenous peoples.

The Ainu share many of the political, cultural, and economic challenges that other Indigenous peoples in the world face. It was only in 2008 that the Japanese government finally recognized the Ainu as Indigenous peoples of Japan (Advisory Council for Future Ainu Policy 2009, 1). This official status continues to be a contentious point since it recognizes neither any right for self-determination nor collective rights. As a backdrop of the 2008 resolution, in September 2007, the government of Japan voted in favor of the United Nations Declaration on the Rights of Indigenous Peoples (UNDRIP) while refusing to recognize the Ainu as Indigenous peoples of Japan according to the standards of international law (see more in Stevens 2014; Uzawa 2020b). This implied not being bound by legal guidelines of self-determination and collective rights provided by UNDRIP and entitled fully as stipulated in the International Labour Organization Indigenous and Tribal Peoples Convention 1989 (No.169). Yet it is fair to state that the 2008 resolution was still a major political shift within Indigenous politics in Japan, where both houses of the Japanese Diet passed a "Resolution Calling for Recognition of the Ainu People as Indigenous People" in June 2008 (see more in Stevens 2008).

The core issues of the Ainu political landscape, however, still remain today. In 2019 the Act Promoting Measures to Achieve a Society in Which the Pride of Ainu Is Respected (or the Ainu Policy Promotion Act) came into force (Ministry of Internal Affairs and Communications 2019). The Ainu Policy Promotion Act was also criticized by the Ainu locals, as the core principle of the law is not favorable to the needs of the Ainu. In general the act aims (1) to establish special measures for the Ainu to collect natural resources such as plants and salmon[4] for ceremonial purposes and for the use in transmitting Ainu culture, and (2) to establish a grant system of financial subsidies for local government regional and industrial development using Ainu culture.[5] A cross-ministerial Headquarters for the Promotion of Ainu Policy has been established within the cabinet. The law aims to enable Ainu people to live in society with pride and dignity wherein each individual coexists in an environment of respect. It is the first time that the Ainu are to be recognized as an Indigenous people within the Japanese law. A prohibition against discrimination toward individuals is also included in the law (see also Uzawa 2019a, 2019b).

However, a close reading of the act reveals no definition of the term *Indigenous*, nor does it mention any collective rights. No concrete details of how the Ainu are to be involved in the planning, implementation, or evaluation of the financial subsidies have been included, nor can one find any concrete penalties for violations of the discrimination clause. The act thus not only fails to recognize Ainu self-determination but also risks neglecting direct Ainu involvement. Furthermore, legislators have specifically expressed expectations regarding the new law's role in bolstering Ainu tourism, a notion that, given the exploitative history of Ainu tourism, has enraged some Ainu activists (*Japan Times* 2019; see also Uzawa 2019b).

Moreover, the act falls far short of recent demands by concerned Ainu groups. *Hokkaido Shimbun* reports that Ainu activists, who had been critical of the process deliberations leading up to the draft bill, stated that the one-sided hearings suggest a notion of colonialism (Murata and Yoshida 2018). *Shuukan Kinyobi* reports that Ainu activists established the lobbying organization called the Realization of Ainu Voices as Indigenous People (Senjū minzoku Ainu no koe jitsugen) in 2018. They formulated a number of demands based on discussions with the Policy Office for Ainu Affairs: (1) an apology for historical wrongs; (2) the establishment of the right to self-determination; (3) the deregulation of the new grants for the Ainu; (4) the right to natural resources, including the return of land; and (5) the ceasing of all further research on Ainu ancestral human remains (Saito 2018). Tahara Ryoko, one of the representatives from the Realization of Ainu Voices as Indigenous People, stated, "It is 150 years since Ainu Mosir (Ainu land) was renamed. For the Ainu, it has been 150 years of struggles. I hope the New Ainu Law to be something that enables Ainu to live as human beings" (Saito 2018; see also Uzawa 2019a). A critical comment on the Hokkaido 150-year commemoration ceremony within the Ainu community is reflected in such a statement where they cannot celebrate such a day without an official apology from the government, and that the development in the land was done under the label of pioneering, which did not recognize the history of suppression of the Ainu (See also Uzawa 2020b). These responses demonstrate fundamental differences between the government's and the Ainu groups' understanding of Ainu livelihood and well-being as affected by colonial history throughout the past century and a half.

A Paradox of Contemporary Japanese Society

Despite the widely held view of Japan being a homogeneous society, it has become more notable in recent years that Japan consists of an ethnically, culturally, and socially diverse population (Lie 2001). Japan today is a mix of the Ainu Indigenous peoples; the Ryukyuans[6] people, who are Indigenous to Okinawa; the Zainichi Korean, born and raised in Japan; and the Burakumin,[7] foreign migrants, and naturalized immigrants (Uzawa 2020b). All of them are now important members of Japanese society.

When it comes to the number of Ainu in the population, however, it remains unclear since Japan does not conduct a survey on ethnicity in the national census. Considering existing prejudice and discrimination toward Ainu, it is reasonable to assume that there are many Ainu who do not wish to reveal their identity and ethnic background. This can be seen, for example, in the vast difference in the numbers of the Ainu population in the governmental surveys both on Hokkaido Ainu and Ainu who reside outside of Hokkaido. Firstly, the Hokkaido Ainu Living Condition Survey,[8] which has been conducted every seven years since 1972 by the Hokkaido prefectural government, shows the vast difference in the Ainu population between 2006 and 2017. The 2017 survey found 13,118 individuals in 5,571 households across 63 municipalities, while in the 2006 survey it was 23,782 individuals in 8,274 households in 72 municipalities, a decline of nearly 45 percent (Department of Hokkaido Environment and Lifestyle 2017, 3). Secondly, the most recent survey, the Ainu Living Condition outside of Hokkaido Survey in 2011, shows a result of only having 210 respondents (Council for Ainu Policy Promotion Working Group on the Survey of Living Conditions of Ainu Outside Hokkaido 2011). In addition to the 2011 survey, the Consciousness Survey on the Degree of Public Understanding for Ainu People in 2016 reports only 28 individual respondents living in the Kanto[9] area (Council for Ainu Policy Promotion 2016, 4). This is significantly lower than the estimation by Ainu in Tokyo, which suggests around 10,000 Ainu who live in and around the capital region (Watson 2014b, 69). This is, for example, similar to the case of the Indigenous population in Canada, where the systematic undercounting of Indigenous peoples is seen as a fundamental challenge (Andersen 2013, 47).

Another important factor to be aware of is the cross-cultural environment in which contemporary Ainu reside. The Ainu and Wajin livelihood and relations are inseparable in contemporary Japanese society; most Ainu marry Wajin or other nationals, have Japanese as a mother tongue, and are educated in Japanese. This signals the complexity of Ainu's everyday life and identity.

Studies of the Urban Ainu

There has been very little research on the urban Ainu. An exception here is Simon Cotterill's (2011) article that examines the contemporary urban Ainu in Greater Tokyo, which shows the struggles and challenges of Tokyo Ainu through a lens of the documentary film *TOKYO Ainu*. Nakamura Naohiro (2015) studied socioeconomic relations and identities of Ainu living outside of Hokkaido, or Dogai Ainu, and describes their experience as "statistical genocide," facing a challenge in finding their Indigenous identity and a lack of social welfare and basic means of life (Nakamura 2015, 661; see also Watson 2010, 2014a, 2014b). My doctoral dissertation, which consists of three academic articles, also contributes to the urban Ainu discussion by highlighting voices of Ainu and Wajin youth. My dissertation focuses on Ainu cultural revitalization in the cities of Sapporo and Tokyo and was based on my ethnography as an urban Ainu myself. I also examine identity politics and relations between Wajin and Ainu youth under an umbrella theoretical term *urban diasporic indigeneity*.

There is even less published in Japanese (but see Sekiguchi 2007; Ogasawara 1990), although there are two publications by Ainu people themselves. A respected Ainu elder, Ukaji Shizue (2011), published a nonacademic essay where she shares her life story from childhood to her adult life in Tokyo, and one of the few Ainu organizations in Tokyo, called Rera no kai (the Association of Rera, 1997) complied stories of the restaurant Rera Cise and its member's life stories (see more in Uzawa 2020b).

What Does it Mean to be Urban Ainu in the Twenty-First Century?

Technological advancements and transportation on a global scale give one a sense of becoming a global citizen. I am an urban Ainu raised both in Tokyo[10] and Hokkaido. I was inspired by the Sami political development in Norway, which led me to pursue higher education there. Mobilization on a global scale challenges one's sense of belonging; it challenges one to remain in touch with one's traditional livelihood, culture, and expression while also giving new possibilities to explore one's world view and to develop one's sense of identity and belonging (Uzawa 2020b, 27).

I was born in Tomakomai, Hokkaido, but spent my childhood and youth in and around Tokyo. As my mother comes from a small Ainu community called Nibutani, located in the southwest of Hokkaido, I spent all my school holidays with my relatives in Nibutani, one of the few Ainu communities that still has active participation in Ainu cultural revitalization. The Nibutani community is unique for two reasons: (1) Nibutani is a historical Ainu community, and (2) more than half of the residents have Ainu heritage. I consider Nibutani as my home community, while I also consider the Tokyo Ainu community as my home where I spent my youth. As a child, I considered both Ainu and Japanese culture valuable resources of my heritage and identity, even though I did not feel any urge to learn either the Ainu language or its culture. This was simply because Ainu culture appeared to me as something natural that is embedded in my body and memory as part of my everyday life. My childhood in Tokyo, on the other hand, was something completely different: there was no sign of Ainu culture, and nobody spoke about it, either. I remember myself adopting these two completely different environments, questioning why no one ever spoke about Ainu culture or language in Tokyo. It felt strange that no one ever spoke about a culture that is supposedly part of the diverse Japanese society. The question grew bigger and more prominent within me during my teenage years.

My grandfather, Tadashi Kaizawa, was a well-known Ainu leader and rights advocate who devoted his life to the landmark court case of the Nibutani dam verdict in 1997.[11] The Nibutani dam verdict changed the political landscape of the discussion of indigeneity in Japan by challenging a deeply rooted image of Ainu as a dying race. A discussion around who is entitled to be considered Indigenous in Japan and the implications of the use of the term *Indigenous peoples*[12] became more widely discussed in public. Ainu appeared more in local news, TV, and social media, which has even drawn international attention.[13]

The court case process had a great impact on my youth. I learned for the first time that to be Ainu was to be discriminated against. This shocked me, as this was in stark contrast to all my warm memories of the Ainu people and culture—the kindest and warmest people I have ever known. I began to search for a reason by involving myself with Tokyo Ainu cultural events and activities as an undergraduate student.

The Tokyo Ainu Community as My Home

I was introduced to an Ainu restaurant in Tokyo at the age of nineteen. Rera Cise[14] (house of wind), located in Waseda, Tokyo, opposite Waseda University, was a commercial restaurant established in 1994 under a successful national fundraising campaign by Ainu and Wajin supporters. This was initiated by Tokyo Ainu to create a place for all Tokyo Ainu to gather and enjoy each other's company with Ainu food. The Rera Cise restaurant was run by the Ainu Association of Rera, an Ainu cultural association established in 1983, and formed of Ainu members who practice Ainu performing art. It aims to disseminate Ainu culture to the public by visiting schools, festivals, and any other venues requested. As I was in search of my Ainu identity and expression, I became fascinated by the restaurant and its activities. I became a member of the Ainu Association of Rera: I participated in almost all activities and events organized by the association and started working as a waitress at the restaurant. Working as a waitress allowed me to meet and talk to many Tokyo Ainu, whom I would not have met otherwise. I learned about their life experiences and challenges, why they left Hokkaido, and what it's like to be Ainu in Tokyo. Some moved to Tokyo for work, and some moved to pursue education. Some wanted to have a new life where they were not concerned about being discriminated against as Ainu in Hokkaido. The meeting with Tokyo Ainu also made me realize how privileged I was, going to university and having a grandfather who inspired me and taught me essential life values as Ainu. As I did not receive any direct discrimination as Ainu in my everyday life in Tokyo, my encounters with Tokyo Ainu taught me a different way to understand what it means to be Ainu in Tokyo in the twenty-first century. I suppose the reason I was not receiving any direct discrimination as Ainu was probably because of my appearance, which more closely resembles Wajin physical features. This was demonstrated—somewhat ironically—by the Wajin audience being puzzled at my appearance whenever I performed in public as a member of the Ainu Association of Rera. They asked, "Are you also Ainu!?" I replied, "Yes." They stared at me, so I thought, "What do you expect the Ainu to look like?" This type of reaction made me feel unsafe and insecure about myself—completely opposite from all the positive feelings I had toward the Ainu culture and people. I was angry and frustrated. On the other hand, I sometimes encountered some who thought having Ainu heritage was something cool and exciting. It was cool because it is different from Japanese culture and exciting because there is something new to learn from.

I learned most of my Ainu songs and dances from the elders in the Ainu Association of Rera in Tokyo and cherish the memories with them even today. For me, learning Ainu performing arts meant much more than learning elements of songs and dances. The time being with elders gave me an opportunity to explore their world views and see their lived experiences. A miracle moment happens when my singing and dancing are synchronized together with them. It is a sense of collective recognition and safety, a moment in which Ainu traditional songs and dances become part of me. I flourish as Tokyo Ainu.

The Rera Cise restaurant was more than a restaurant for many Tokyo Ainu. It offered a sense of home where all Tokyo Ainu rest their mind from very busy everyday life in Tokyo. The Rera Cise was located in the basement of a building that was only about fifty square meters. As one walks down to the restaurant, the Ainu music welcomes the guests. Most of the restaurant's furniture is wooden, which gives a warm, homey feeling. A slightly dim room decorated with *cikoro-inaw*, Ainu homemade wood-shaving sticks used for Ainu ceremony, gives a sense of being in Ainu cultural space (see more in Uzawa 2018).

I spent more time at the restaurant than my university campus, and even considered Rera Cise as a better learning space than a university. What was fascinating about working at Rera Cise was that I learned the Ainu food culture, which I never had a chance to learn properly when I was in Nibutani. The first thing I learned was that there are no written recipes (as far as I can remember). All recipes were in the memories of the Ainu elders who worked in the kitchen. What one had to do is to observe and learn from the elders. Everything was homemade with important Ainu ingredients delivered directly from Hokkaido. Dishes prepared with warm thoughts and inspiration from the elders tasted better than anything that I have ever experienced in the past. Because of Rera Cise, Tokyo was no longer a place where no one speaks about the Ainu. From this moment on, Tokyo became a *home* to me (see also Uzawa 2018).

By learning more about the Ainu food culture, I discovered how food can trigger memories of a colonial history. For example, *kitopiro* (*gyoja ninniku* in Japanese and *pukusa* in Ainu) is a good example. *Kitopiro* is known in the Ainu community as a green edible plant that has medicinal properties. It has a strong garlicky taste, and locals are extremely careful when and when not to eat it. In the past, its powerful smell fed a prejudice against the Ainu, who were referred to as "smelly Ainu." This is reminiscent of the incident I mentioned earlier of a Japanese comedian's commentary on *ah inu,* meaning "oh dog" in Japanese (see also Uzawa 2020a). This *kitopiro* was my grandfather's and my favorite that we used to have in his garden. *Kitopiro* was one of the more popular dishes at the Rera Cise and something that I regularly had to explain to customers. This was a moment in which I felt my knowledge on the Ainu food was finally recognized and appreciated. It was also a moment in which I could connect myself to warm memories of my grandparents and how our family enjoyed sharing the meal together.

Rera Cise became more and more popular for all Ainu supporters, university students, and anyone who read about it in newspapers and food magazines. It was also obvious that it became a hub for Tokyo Ainu who searched for their home in Tokyo. Rera Cise offered a free cultural learning space for Ainu living in and around Tokyo—a venue to find a sense of community and belonging. On the other hand, it was a kind of "come as you are" environment that allows one to engage and disengage with one's identity and commitment to Ainu culture. This created space to regenerate identity making and cultural revitalization in Tokyo (see more in Uzawa 2020b).

Through Rera Cise I encountered many Tokyo Ainu who had diverse backgrounds, and I learned the various reasons they moved to Tokyo: some because of better employment and education opportunity and some to start a new life, sometimes escaping from discrimination in Hokkaido (see more in Council for Ainu Policy Promotion 2016; Association of Rera 1997; Ukaji 2011). What struck me most was not their social or financial struggles, which tend to be a focus of Ainu issues in the general discourse, but rather their efforts to solidify a strong sense of community and belonging through food culture and cultural practices. Through this experience, I also learned a way to explore my Ainu identity and what it means to be urban Ainu in Tokyo. My time with Tokyo Ainu became a treasure in my life.

What Makes Us Indigenous?

What is the discursive challenge within the discourse of urban Indigenous peoples? This addresses a key question of how to come to terms with what "authentic" indigeneity is and is not. Is this a question in relation to essentialist claims to land and boundary making, or a question of diasporic[15] Indigenous lifestyle that is more based on genealogical claims and one's identity making in cities (see more in Uzawa 2020b, 40–44)? James Clifford, for example, uses Indigenous diaspora to demonstrate the complexity of Indigenous people today, which does not always require continuous residency in the homeland, as most Indigenous peoples reside in cities in countries like the United States, Canada, Australia, and Aotearoa New Zealand (2013, 70; see also Uzawa 2020b). This is applicable to the Ainu case as well, where many Ainu migrate to larger cities from Hokkaido for various reasons. According to the Ainu Living Conditions Outside of Hokkaido Survey, the reasons for migration are 50 percent for work, 11.4 percent because of discrimination toward the Ainu, and 10.1 percent for education (Council for Ainu Policy Promotion Working Group on the Survey of Living Conditions of Ainu Outside Hokkaido 2011, 27; see also Uzawa 2020b, 7–8). Commuting to larger cities for work is generally considered part of contemporary Ainu lifestyle. In other words, the man in the household supports the family in Hokkaido by seasonal or permanent work in cities. This lifestyle has become the contemporary livelihood of the Ainu, which is more of necessity than choice, to improve their life and future (Uzawa 2020b, 7–8).

Yet the homeland-based discussion has an important ground for claiming Indigenous rights, such as collective rights and rights to self-determination. It gives Indigenous peoples legitimacy to claim what was once their territory and space for traditional livelihood. This also enables them to discuss what is essential for their sustainable livelihood, such as access to natural resources, traditional knowledge of food, biodiversity, and cultural practices. These issues deserve significant attention for further discussion on a global scale. However, it is also crucial to expand our understanding of contemporary Indigenous livelihood that does not only depend on a tie to ancestral land, which has been widely used as one of the key indicators defining who is Indigenous and who is not (see also in Martínez Cobo 1987, esp. 22–23; Uzawa 2020b). The term *Indigenous* is political and has legal implications,[16] as Richard Siddle explains: "Indigenous people is not an objective anthropological category, but a political construct explicitly linked to international law and human rights movements" (2006, 114).

The homeland discussion has its own limitation when it comes to a question of diasporic Indigenous peoples in cities who may not have a strong connection to their homeland. It excludes those who have lost a connection to the homeland or do not fall into categories of national survey and census.[17] This is also a trigger for underlined tension between Hokkaido Ainu and Ainu living elsewhere (Uzawa 2018, 2020b). They become invisible from the public eye, or Other in the Japanese society (see more in Siddle 2006). Within the Ainu context, anyone who resides outside of Hokkaido can be considered as diasporic Ainu. In Japanese, it is referred to as Dogai Ainu, which has a negative connotation: Ainu outside of their homeland (see Nakamura 2015). In other words, it implies a lack of authenticity (Brablec and Canessa, introduction to this volume; Watson 2010, 2014a, 2014b; Hudson, Lewallen, and Watson 2014). This is the paradox of contemporary Ainu life, where many Ainu rely on their livelihood outside of Hokkaido, mainly in larger cities. While the term *Dogai Ainu* challenges the authenticity of Ainu living outside of Hokkaido, the term *diasporic* opens more space for Dogai Ainu opportunities in cities and a new way to craft their culture and identity. This can be seen from an example of different claims made by Hokkaido Ainu and Dogai Ainu to the government. The claims by Hokkaido Ainu focus on more access to natural resources and liberty to exercise Indigenous rights, which are still restricted by the local government, while Dogai Ainu place more focus on strengthening cultural aspects by creating shared spaces, such as a community center to foster Ainu youth, culture, and language (see more in Uzawa 2018; 2020b, 40–45).

What we refer to as *space* can be described as *iwor* in the Ainu culture. *Iwor* denotes a geographical space in nature and land used for maintaining Ainu traditional livelihood, such as gathering edible plants, fishing, and hunting (Oono 2017). Since the Ainu traditionally did not have a modern notion of individual land ownership, a concept of *iwor* may be more suitable for understanding urban space and place where Dogai Ainu foster and nurture Ainu culture, language, and people.[18]

Concluding Remarks

What makes me Indigenous? What makes me Ainu? All memories of dancing and singing Ainu songs and tasting warm salmon soup, *ohaw*, with Tokyo Ainu, smelling the forest, and gathering edible plants in Hokkaido are important parts of who I am today. I am someone from the Ainu diaspora who has lived overseas for over a decade but still cherishes all these memories even today. I do not see being part of the Ainu diaspora as the end of my indigeneity but rather as a new way to nurture my own Ainu-ness. This has challenged my capacity to find a new way to express and share inspiration, which I once received from Ainu people and culture. The most recent example is an establishment of my own website, together with like-minded colleagues and friends, called *AinuToday*.[19] It is the first English-language knowledge-sharing platform for an international audience to learn about contemporary Ainu voices, issues, and arts. *AinuToday* aims to deliver Ainu voices through literature, news, stories, online language courses, and art. With *AinuToday*, I attempt to go beyond an essentialized notion of the Ainu as a dying race or Indigenous people who live in the wilderness by delivering living stories of the Ainu. This is my contribution to the Ainu and other global Indigenous communities.

Within this framework, I produce contemporary dance and song, inspired by the Ainu traditional songs and dance, together with Ainu and non-Ainu artists. I use a Norwegian landscape and refer to this space as *iwor*, where I foster and nurture my Ainu-ness and express my contemporary development as a diaspora Ainu. This was something unthinkable when I was a Tokyo Ainu. What was considered as authentic was something we were all expected to respect and follow; there was no space for the youth to experiment with something innovative and new. At least, that was my understanding during my youth. When it comes to food culture, there is limitation of sustaining food culture in Norway where I reside. However, a fundamental understanding of food culture that respects relation and connection between human beings and nature is deeply rooted within me, and I wish to carry that onto my children.

I often refer to the Ainu word *Aynupuri* as indigeneity in my own interpretation. The Ainu traditionally use this term *Aynupuri* when one is expected to perform in a certain way or practice the Ainu culture in a traditional manner. The term *Aynupuri* is respected and used with the most care. As a diasporic Ainu, I interpret it differently: I interpret *Aynupuri* as *indigeneity*, which frees us from essentialized representation of the Ainu. This is an act of exercising the rights to self-determination and contribution to a decolonization process without external interference. The right to self-determination provides an opportunity for Indigenous peoples to make individual decisions. This can eventually contribute to form the foundation of the collective right, which translates to wider-scale cultural, economic, and social development.

Notes

This chapter is a slightly modified version of my doctoral dissertation (Uzawa 2020b).

1. I capitalize Indigenous referring to the global Indigenous rights movement and its discourse, which implies the rights to self-determination and collective rights.
2. A large number of Indigenous peoples refer to themselves as *people*, such as many of the Indigenous peoples of the Americas.
3. The concept of erasure—ignoring the Indigenous inhabitants as a nuisance or a hindrance to the project of colonization—was used during the latter half of the nineteenth century. By treating the Ainu as insignificant, the avenue was thus opened for the settlement and development of Hokkaido.
4. Salmon used to be a staple food for the Ainu.
5. "Overview of Ainu Policy in Japan," https://www.kantei.go.jp/jp/singi/ainusuishin/index_e.html.
6. Ryukyuans have been claiming to be Indigenous to Okinawa but are not yet recognized as Indigenous people of Japan by the Japanese government.
7. Burakumin were once considered an outcast group, people who were placed forcibly at the bottom of the traditional Japanese feudal order.
8. The survey states that the number does not represent the total population of the Ainu in Hokkaido but rather gives an indication of numbers each city managed to count. The criteria used for the survey is for individuals who identify themselves as Ainu, those who are believed to have Ainu bloodlines in their communities, and those who reside with Ainu because of marriage and adoption (Department of Hokkaido Environment & Lifestyle 2017, 1, 3).
9. The Kanto region is the largest island of Japan, which also includes the Greater Tokyo area.
10. Tokyo is one of the world's largest metropolitan cities with an estimated population of 13 million in 2015 (Tokyo Metropolitan Government, n.d.)
11. The Sapporo District Court for the first time in history recognized the Ainu's individual rights, stipulated in Article 13 of the Japanese Constitution, as well as a right to enjoy their own minority culture, stipulated in Article 27 of the International Covenant on Civil and Political Rights (Stevens 2014, 205).
12. James Anaya argues that the legal term *Indigenous peoples* with an *s* denotes a collective right following international law standards (2004, 100).
13. Ainu also became more known internationally through their participation in the UN arena since 1987, such as the United Nations Working Group on Indigenous Populations.
14. Rera Cise is now closed, but there is a new Ainu restaurant in Tokyo called Harukoro.
15. William Safran describes the term *diaspora*, referring to Jews, this way: "The Jews are the oldest diaspora; they lacked a 'homeland' for two millennia but thought about it constantly and the idea of a return to it—at first an escha-

tological conception and much later a concrete one—remained part of their collective consciousness" (2005, 36–37).

16. The discussion on the term *Indigenous* or *Indigenous peoples* is beyond the scope of this chapter. (See more in Anaya 2004; Dahl 2012; Niezen 2003; Uzawa 2020b).
17. For further discussion on the complexity of urban Indigenous identities, see Chris Andersen's explanation of a case from Canada (2013 47).
18. For further discussion on the relationship between Ainu and land, see the explanation of the Chikabumi Land Dispute at the beginning of the twentieth century in Uzawa (2020b, 43).
19. *AinuToday*: https://ainutoday.com. Dr. Uzawa founded AinuToday in 2021, supported by people throughout the Ainu community and like-minded colleagues Prof. Makiko Kimura; Dr. Scott Harrison; Sabra Harris, MA; Michael J. Ioannides, MA; and Maria Victoria Diaz-Gonzalez.

References

Advisory Council for Future Ainu Policy. 2009. *Final Report.* Tokyo: Government of Japan.

Anaya, J. 2004. *Indigenous Peoples in International Law*. New York: Oxford University Press.

Andersen, C. 2013. "Urban Aboriginality as a Distinctive Identity, in Twelve Parts." In *Indigenous in the City: Contemporary Identities and Cultural Innovation*, edited by C. Andersen and E. Peters, 46–68. Vancouver: University of British Columbia Press.

Association of Rera. 1997. *Rera Cise e no Michi—Kōshite Tokyo ni Ainu Ryōriten ga Dekita* [The Road Toward the Rera Cise: The Making of an Ainu Restaurant in Tokyo]. Tokyo: Gendai Kikakushitsu.

Clifford, James. 2013. *Returns: Becoming Indigenous in the Twenty-First Century.* Cambridge, Mass., and London: Harvard University Press.

Cotterill, Simon. 2011. "Documenting Urban Indigeneity: *TOKYO Ainu* and the 2011 Survey on the Living Conditions of Ainu Outside Hokkaido." *Asia-Pacific Journal: Japan Focus* 9 (45): 2. https://apjjf.org/2011/9/45/Simon-Cotterill/3642/article.html.

Council for Ainu Policy Promotion. 2016. *Consciousness Survey on the Degree of Public Understanding for Ainu People.* https://www.kantei.go.jp/jp/singi/ainusuishin/pdf/rikaido_houkoku160322.pdf.

Council for Ainu Policy Promotion Working Group on the Survey of Living Conditions of Ainu Outside Hokkaido. 2011. *The Report of the Working Group on the Survey of Living Conditions of Ainu Outside Hokkaido.* www.kantei.go.jp/jp/singi/ainusuishin/dai3/siryou3_3.pdf.

Dahl, J. 2012. *The Indigenous Space and Marginalized Peoples in the United Nations.* New York: Palgrave Macmillan.

Department of Hokkaido Environment & Lifestyle. 2017. *The Report of Hokkaido Ainu Living Conditions Survey*. http://www.pref.hokkaido.lg.jp/ks/ass/H29_ainu_living_conditions_survey_.pdf.

Hudson, M. J., A. E. Lewallen, and M. K. Watson, eds. 2014. *Beyond Ainu Studies: Changing Academic and Public Perspectives*. Honolulu: University of Hawai'i Press.

Japan Times. 2019. "'Empty words': Rights Groups Say Japan's Bill Recognizing Ainu as Indigenous Group Falls Short." March 2, 2019. https://www.japantimes.co.jp/news/2019/03/02/national/empty-words-rights-groups-say-japans-bill-recognizing-ainu-indigenous-group-falls-short/#.XKiKey2B1-U.

Lie, J. 2001. *Multiethnic Japan*. Cambridge, Mass., and London: Harvard University Press.

Martínez Cobo, J. R. 1987. *Study of the Problem of Discrimination against Indigenous Populations*. http://undocs.org/en/E/CN.4/Sub.2/1986/7/Add.4.

Ministry of Internal Affairs and Communications. 2019. Act Promoting Measures to Achieve a Society in Which the Pride of Ainu Is Respected. Retrieved from https://elaws.e-gov.go.jp/document?lawid=431AC0000000016 (Japanese only).

Miyata, Y., and T. Ono. 2021. "TV Network Apologizes for Slur toward Ainu People." *Asahi Shimbun*. https://www.asahi.com/ajw/articles/14266148.

Murata, R., and Yoshida, N. 2018. "Ainu New Law: Special Measure for Tree Collection and Salmon Fishing." *Hokkaido Shimbun*.

Nakamura, Naohiro. 2015. "Being Indigenous in a Non-Indigenous Environment: Identity Politics of the Dogai Ainu and New Indigenous Policies of Japan." *Environment and Planning A* 47 (3): 660–675. https://doi.org/10.1068/a130003p.

Niezen, R. 2003. *The Origins of Indigenism: Human Rights and the Politics of Identity*. Berkeley: University of California Press.

Ogasawara, Nobuyuki. 1990. *Shōppai kawa—Tokyo ni ikiru Ainutachi* [Crossing the Salty River: The Stories of Ainu Living in Tokyo]. Tokyo: Kirokusha.

Oguma, E. 1998. *"Nihonjin" no kyokai: Okinawa, Ainu, Taiwan, Chosen, shokuminchi shihai kara fukki undo made*. Tokyo: Shinyosha.

Oono, T. 2017. *Apoi no Fumoto kara: Ainu minzoku no Bunka to Rekishi eno Izanai* [From Apoi moutain: Invitation to Ainu Culture and History]. Samani, Hokkaido: Apoi dake fun club.

Osakada, Y. 2020. "An Examination of Arguments over the Ainu Policy Promotion Act of Japan Based on the UN Declaration on the Rights of Indigenous Peoples." *International Journal of Human Rights* 25 (6): 1053–1069.

Safran, W. 2005. "The Jewish Diaspora in a Comparative and Theoretical Perspective." *Israel Studies* 10 (1): 36–60.

Saito, M. 2018. "Ainu Make 12 Demands on New Law Including 'Government Apology.'" *Shuukan Kinyobi*, December 6, 2018. http://www.kinyobi.co.jp/kinyobinews/2018/12/06/antena-381/.

Sekiguchi, Yoshihiko. (2007). *Shutoken ni Ikiru Ainu Minzoku: 'Taiwa' no Chihei kara* [The Ainu Who Live in the Metropolitan Area: From the Horizon of "Dialogues"]. Urayasu, Japan: Sohukan.

Siddle, R. 1996. *Race, Resistance and the Ainu of Japan*. New York and Oxfordshire: Routledge.

———. 1999. "Ainu History: An Overview." In *Ainu: Spirit of a Northern People*, edited by W. W. Fitzhugh and C. O. Dubreuil, 67–73. Los Angeles: Smithsonian Institution in association with University of Washington Press.

———. 2002. "An Epoch-Making Event? The 1997 Ainu Cultural Promotion Act and Its Impact." *Japan Forum* 14 (3): 405–23. https://doi.org/10.1080/095558002200 0008763

———. 2003. "The Limits to Citizenship in Japan: Multiculturalism, Indigenous Rights and the Ainu." *Citizenship Studies* 7 (4): 447–462. https://doi.org/10.1080/1362 102032000134976.

———. 2006. "The Making of Ainu Moshiri: Japan's Indigenous Nationalism and Its Cultural Fictions." In *Nationalisms in Japan*, edited by Naoko Shimazu, 122–142. London: Routledge.

Sonohara, T. 1997. "Toward a Genuine Redress for an Unjust Past: The Nibutani Dam Case." *Murdoch University Electronic Journal of Law* 4 (2): 1–43. http://classic .austlii.edu.au/au/journals/MurUEJL/1997/16.html.

Stevens, G. 2008. "Resolution Calling for Recognition of the Ainu People as an Indigenous People." *Asia-Pacific Journal on Human Rights and the Law* 9 (1): 49–50.

———. 2014. "The Ainu, Law, and Legal Mobilization, 1984–2009." In Hudson, Lewallen, and Watson 2014, 200–222.

Tokyo Metropolitan Government. n.d. *Tokyo's History, Geography, and Population*. Accessed November 25, 2022. http://www.metro.tokyo.jp/ENGLISH/ABOUT /HISTORY/history03.htm.

Ukaji, Shizue. 2011. *Subete wo Asu no Kate toshite: Imakoso Ainu no Chie to Yuki wo* [Making Everything Resources for Tomorrow: Knowledge and Courage of the Ainu]. Tokyo: Seiryu shuppan.

Uzawa, K. 2018. "Everyday Acts of Resurgence and Diasporic Indigeneity among the Ainu of Tokyo." In *Indigenous Efflorescence: Beyond Revitalization in Sapmi and Ainu Mosir*, edited by G. Roche, H. Maruyama, and Å. V. Kroik, 179–203. Canberra: Australian National University Press.

———. 2019a. "Japan." In *The Indigenous World 2019*, edited by D. Berger and S. Leth, 269–74. Copenhagen: International Work Group for Indigenous Affairs.

———. 2019b. "What Does Ainu Cultural Revitalisation Mean to Ainu and Wajin Youth in the 21st Century? Case Study of Urespa as a Place to Learn Ainu Culture in the City of Sapporo, Japan." *AlterNative: An International Journal of Indigenous Peoples* 15 (2) 168–79. https://doi.org/10.1177/1177180119846665.

———. 2020a. "Being Ainu Today: Living in the Past, Present, and Future." *Kyoto Journal*, no. 98, 62–65.

———. 2020b. *Crafting Our Future Together: Urban Diasporic Indigeneity from an Ainu Perspective in Japan*. PhD dissertation, UiT Arctic University of Norway. https://munin.uit.no/handle/10037/17182.

Uzawa, K., and Gayman, J. 2022. "Japan." In *The Indigenous World 2020*, edited by Dwayne Mamo, 220–24. Copenhagen: International Work Group for Indigenous Affairs.

Watson, M. K. 2010. "Diasporic Indigeneity: Place and the Articulation of Ainu Identity in Tokyo, Japan." *Environment and Planning A* 42 (2): 268–84. https://doi.org/10.1068/a41112.

———. 2014a. *Japan's Ainu Minority in Tokyo: Diasporic Indigeneity and Urban Politics*. London: Routledge.

———. 2014b. "Tokyo Ainu and the Urban Indigenous Experience." In Hudson, Lewallen, and Watson 2014, 69–85.

CHAPTER SIX

The Politics of Ese Eja Indigenous Urbanite Images in Distinct Nation States

The Bolivian and Peruvian Amazon

DANIELA PELUSO

Diverging River: Distinct Nation States

Recent focus on Indigenous urbanization in Lowland South America has rightfully drawn attention to the dangers of strictly rural images for Amazonians (Alexiades and Peluso 2015, 2016; Peluso and Alexiades 2005a, 2005b). This chapter is premised on the importance of understanding Indigenous peoples as diversely participating in rural-urban flows, yet it also pays close attention to the particular complications that urban images pose as many conscientiously uphold them. Such an examination does not question the significance of stressing urbanization in the way that Indigenous peoples are represented, yet it aims to be cognizant that such images are often manipulated by agents with vested interests in divesting rural areas of its inhabitance.

Indigenous people "living at the borders" in Amazonia actually, apart from the symbolic underpinnings of the phrase as intended in this volume, do often tend to live on physical borders and have a long history of rural-urban flows that might not immediately seem apparent. Indeed, archeologists have now verified that pre-Columbian Amazonian settlements were large-scale and urban, centralized, densely populated, and stratified (Denevan 1992; Erickson 2006; Heckenberger et al. 2008) and were thus metropolises in their own right. Such findings expose large and expansive trade networks and challenge deeply rooted misconceptions of Amazonia as an area of pristine wilderness with minimal human impact on the environment and settlements (Fausto and Heckenberger 2007; Alexiades 2009).

Yet in more recent history, the overall human trafficking during the rubber boom alongside the debt peonage systems that preceded and outlasted it resulted in the multidirectional movements of people. Various groups either moved toward the headwaters or the interior to avoid infringements on their freedom, moved downriver toward the commodities and novelties that centers or cities offered, attacked the rubber labor camps, worked for rubber and gold mining barons, or traversed rural and more populated areas (Alexiades 2009; Alexiades and Peluso 2003; Fifer 1970; Peluso 2014). What is noteworthy here is that even if individuals and groups had never been part of the urban milieu, they were importantly responding to the emergence of "the urban" as an impactful space and presence; furthermore, these urban spaces are often territorial areas that many groups may have had historical access or claims to. Hence, Indigenous peoples have not and are not disconnected from urban spaces.

Amazonian Ese Eja settlements and mobility have forged their decisions, like many other groups, around activities that emerge from non-Indigenous dominated spaces, particularly economic and extractive regimes, the establishments of nation states, and the dynamics of populations in urban centers. Ese Eja, a self-denominated ethnonym, are a group of approximately three thousand individuals living in eight communities along the Beni, Madre de Dios, Heath, Orton, and Tambopata Rivers in the Beni, Pando, and La Paz border regions of Bolivia and Madre de Dios, Peru. Most Ese Eja plant swidden horticultural fields, hunt, fish, gather, extract and process forest resources for their own consumption and commercial trade, and variably engage in labor with townsfolks, as well as variably circulate and reside between rural and urban centers. They have ongoingly come together and apart across physical and symbolic borders that over time evolved into the distinct nation states that they now inhabit.

Ese Eja origin myths of Bawaja locate their point of origin at the headwaters of the Madidi River (Bolivia), which bifurcated naturally into two opposite downriver directions that ended up eventually spreading Ese Eja (Madidikwinaji, people of the Madidi River) communities over five hundred kilometers apart from each other. As such, their settlements became increasingly separated, and contact and communication between the various resident groupings mostly ceased as it became more difficult and inconvenient to retrace their own steps.

The majority of Ese Eja were created communities that were clearly located within what only later became known as the Bolivian or Peruvian

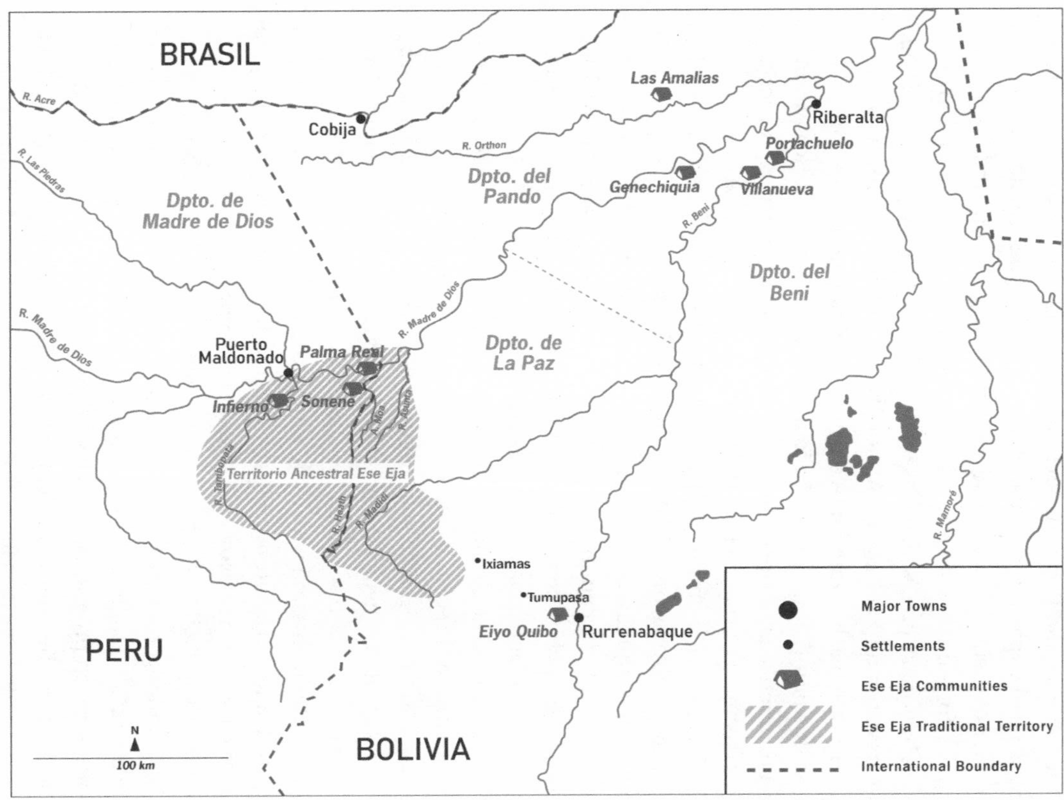

FIGURE 6.1 Map of Ese Eja Communities, Bolivia and Peru. Crafted by Miguel Alexiades.

nation states, with the exception of those who live on the Heath (Sonene) River. Roughly twenty years before the separation of the Heath River Ese Eja (Sonenekwinaji, people of the Sonene River) from the rest of the Madidikwinaji, the Bolivian and Peruvian governments, utilizing the expertise of their commissioned explorers and mapmakers and the political and armed maneuverings of their key traders and powerful rubber barons and institutions, vigorously forged toward each other to eventually establish the Peruvian-Bolivian boundary line, which was finalized between 1909 and 1912 (Toppin 1916; Chavez, n.d.; Fifer 1970). Although the Heath River forms a natural boundary of what became known as two separate countries, Bolivia and Peru, at this point, Sonene Ese Eja found themselves to technically, though not yet in practice or performance, have no option other than to subscribe to the citizenship of the land where they found themselves as Peruvian citizens.

Ese Eja still living on the Heath River, which separates Peru and Bolivia in southeastern Amazonia, had long lived on both sides of the river, utilizing both sides equally as one territory. When national documents began to be issued in both countries from the 1940s onward, Ese Eja were forced to choose citizenship, something that they had resisted doing up until that point. Despite identifying themselves as being more related to Ese Eja in the nation state of Bolivia, sharing the same language variant as well as a history of antagonism and recent warfare with Ese Eja groups in Peru, they made their nation state allegiance solely on the basis of where the closest urban center was located—hence the official maintenance of their community on the Peruvian side of the river. This choice was further limited by the Dominican Catholic mission who took it upon themselves to register all Heath River Ese Eja as Peruvian born. Urbanity and its proximity for the sake of bureaucratic ease was the overall guiding principle.

Nationality and citizenship were a matter of convenience. It was indeed their only option, given the kinds of articulation with the nation state that are required by citizenship, such as education, military conscription, and development outreach programs. The Heath River Ese Eja's choice made further logistical sense when one considers that the Bolivian side of the Heath River pertained to the large province of La Paz and did not and still does not have nearby urban settlements. Ixiamas, an Amazonian merchant outpost, would be the closest Bolivian urban center, at a distance of 150 kilometers (if one were to draw a straight line across rainforest terrain). The city of La Paz, capital of the province, is 3,640 meters above sea level and 370 kilometers from the Heath River, and only has routes that include steep mountainous terrain that is difficult to cross; indeed, the main road from Rurrenbaque remains dubbed as Ruta de la Muerte (The Death Route). Even today, if one had no worries about finances, optimal technology, and favorable weather at one's disposal, it would take over a week to travel from the Heath to La Paz. For Ese Eja, such a trip to their regional capital would take months of travel and consume considerable resources, making it an untenable urban destination for the necessary back-and-forth that regional urban capitals often demand from their rural inhabitants.[1]

On the Heath River, for Ese Eja peoples, the national border becomes an urban-Peruvian border facing rural Bolivia. In this sense their choices emphasize an ethno-cultural border, as Brablec refers to (chap. 4, this volume)—one that is geographically, though not culturally, fully moving away from the composition and social relations of the original residential group with whom they still identify. Yet the Heath River is also a symbolic border that reflects living at the margins and living on the edges of society, irrespective of whether or not individuals and families are living in their community or in towns. As individuals circulate across these landscapes, the idea of a definable urban and rural border has long dissolved, if we are ever to accept that they are or were indeed separate. When examining Indigenous urbanization, it is important to be precise about what is meant by this term.

Indigenous Urbanization Today

In recent work, Miguel Alexiades and I have examined Indigenous urbanization in Amazonia as sets of multidirectional processes that are "often highly contingent and situational not as a simple or a permanent migration to a city, but rather as part of an ongoing circulation of people that connects different communities, towns and multiple-sited dwellings" (Alexiades and Peluso 2015, 1; see also 2016). As such, these urbanization choices can be opportunistic and are inspired by an ever-increasing wide range of reasons such as labor, education, social rifts, exploration, entrepreneurship, political work, and so forth (Peluso 2015). Elsewhere, I have described how urban areas become villages and how villages become urban, but most importantly how ultimately these processes begin in people's minds long before they physically take place, hence this idea that "urbanization begins at home" (Peluso and Alexiades 2005a, 1).

Here I discuss how the sociopolitical stakes and impact entailed in particular forms of representation, outreach, and development trap Indigenous Lowland South American peoples, like Amazonian Ese Eja and their neighbors, into "urban" images that are by default seen as anti-"traditional" or anti-rural, while also paying heed to interactions with respective nation states. By this I mean that images that portray Indigenous peoples as urbanites simultaneously carry the threat of portraying them as people disassociated from their lands and the ongoing practices and transformations of their traditions and as having lost or being in the process of losing their vital claims to Amazonian livelihoods. While there are surely some migrations that might be reflective of such instances, overall, generalized reactions to the urban portrayal of Indigenous peoples serve to individually and/or collectively destabilize them in many instances. Indeed, as Brablec and Canessa (introduction to this volume) state, Indigenous people are "vulnerable to the pressure to conform but also made invisible by dominant societies unwilling to recognize them."

Geographers such as McSweeney and Jokisch (2015, 14) have persuasively put forward the argument that adverse reactions to urban Indigenous peoples are rife in policy documents that are "generic, inevitable, and ultimately disempowering to natives' territorial positions" and that, in turn, these policies create their affect. Such positions lean heavily on unsuitable applications of migration push-pull theories about Amazonian populations (Peluso 2015). Policy documents endorse the idea that urbanization entails the abandonment of territories. Yet apart from ethnographic examples used to elucidate migration to cities, permanent or otherwise, there is very scant ethnographic detail on how such misuse of urban images is operationalized, despite its insidious presence in what underlies commonplace perceptions of urban Indigenous peoples and how these viewpoints influence decisions that are made that affect their livelihoods and futures.

The multisited-ness of Amazonian Indigenous urbanization reflects an ongoing refashioning of Indigenous social and political identities, and the coproduction of new forms of territoriality provides a contrast with preestablished notions of urbanization as entailing and generating its opposite: social, cultural, territorial, and political dilution and disenfranchisement. Yet the disjuncture between these emergent and orthodox views of Indigenous urbanization has direct on-the-ground implications. This is particularly the case given that Indigenous claims to rights, resources, and territories are commonly substantiated through claims to ancestry, emplacement, and tradition, and often directly linked to environmental conservation and to territories that are adjacent to or within natural protected areas (Fisher 1994).

The presence of Lowland South American Indigenous territories has complicated the agendas of the aggressive and expanding neoliberal agro-extractive frontier organized around energy (oil and gas, hydroelectric, biofuels), mining, transport, and agro-industrial sectors. The extent to which Indigenous peoples can retain control over vast territories—many of them within or around natural protected areas—is in large part dependent on the kinds of relationships they form with both cities and forests and, most importantly, how these are understood, represented, and communicated. If urbanized Indigenous peoples, as some layperson and media representations contend, are not "really" Indigenous, then their claims to highly contested lands, resources, and rights become problematic. The politics of authenticity and the issue of Indigenous urbanization do not escape the manipulation of external interested actors. For instance, the politically powerful Confederation of Agriculture and Livestock of Brazil used evidence of TV and DVD use as proof of Indigenous peoples' "urbanization" and, therefore, diminished need for their lands (McSweeney and Jokisch 2015).

As stated earlier, due to a combination of geographical, ecological, historical, and circumstantial factors, Peruvian and Bolivian communities have access to different kinds of resources and affordances for interacting with regional markets (Alexiades 1999; Peluso 2003). In Madre de Dios the outreach teams of extractive industries, such as Petro Peru, specifically target the ambiguous and sometimes tense politics between communities and their more urbanite members. In the Pando, Beni, and La Paz departments of Bolivia, Indigenous mobility can be misrepresented as the abandonment of their territories by land-hungry adjacent ethnic groups and their enabling NGO supporters (Alexiades, Machuqui, and Monje 2009; Alexiades et al. 2009). It is common for oil and gas development companies to employ teams that arrive in the potentially affected communities in advance of the extractive activities in an attempt to get them to buy in to the company's desired future presence in their communities. These teams are similar to development organizations in that they offer community projects and infrastructural improvements in exchange for extractive activities. In many cases they offer transitory benefits that do not reflect an equitable exchange of resources. As Suzanne Sawyer has stated, "The high social and environmental stakes of oil operations cannot be exchanged for trinkets—be they pencils or buildings, metal roofing or high school scholarships" (1998, 43).

Some organizations disingenuously label any conversation that they engage in as a "community consultation" even if it is with one person and does not engage with the community's structure and protocols for representation or consent. This allows organizations to tick off the community consultation box that they need to satisfy in order to proceed with their simulation of consent. In the case of Madre de Dios, it has millions of hectares of land protected as national parks and heavily depends upon natural products and raw materials for its economy. No manufacturing industries are present in this region of cross-border trading. Informal economies are committed to the extraction and exportation of mahogany, gold, oil, and gas (Peluso 2018). The area's reputation as a lawless land rings true when informal economies here are further linked to invisible drug economies (allegedly as a transit region), continuing debt-peonage systems, and, as in the case of gold extraction, the nearly annual discovery of the mass graves of unidentified children. Regional attitudes toward Ese Eja are highly contingent upon poor Andean migrants in the region (who tend to view them harshly, typically enlisting the culture of poverty explanations for Ese Eja marginality) combined with a more recent migration of middle-class individuals and families from both Cusco and Lima (who view them with a greater degree of sympathy and, at times, idealization).

In Bolivia regional politics toward Indigenous peoples are starkly different in cities such as Riberalta, where people see themselves as being local Amazonians (*cambas*) even if they are not Indigenous Amazonians. Residents tend not to be recent migrants, or at least have histories that are more rooted in the region when compared to Peruvian counterparts, even if such rootedness began and solidified with the extractive economies that exploited Indigenous peoples. While I am not ignoring that Indigenous Amazonians are often considered to be inferior by their Andean neighbors (Canessa 2007), the appreciation of the Amazon region itself by the people that reside there, as well as their sense of belonging to it, have translated into an overall appreciation of Indigenous activities in some arenas. For instance, townsfolk's appreciation and consumption of food crops such as plantains (an Ese Eja food staple) and artisanal products have allowed Bolivian Ese Eja to productively expand their local horticultural practices toward income-producing opportunities, whereas the production of plantains in Peru is not an economic activity.

Where they are found, Brazil nuts often constitute the most commercially valuable and coveted, and thus often contested, forest resource. Access to Brazil nuts in the communities of Sonene and Palma Real (Peru) is mostly well regulated and organized through a combination of de jure and de facto rules. In Bolivia, Brazil nut extraction and trade are more complex and tense, in part because the Ese Eja in four communities (Portachuelo Alto, Portachuelo Bajo, Villanueva, and Genechiquía) are in a multiethnic Indigenous territory, with shared forest usufruct rights with Cavineño and, especially, Tacana, who according to the Ese Eja have managed to secure access to the most productive stands (Alexiades, Machuqui, and Monje 2009; Alexiades et al. 2009). Indeed, as in other parts of Amazonia, unequal access to Brazil nuts constitutes a source of social tension and conflict within and between communities (Ubiali and Alexiades, forthcoming). In the Bolivian Ese Eja case, claims to land, and hence Brazil nut access, hinge upon a rural, nonurban presence that is surveilled by neighboring competing Indigenous leadership and overseen by regional politicians with vested interests.

There are additional geographical resource differences that affect Ese Eja individual and community articulations with urban centers. Bolivian communities are located on the lower reaches of the Beni or Madre de Dios Rivers and have historically and ongoingly had access to much larger stocks of fish. However, through overfishing and contamination with mercury from the increasing alluvial gold mining industries, these resources are increasingly diminishing in importance. While goldmining has been environmentally damaging to the area, it has not produced broader public leveraging of rural versus urban indigeneity by goldmining stakeholders.[2]

Community-Facing Indigeneity

The posturing, strategizing, misuse, or overuse of rural "Indigenous" Amazonian images by Indigenous leadership as forms of promoting their indigeneity toward outsiders in order to confront the assault of extractive economies and gain allies in environmental service economy is well documented (Turner 1991, 1992; Peluso 1993; Conklin and Graham 1995). Indigenous leaders who need to travel or reside outside of their communities as members of local Indigenous federations or as representatives of their communities have long been commonly critiqued within their home communities for being corrupt or corruptible (Murphy 1974). For instance, most of these outward-facing roles require literacy, which by default has often excluded elders, and are accompanied by the everyday adoption of the national language and customs (Peluso 1993; Alexiades and Lacaze 1996). However, a new phenomenon that I wish to call attention to is how Indigenous leaders are projecting their indigeneity toward their own community or group as a way of evidencing their dedication and leadership. This is often the outcome or desire to deflect gossip, misinformation, and misunderstandings that are propelled by their residence in urban centers and their ensuing urban lifestyles. In this sense, the community is not only whom Indigenous leaders represent but also, in effect, their audience.

The need for leaders to project indigeneity onto the community indicates that there is an emerging set of challenges to the Indigenous urban image. My example here, while anonymized, should nonetheless be familiar to anyone working with Indigenous groups. In both Bolivia and Peru, Indigenous peoples have rightfully learned to use indigeneity as a resource. This is certainly evidenced by processes of ethnogenesis (Hill 1996; Hornborg 2005; Peluso and Alexiades 2005a, 2005b) and the reindigenization of some Amazonian groups (Jackson and Warren 2005; Chaves and Zambrano 2006; Lopez Pila 2014). Among Ese Eja in Bolivia, community-facing efforts to perform indigeneity are mostly subtle. The 2005–2019 Evo Morales government—in their quest to bring water, roads, and communications to all rural areas—installed telecommunication antennas in all communities and laid the ground for the popularity and use of internet phone apps that allow for communication within and among different Ese Eja communities. For instance, multiple WhatsApp groups formed that allowed for the open and ongoing exchange of information.[3] While the content of WhatsApp mobile phone messages embrace a vast array of topics, from the most silly to the most serious, there is a particular form of communication that has been helpful to Indigenous leadership and the communities they represent. Among Bolivian Ese Eja, there is an unwritten mandate that any document that is intended to be signed by any Ese Eja representative, even if they are employed outside of their community as a government representative, must be posted on WhatsApp. These posts are often followed by texts and audio recordings and can become long conversations between multiple individuals asking questions about the document and the arrangements and implications that it entails. Furthermore, Indigenous leaders send photos of their meetings and their whereabouts when they are away from their communities, allowing them to remain connected to community members and other leaders.

This is not the case for many Indigenous groups in Madre de Dios, Peru, where leaders tend to live in urban centers and are often isolated from their communities. Internet communication towers have only recently been built in 2021 and have not yet formed such open-access communication among communities. It is not customary for representatives to share actual documents and their daily whereabouts and conversations. Nor is it customary to provide people with an update of activities unless a formal meeting is called. With this in mind, it has therefore always been easier for the development efforts of extractive industries to be able to siphon off a few individuals for either community "consent" or as intermediaries who do not have the full backing of their communities but will oblige. Concurrently, when Indigenous leaders resist development outreach, some outreach officers try to either create new or exacerbate existing rifts between Indigenous people and their leaders, particularly taking advantage of a rural/urban divide. They do this by insinuating that their leaders have tried to negotiate with the organizations one-on-one for their own personal interests but that the officers prefer speaking directly with the community.

I will illustrate this point through the anonymized story of a Peruvian Amazonian leader who I will refer to as Roberto. He works with the local Indigenous federation in his region. Roberto's presence in the Puerto Maldonado is increasingly typical of someone in a leadership position, and indeed leadership roles are a prominent cause and justification for multisited Indigenous residence and urbanization (Peluso 2015). Roberto still maintains a home in his Native community alongside his home in the city, and he is caught in what has now become a classic predicament of residing outside his community while aiming to defend the rights of his community. He is also someone who has received international recognition for his initiatives, and although twenty years ago he did not don Indigenous attire to emphasize and perform his indigeneity, this is indeed what he routinely and consistently does today. In today's Indigenous politics, dressing up your indigeneity is commonplace and expected. There is a long history of scholarly work on dressing indigeneity as a resource in Lowland South America (Veber 1992, 1996; Peluso 1993; Conklin and Graham 1995; Conklin 1997; Santos-Granero 2009) that documents and argues that Indigenous dress has been used not as a form of submissiveness or assimilation but rather as a political tool. In addressing Roberto's Indigenous attire as a form of projecting his indigeneity in his home community, I hope to stress why such a political device has arisen and what its relationship is to Indigenous urbanity.

The need for urban Indigenous leaders to reiterate their indigeneity through dress and other actions toward their own communities has emerged in the last decade. While Indigenous communities have long scrutinized their own leaders and representatives over the proper use of external resources—be it development projects, regional distributions, or rights over natural resources—these had not resulted in their overutilizing indigeneity toward their own communities. Whereas previously indigeneity was an outward-facing exercise, it has increasingly become an inward-facing performance. In Peru this can be understood within the context of an emerging set of external actors from extractive or government agencies that began to recognize and employ ways in which they could swerve the Indigenous urban image toward a narrative of excess and distrust, precisely at the time that this image began to emerge in ways that were meant to unhinge urbanity from its negative stereotype. Such suspicions are not difficult to foster, as there has been much distrust in general toward Indigenous leaders. Indigenous leaders are caught amid a paradoxical set of power relations: they must both represent their communities to the Indigenous federations they are elected to and simultaneously represent the Indigenous federation to the communities they represent (Rubenstein 2001).

In the case of Roberto, the identity politics of indigeneity that began for one set of reasons (projecting to the non-Indigenous world as a political platform) continues for another set of reasons. Roberto dresses in Indigenous attire for all of his meetings, and now also does so when he visits his own or other communities. He cannot afford to be an invisible urbanite but instead wishes to continually remind his communities that he is intrinsically Indigenous. He does this by showing that his indigeneity is embedded in his everyday presentation no matter where he is—that it is not something that is put on solely for outside agents and taken off at will but rather that the marking of his Indigenous clothing shapes the making of his person and reflects his commitment to Indigenous communities in all settings.

Outside agents, particularly of natural oil and gas companies, approach Indigenous communities and operationalize their agenda by simultaneously employing two strategies. They create or build upon a rift within and between communities and their leaders over a perceived urban/rural divide despite Indigenous circulations between communities and towns. Manipulative jokes are made to community members about how their leaders are getting fat, living well while all the while depriving their community members of resources associated with modernity. At the same time and with the same tone, to the larger public they describe how *all* Indigenous peoples have now become fat, Coca-Cola drinking, deterritorialized urbanites. Such agents are extremely skilled and know precisely what they are doing, and do it effectively. Indeed, the lapses in judgment on behalf of community members and townsfolk have been provoked by the disingenuous misuse of the urban image.

The tactics I have described use urbanity against Indigenous peoples precisely as they become more at ease with their urban profiles. Such strategies expose and address existing public and political misuse of Amazonian urban images by portraying them as anti-"traditional." It is the inverse of the political wielding of "traditional" images as tools to undermine the urban reality of many Indigenous peoples that manipulates public opinion by rejecting either urban aspects of Indigenous lives or the possibility that Indigenous peoples can be both urban and Indigenous. If strategies like those of some of the oil and gas companies have traction, they are intensified when Indigenous peoples are increasingly residing in cities. The need for Indigenous peoples and their allies to readily combat discursive antiurban strategies is urgent. Clearly, community dwelling and Indigenous urbanization occur alongside each other and not in opposition. Indigenous urbanization coproduces both city and territory as Indigenous political space (Alexiades and Peluso 2015; McSweeney and Jokisch 2015), and indeed there is much to suggest that this urban—even cosmopolitan—mobility has been critical to Indigenous political resurgence over the past three decades in old and new spaces.

Conclusion

This chapter has contemplated the complexity of Indigenous urban images among the leaders of the same Amazonian ethnic group across distinct nations states at a moment in time when urbanity is generally more uncritically accepted as being part of Amazonian indigeneity. Yet it has also examined how the emerging surge in urban images and their ensuing urban lifestyles can be repurposed as political tools against Indigenous leaders toward both the public and their own communities. In this discussion, the historical and contemporary particularities of regional differences among dissimilar nation states have shown how technological infrastructures and advances in Bolivia have served to strengthen Ese Eja community trust in their leaders while Peruvian leaders must cope with the heavy targeting of their communities by outside agents who want to position themselves advantageously so as to serve their own extractivist self-interests. While it is well-documented that Indigenous leaders have strategically positioned their indigeneity as a political resource when dealing with outsiders or building alliances, what I have paid attention to here is how Peruvian Indigenous leaders increasingly use outwardly noticeable Indigenous symbols such as dress when returning to their communities. They do this to emphasize their indigeneity as a public counterpoint to their own urban lifestyles. This approach ensures their public dedication as representatives who are ideally immune to corruption and protects them from the deployment of any "fat cat" image that outside agents might strategically deploy to show them as weak and excessive both to their communities and to the larger regional public. The outward display of their indigeneity toward their own communities promotes them as individuals who maintain an implicit association with Indigenous territories and rights. Both in Bolivia and Peru, Indigenous leaders are surveilled and scrutinized by the many, whether it is by posting documents and photos of their whereabouts on WhatsApp or by navigating city streets or community paths donned in Indigenous symbols. A leader's awareness of being watched by his community members supports Pierre Clastres's (1987) assertion that it is difficult for Amazonian leaders to exert their personal will on people. In this way, Amazonian Indigenous leaders cannot separate power from the group even when they are immersed in urban lifestyles; if a leader desires power for him or herself, then he or she is simply ignored and eventually abandoned by the group (Clastres 1994).

Diverse historical and current nation state politics in Peru and Bolivia have led to distinct political and economic relations with Indigenous peoples across urban centers. These dynamics have contributed to shaping who Ese Eja are today in these distinct spaces. Indigenous urbanization is part of the ebb and flow of community and urban center articulations, flows, and circulation. In the case of city-centered Indigenous leadership, it raises ontological challenges for how individuals can continue to live their Ese Eja–ness in ways that keep them connected to their communities. The ongoing iteration of Ese Eja conviviality, consubstantiality, and commensality are fundamentally associated with being a proper human (Peluso 2003). It is not only how you clothe your body (Gow 1999; Viveiros de Castro 1998; Veber 1996) or how you attain and share your food (Fausto 2007) that constitutes the social person but also how the qualities of these substances and social relations (Vilaça 2002) are pivotal for crafting who you are and thus how you are expected and predicted to act. The risk of losing these habits puts one in the position of potentially becoming Other. In this sense, Indigenous ideas about power relations between leaders and community members amid urban and rural flows also become aspects of self and Other making.

With the increased urbanity of Amazonian leaders in a contentious space as outsiders approach them for favors that can have dire consequences in the rural areas they represent, the projection of traditional images as a form of facing inward toward communities also confronts the danger of transformation from one type of person and leader to another. In doing so, leaders position themselves against the potential rifts that can arise through the portrayal by others of images of urban excess or self-serving political temptations. As McSweeney and Jokisch (2015) have also pointed out, there is a paradox in the political dynamics that ensue from intensified links between Indigenous peoples and urbanization: while the intensified links with urban spaces have opened up spaces for their collaboration in political processes and allowed them to project their agendas, the very same movements can also undermine their own legitimacy in the eyes of certain outsiders with their facile assumptions about what is compatible and not with tradition. Indigenous peoples themselves become caught up in these complex dynamics as on the one hand they draw on powerful tropes as tradition and emplaced territoriality in order to substantiate claims and rights, while on the other hand navigating social realities that are visibly at odds with these simplified representations.

The trend of Indigenous leaders being preoccupied with tradition in their interactions with their own communities is part of the ongoing processes that engage with new interactions and challenges in ever-increasing rural-urban flows. With cities reflecting possibilities for people to traverse ways of being (though new life and leadership styles, dressing, and eating choices) as well as spaces, then it should follow that, in theory, urbanity offers possibilities for transformation that are kept in place by acts that reflect one's desires to be Ese Eja. While this is not usually a troubling aspect of such ongoing movement and exchange among community members who either temporarily or permanent live in cities, it can be problematic for leaders whose livelihoods are now tied to cities by virtue of being unambiguously Indigenous. Lowland South American Indigenous individuals and groups share cities through proximity and residence, participating in diverse spatial mobility practices that seek to define and appropriate or reappropriate urban space on their terms and for their benefit, all while becoming, maintaining, or transforming how they represent themselves in response to the economic opportunism and inequalities that they both resist and reveal.

Acknowledgments

I am indebted to Ese Eja peoples for their ongoing hospitality and kinship. I greatly appreciate the support of the FENAMAD, the British Academy Small Research Grant, the Wenner-Gren Foundation for Anthropological Research, Social Science Research Council, Fulbright, and American Women in Science. Many thanks to the editors of this volume, Dana Brablec and Andrew Canessa, as well as to two anonymous reviewers for their feedback. I am grateful to Dimitri "Chijiyo" Alexiades for always bringing the obscured obvious into the foreground of any analysis, and to Miguel Alexiades for his comments and our many insightful conversations on Indigenous urbanization and nation state differences among Ese Eja communities over the last few decades.

Notes

1. Within Bolivia it is only the Bolivian side of the Heath River that is part of the province of La Paz. Ese Eja communities in Bolivia are located in the provinces of Pando and the Beni.
2. Another marked resource that shapes differences in urban interactions are the plant resources that Ese Eja women use to craft both functional and artisanal products. In Bolivia the Ese Eja make mats (*esteras*), woven with the dried leaves of the palm *yokise* (*Chelyocarpus sp.*), for which there is a strong demand in the town of Riberalta. While there are other palm fibers that can also be used to weave mats, according to the Ese Eja, none compare in quality and durability to *yokise*, a plant that is not found along the rivers where the Ese Eja in Peru live. This demand articulates Bolivian Ese Eja women with the town more than their Peruvian counterparts. Indeed, Peruvian Ese Eja do not generally weave mats. They do, however, make baskets from *tamishe* (*Heteropsis sp.*), a resource not available in Bolivia. However, the demand for baskets is not significant; they

are sold as specialty items for tourists, and only a fraction of women in each Peruvian community weave these, whereas in Bolivia all Ese Eja women make mats for sale.

3. WhatsApp Messenger is an American freeware, cross-platform, centralized messaging and voice-over-IP service owned by Meta Platforms that is widely used throughout South America.

References

Alexiades, Miguel N. 1999. "Ethnobotany of the Ese Eja: Plants, Health and Change in an Amazonian Society." PhD dissertation, City University of New York.

———, ed. 2009. *Mobility and Migration in Indigenous Amazonia: Contemporary Ethnoecological Perspectives*. Environmental Anthropology and Ethnobiology 11. New York: Berghahn Books.

Alexiades, Miguel N., and Didier Lacaze. 1996. "FENAMAD's Program in Traditional Medicine: An Integrated Approach to Health Care in the Peruvian Amazon." In *Medicinal Resources of the Tropical Forest: Biodiversity and Its Importance to Human Health*, edited by M. J. Balick, E. Elisabetsky, and S. A. Laird, 341–65. New York: Columbia University Press.

Alexiades, Miguel N., Alejandro Machuqui, and Javier Monje. 2009. *Proceso de Reivindicación Territorial del Pueblo Indígena Ese Ejja en el Bajo Heath Boliviano. Bases para su Sustentación, Diagnóstico Situacional y Memoria Actualizada (2006–2008)*. Portachuelo, Bolivia: CIPEA (Capitanía Indígena del Pueblo Ese Ejja de la Amazonía); Riberalta, Bolivia: CIRABO (Central Indígena de la Región Amazónica Boliviana).

Alexiades, Miguel N., and Daniela M. Peluso. 2003. "La sociedad Ese Eja: Una aproximación histórica a sus orígenes, distribución, asentamiento y subsistencia." In *Los pueblos indígenas de Madre de Dios. Historia, etnografía y coyuntura*, edited by Alfredo García and Beatriz Huertas, 91–110. Sweden: IWGIA.

———. 2015. "Introduction: Indigenous Urbanization in Lowland South America." In "Indigenous Urbanization: The Circulation of Peoples between Rural and Urban Amazonian Spaces," edited by D. M. Peluso. Special issue, *Journal of Latin American and Caribbean Anthropology* 20 (1): 1–12.

———. 2016. "La urbanización indígena en la Amazonia: un nuevo contexto de articulación social y territorial." In "Minorías étnicas, procesos de globalización." Special issue, *Gazeta de Antropología* 32 (1): 1–22.

Alexiades, Miguel N., Roberto Quioshe, Antonio Quioshe, Mateo Biaeja, David Biaeja, Benjamín Huajohuajo, Edy Manrique Huajohuajo, Daniel Rodríguez, and Daniela Peluso. 2009. "La Reconstrucción Del Territorio Ancestral Ese Eja Sobre El Río *Sonene* (Heath): Contexto Histórico Y Recuento De Una Experiencia (2003–2009)." Unpublished report, property of CIPEA (Portachuelo, Bolivia) and CIRABO (Riberalta, Bolivia): CIRABO.

Canessa, Andrew. 2007. "Who Is Indigenous? Self-Identification, Indigeneity, and Claims to Justice in Contemporary Bolivia." *Urban Anthropology and Studies of Cultural Systems and World Economic Development*, no. 3, 195–237.

Chaves, Margarita, and Marta Zambrano. 2006. "From Blanqueamiento to Reindigenización: Paradoxes of Mestizaje and Multiculturalism in Contemporary Colombia." *Revista Europea de Estudios Latinoamericanos y del Caribe* 80 (April): 5–23.

Chavez, Mercado. n.d. *Buscando el Eldorado*. Unpublished manuscript, property of the Estate of Vaca Diez. Riberalta, Bolivia.

Clastres, Pierre. 1987. *Society Against the State: Essays in Political Anthropology*. Translated by Robert Hurley. New York: Zone Books.

———. 1994. *Archeology of Violence*. Translated by Jeanine Herman. New York: Semiotext.

Conklin, Beth. 1997. "Body Paint, Feathers, and VCRs: Aesthetics and Authenticity in Amazonian Activism." *American Ethnologist* 24 (4): 711–37.

Conklin, Beth, and Laura Graham. 1995. "The Shifting Middle Ground: Amazonian Indians and Eco-Politics." *American Anthropologist* 97 (4): 695–710.

Denevan, William M. 1992. "The Pristine Myth: The Landscape of the Americas in 1492." *Annals of the Association of American Geographers*, no. 82, 369–85.

Erickson, Clark L. 2006. "The Domesticated Landscapes of the Bolivian Amazon." In *Time and Complexity in Historical Ecology: Studies in the Neotropical Lowlands*, edited by William Balée and Clark Erickson, 235–78. New York: Columbia University Press.

Fausto, Carlos 2007. "Feasting on People: Cannibalism and Commensality in Amazonia." *Current Anthropology* 48 (4): 497–530.

Fausto, Carlos, and Michael Heckenberger. 2007. *Time and Memory in Indigenous Amazonia: Anthropological Perspectives*. Gainesville: University Press of Florida.

Fifer, J. Valerie. 1970. "The Empire Builders: A History of the Bolivian Rubber Boom." *Journal of Latin American Studies* 2 (2): 113–46.

Fisher, William H. 1994. "Megadevelopment, Environmentalism, and Resistance: The Institutional Context of Kayapó Indigenous Politics in Central Brazil." *Human Organization* 53 (3): 220–32.

Gow, Peter. 1999. "Piro Design: Painting as Meaningful Action in an Amazonian Lived World." *Journal of the Royal Anthropological Institute* 5 (2): 229–47.

Heckenberger, Michael J., J. Christian Russell, Carlos Fausto, Joshua R. Toney, Morgan J. Schmidt, Edithe Pereira, Bruna Franchetto, and Afukaka Kuikuro. 2008. "Pre-Columbian Urbanism, Anthropogenic Landscapes, and the Future of the Amazon." *Science* 321 (5893): 1214–17.

Hill, J. D., ed. 1996. *History, Power, and Identity: Ethnogenesis in the Americas, 1492–1992*. Iowa City: University of Iowa Press.

Hornborg, Alf. 2005. "Ethnogenesis, Regional Integration, and Ecology in Prehistoric Amazonia: Toward a System Perspective." *Current Anthropology* 46 (4): 589–620.

Jackson, Jean E., and Kay B. Warren. 2005. "Indigenous Movements in Latin America, 1992–2004: Controversies, Ironies, New Directions." *Annual Review of Anthropology*, no. 34, 549–73.

Lopez Pila, E., 2014. "'We Don't Lie and Cheat Like the Collas Do': Highland-Lowland Regionalist Tensions and Indigenous Identity Politics in Amazonian Bolivia." *Critique of Anthropology* 34 (4): 429–49.

McSweeney, Kendra, and Brad Jokisch. 2015. "Native Amazonians' Strategic Urbanization: Shaping Territorial Possibilities through Cities." *Journal of Latin American and Caribbean Anthropology* 20 (1): 13–33.

Murphy, Robert. 1974. "Deviance and Social Control: What Makes Waru Run?" In *Native South Americans: Ethnology of the Least Known Continent*, edited by P. Lyons, 195–202. Boston: Waveland Press.

Peluso, Daniela. 1993. "Conservation, Indigenismo and Mimesis." *Hemisphere* 5 (2): 6–11.

———. 2003. "Ese Eja Epona: Woman's Social Power in Multiple and Hybrid Worlds." PhD dissertation, Columbia University.

———. 2014. "Shajaó: Histories of an Invented Savage." *History and Anthropology* 25 (1): 102–22.

———. 2015. "Circulating between Rural and Urban Communities: Multi-Sited Dwellings in Amazonian Frontiers." *Journal of Latin American and Caribbean Anthropology* 20 (1): 57–79.

———. 2018. "Traversing the Margins of Corruption amidst Informal Economies in Amazonia." In "The Social Life of Corruption in Latin America," edited by D. Goldstein and K. Drybread. Special Issue, *Culture, Theory and Critique* 59 (4): 400–418.

Peluso, Daniela M., and Miguel N. Alexiades. 2005a. "Urban Ethnogenesis Begins at Home: The Making of Self and Place amidst Amazonia's Environmental Economy." *Traditional Dwellings and Settlements Review* 16 (2): 1–10.

———. 2005b. "Indigenous Urbanization and Amazonia's Post-Traditional Environmental Economy." *Traditional Settlements and Dwelling Review* 16 (11): 7–16.

Rubenstein, Steven L. 2001. "Colonialism, the Shuar Federation, and the Ecuadorian State." *Environment and Planning D: Society and Space* 19 (3): 263–93.

Santos-Granero, Fernando. 2009. "Hybrid Bodyscapes: A Visual History of Yanesha Patterns of Cultural Change." *Current Anthropology* 50 (4): 477–512.

Sawyer, Suzana. 1998. Review of "Seeking Common Ground: Petroleum and Indigenous Peoples in Ecquador's Amazon," by Sixto Mendez, Jennifer Parnell, and Robert Wasserstrom. *Environment: Science and Policy for Sustainable Development* 40 (5): 12–45.

Toppin, Henry S. 1916. "The Diplomatic History of the Peru-Bolivia Boundary." *Geographical Journal* 47 (2): 81–95.

Turner, Terence. 1991. "The Social Dynamics of Video Media in an Indigenous Society." *Visual Anthropology Review* 7 (2): 68–76.

———. 1992. "Defiant Images: The Kayapo Appropriation of Video." *Anthropology Today* 8 (6): 5–16.

Ubiali, Bruno, and Miguel Alexiades. 2022. "Forests, Fields and Pastures: Unequal Access to Brazil Nuts and Livelihood Strategies in an Extractive Reserve, Brazilian Amazon." *Land* 11 (7): 967–87.

Veber, Hanne. 1992. "Why Indians Wear Clothes: Managing Identity across an Ethnic Boundary." *Ethnos* 57 (l–2): 51–60.

———. 1996. "External Inducement and Non-Westernization in the Uses of the Asheninka Cushma." *Journal of Material Culture* 1 (2): 155–82.

Vilaça, Aparecida. 2002. "Making Kin out of Others in Amazonia." *Journal of the Royal Anthropological Institute* 8 (2): 347–65.

Viveiros de Castro, Eduardo. 1998. "Cosmological Deixis and Amerindian Perspectivism." *Journal of the Royal Anthropological Institute* 4 (3): 469–88.

CHAPTER SEVEN

Spaces of Indigeneity and the Impossibility of Mapuche Citizenship in the Urban Neoliberal Modernity of Santiago de Chile

The Case of the Film Play

SANDRA DEL VALLE CASALS

> Eran tiempos duros, pero modernos.
> *They were hard times, but modern ones.*
>
> —*Italian proverb, cited in* Play

This chapter looks at *Play*, a post-dictatorship Chilean film by Alicia Scherson (2005) that introduces, in a novel way within contemporary Chilean filmmaking, the tensions between being Mapuche in neoliberal Chile and the nation's racial paradigm, which privileges a white European physiognomy. For this examination, this chapter follows two lines of inquiry: the first is related to the construction of the Mapuche Indigenous identity within the Chilean neoliberal project of modernization, and the second concerns the implications of the neoliberal character of the nation for the exercise of Mapuche citizenship. In *Play* the Mapuche character is positioned as fundamental to the story, enabling the exploration of cinematic narratives of indigeneity and of the tensions of the emergence of an urban Mapuche identity. Nonetheless, the particular forms of representation used by the film engage in an ambivalent way with the social structures and symbolic frameworks that relegate the Mapuche to the space of Otherness in Santiago's urban setting. In the context of the Chilean neoliberal racial project, the film suggests the impossibility for the Mapuche subject to transcend the racialized filters of difference operating in society, which continue to lock them into a position of marginalization as *indios* (Indians). Within this Othering framework, the Mapuche also struggle to embody the figure of a modern citizen. Drawing on José Rabasa's (1997) articulation of the notion of "the impossible" in relation to the Zapatista Indigenous movement in Mexico, I argue that the impossibility of Mapuche citizenship points to the incompatibility of being Mapuche with prevailing narratives of the modern citizen in neoliberal Chile. For Rabasa (1997, 40), the claim "Exigir lo imposible (Demand the impossible)" made by the movement suggests the impossibility of reconciling the Zapatistas' divergent model of citizenship with dominant national discourses that confine the Indigenous to a premodern subaltern status. Equally, this demand also alludes to the process through which Indigenous people attempt to reframe modernity and reclaim their belonging to an alternative project, similar to the way in which Cristina, the Mapuche protagonist, pursues the same through different degrees of agency to carve out an alternative space of belonging.

In order to investigate the narratives of Otherness around indigeneity and modernity in *Play*, my exploration pays attention to the articulations between space, mobility, and belonging. The praxis of racial politics of citizenship in neoliberal Chile takes the form of control over space, limiting or favoring regimes of mobility and establishing the boundaries of belonging. In the film, different forms of contestation over both the material space and the symbolic one produce conflicting meanings of indigeneity. Additionally, examining the cinematic representation of the spatialization of difference reveals how the historical privileges associated with racial regimes of difference continue to be embedded in the neoliberal notion of the citizen. The rights once assigned to racial superiority are transferred onto the exercise of citizenship. Racial difference still operates through producing citizens entitled to inhabit and move through certain spaces to which Indigenous people, as indios, do not have access.

This study locates the category of the *indio* within the larger framework of dominant narratives of the nation and the historical forms of Othering the Mapuche people. This framework is helpful to show the current entanglement of the discourse of racial belonging to the imagined nation with those of neoliberal politics. Although with the rise of Indigenous rights movements across Latin America the term *indio* has been appropriated as a form of political self-identification, historically it has been used to refer to

Indigenous in a demeaning tone. In my analysis, the notion of the *indio* is approached not as an ethnic one but rather as one that reflects the complex racial and class formations in Chile, in which forms of racial discrimination have been subsumed in discourses of class difference. This dynamic echoes Judith Friedlander's (2006, 71) encapsulation of similar historical processes of the conflation of racial and class discourses in Latin America, suggesting that Indigenous people in Mexico were considered indios because they were poor, and they were poor because they were indios. In the context of neoliberalism in Chile, while being indio carries racial connotations, this notion is disguised under an epistemic justification of why Indigenous people do not fit into the elite project of neoliberal modernity by defining them as lazy, backward, antimodernity.

As *ethnicity* became a more acceptable term for what had previously been understood as race, it continued to be applied to groups—especially Indigenous ones—that did not conform to the racialized national project and which were generally officially presented in Latin American as either mestizo or white (Appelbaum, Macpherson, and Rosemblatt 2003, 8). This language perpetuated the "absent presence" of racialized concepts in the region, as Peter Wade et al. (2014) describe what David Goldberg (2008) has called the purge of racial lexis from the public sphere effected by the neoliberal ideology. In Chile, while this "purge" was already taking place due to the subsumption of race into class, neoliberalism certainly imposed the rhetoric that disguised the exclusion of racialized subjects on the grounds of their "incapacity" for success in the capitalist market. As Patricia Richards (2013, 8) argues, the historic "absent presence" of racial discourses in Chile fostered the idea of the country as a "raceless" nation, an understanding that has epistemological and practical consequences through to the present. In the Chilean case, the racial project excluding Indigenous Otherness from the nation intertwines with neoliberal narratives of "raceless racism" (Goldberg 2008) that justifies the barring of racialized subjects in terms of their individualized performance within market relations.

Acknowledging that in the neoliberal modern project the practice of citizenship and the formation of national identity are bound to the market and the act of consuming, one may ask how, according to the film, the Mapuche are integrated into the nation. Bolivian intellectual Silvia Rivera Cusicanqui (2010, 64–65) claims that the Indian component of societies like Bolivia should be understood as a part of modernity, and not as stagnant, static, and petrified tradition. However, as Rivera Cusicanqui also notes, the first step is not only to counter the idea of Indigenous people as an essentialized alterity but also to recognize them as subjects whose political identity proposes both a dialogue with and dispute over the notion of modernity. In order to address Rivera Cusicanqui's interpellation, it is critical to examine to what extent the inclusion of a Mapuche character as protagonist of the film authorizes her as subject of the modernity advanced by the neoliberal nation or of the Mapuche's own model of engaging modernity. As various Latin American scholars have explained (Quijano 1989, 1993, 2007; Mignolo 2011; Escobar 2007, 2010), the notion of *modernity* is problematic in itself as a complex narrative that celebrates Western civilization while hiding the colonialist principles through which its application and adoption occurred in Latin America. "Coloniality"—what Walter Mignolo has called the darker side of Western modernity—"is constitutive of modernity—there is no modernity without coloniality" (2011, 2–3).

Mignolo makes a notable contribution to the discussion on modernity in his book *The Darker Side of Western Modernity: Global Futures, Decolonial Options*, where he builds upon the argument made by Aníbal Quijano about the inherent relationship between modernity and coloniality.[1] Drawing on Quijano, Mignolo explores the possibilities for rethinking the idea of modernity by uncoupling the concept from its inherent coloniality in order to give space to the emergence of decolonial modernities. According to Mignolo (2011, 122), challenging the colonialist foundations of the rhetoric of modernity entails a process of epistemic disobedience. *Play* problematizes stereotyped but entrenched ideas on indigeneity that delegitimize Mapuche people as subjects of modernity. Nonetheless, the ambiguity through which *Play* introduces the Indigenous character's relationship with the Chilean modernization project means that she is not fully able to circumvent dominant narratives of the Mapuche as Other.

Neoliberal Modern Citizenship

In 2005 Alicia Scherson premiered her debut film *Play*, which tells the story of Cristina (Viviana Herrera), a young Mapuche woman who migrates to the capital, Santiago, seeking to experience the "benefits" of the modern urban city. Cristina nurses an elderly man of Jewish-Hungarian origin, Milos, and lives in his apartment as a *nana puertas adentro*, a live-in maid, from which position she is able to explore the promised modernity of the so-called Chilean miracle.[2] The question of modernity as organizing social relations and structuring cultural difference arises as central to the narrative of the film. The piece starts off with a proverb declaring, "They were hard times, but modern ones." With this saying, the film synthesizes the character of the postdictatorship period in which Chile experienced an avalanche of modernizing projects under the sign of neoliberalism and the globalized impetus. The 1992 Seville Expo was a key moment in establishing the image of Chile as a modern nation that was closing off its ominous dictatorial past to be a new country, open to the world (Vidal Valenzuela 2017). For the exhibition, the chief attraction of the Chilean pavilion was a monumental installation: a sixty-eight-ton iceberg brought directly from Chile's Antarctic Territory. The aim of the piece was to convey an idea of Chile contrary to preconceptions of it as an exotic, tropical country, notions that could be used to read the nation as primitive, rudimentary, or backward. In consequence, the exhibition at the expo also sought to challenge racial and civilizational stereotypes historically attached to Latin American territories as dark-skinned, Indigenous, and premodern. In fact, the project sought to identify Chileans as equals to Europeans. According to Fernando Léniz, commissioner of the Chilean Pavilion (and minister of the economy under Augusto Pinochet), "The idea is for Chile to be seen as a modern country. There are no ethnic problems here, we do not have a great pre-Columbian tradition. Chile is basically a new country. . . . We are not interested in impacting the European with the image of an exotic country because we are not. . . . It is simply the need for them to see us the same as them and not as an exotic curiosity"[3] (Subercaseaux 1996, 60). With this official statement, the government position endorsed the erasure of Indigenous groups and their possibility of belonging within the nation.

The inclusion of Mapuche Indigenous people into this project of neoliberal modernity has been denied since the outset of the nation-building project and reinforced by the postdictatorship discourse of the Chilean modern entrepreneurial elite, who have focused on portraying Chile as a winning modern nation, the jaguar of Latin America (Larraín 2001, 164).[4] Chile has been heralded as the first project of neoliberal state formation and one of the major laboratories of political and economic experiments advanced by the Chicago Boys, the group of economists formed in the University of Chicago under the teachings of Milton Friedman and who the dictatorship gave the opportunity to implement their knowledge of and belief in economic monetarism. The transition to democracy did not entail the dismantling of the neoliberal system in Chile. In fact, the *concertacionista* democratic governments that took power after the end of the military regime[5] went further with the privatizations it had started.[6] The transition left untouched the bases of the economic system introduced by the Chicago Boys, and it also showed the advent of a neoliberal subjectivity, particularly during the Seville Expo mentioned above that disregarded the existence of Indigenous groups in the country.

Mapuche Indigenous people went from fulfilling the paradigm of warrior figure praised during the independence struggles—the Spanish colonizers were never able to conquer the Mapuche—to becoming the embodiment of the savage, the primitive, and the backward, connotations that remain in place today under the colonialist policies of the Chilean state. Historically rejected and inferiorized in dominant narratives of Chilean identity formation, the Indigenous body has been portrayed as a cultural racialized Other because of the racial project upheld by the postindependence Chilean elite, whose policies promoted white European immigration and conceived Indigenous groups as inferior and uncivilized and, thus, available for colonization. Within this entrepreneurial identity of the modern nation, drawing on Jorge Larraín's interpretation (2001, 162),[7] Indigenous groups remained confined to a remote and exotic south, arguably trapped in historical territorial claims, with a set of social values attached to land, nature, and ancestral culture. This imagination is challenged by *Play* through the construction of the character of Cristina, a Mapuche prone to the allure of modernity, who is seen as a *rara* (weirdo) in the film. Her "weirdness" is also reinforced in the poster (fig. 7.1), where a backlit Cristina wearing headphones makes us think of an extraterrestrial being. Cristina does not fit the stereotypical representation of Mapuche people as fixed in a monolithic tradition. She likes playing the arcade beat-'em-up *Street Fighter II*, and she fantasizes about being an anime character, suggesting the overarching impact of a technologized and globalized paradigm in Chilean post-transition identity. While her portrayal as a domestic worker reproduces the traditional spaces of invisibility and subordination allocated to Mapuche female migrants in the capital, in the film this status operates as a gateway for Cristina's insertion into the modern lifestyle that she cannot enjoy in the south where her family still lives (probably La Araucanía region),[8] a possibility of learning how to perform modernity.

Cristina is curious and adventurous, crucial qualities in navigating the modern yet segregated city. Her wanderings seem to be limited to central

FIGURE 7.1 Image used in poster. *Play*, Alicia Scherson, 2005.

Santiago, the area around the central station, until the moment she finds a briefcase, which opens the door to the modernized part of Santiago that was previously alien to her, given her class status and racialized appearance. The briefcase belongs to Tristán (Andrés Ulloa), a young upper-middle-class architect, who represents the entrepreneurial identity of the modern capital. Cristina explores the contents of the briefcase: documents, cards, cigarettes, and an iPod with over-ear headphones, a pioneering artifact for the time. As

FIGURE 7.2 Objects of modernity on display. *Play*, Alicia Scherson, 2005.

she lays them out on the floor (fig. 7.2), they seem to constitute the material objects that are required for belonging to modernity and that she is now able to access. The briefcase, as narrative device, helps to connect the two different social realities embodied by these characters, Tristán and Cristina, the entrepreneurial upper class of Santiago and the invisibilized Indigenous migrant.

Like other Mapuche migrants forced to move to the city to find a job, Cristina gets ready to *play* with the modern codes she obtains from the items in the briefcase. As noted by Chilean scholar Nicolás Gissi (2004, 6), the uninterrupted migratory movements of Mapuche people to Santiago has not been a result of recent modernization policies or the effects of globalization. Rather, the need to emigrate to the capital goes back to the colonialist relationship between the Chilean State and the Mapuche people, and it has been perpetuated through different laws that legitimized the appropriation of Mapuche ancestral territories and forced the reconversion of agriculture in the area. In the city space, many Mapuche adopted various strategies to eschew discrimination, for example by hiding their Mapuche-ness by using "modern" looks. Similarly, Cristina begins to "modernize" her image. Nonetheless, what has been assumed as a tactic to avoid discrimination is presented as a ludic act for Cristina, emphasized by the joyful music and the vibrant colors

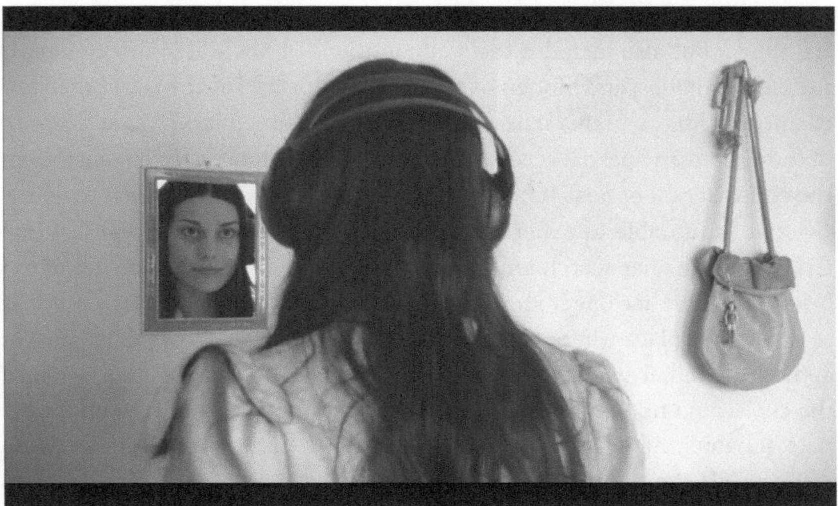

FIGURE 7.3 Cristina and her new image. *Play*, Alicia Scherson, 2005.

of the scenes. She tries the headphones on, starts smoking the cigarettes, and looks at her updated image in the mirror, as pictured in figure 7.3. Moreover, she stops her habit of whistling to herself and adopts the technological device, the iPod, as her source of music. The appropriation of these material objects allows her to experience a sense of belonging to modernity. The focus on the iPod in the film denotes the irruption of technology into the country and the adoption of a symbol of global standards of progress. At the same time, the iPod signals class difference, given that in the early 2000s it was an expensive and hard-to-come-by product. Accordingly, the music that people would listen to on it was not accessible to everyone either, in the democratizing way the internet and apps such as Spotify allowed later on. For the director of the film, this process of technologization and globalization was very tangible in the 1990s in Chile. Scherson has commented that when she was writing the script, it was "era la idea de que entraba todo. En los noventas se abre todo [en el país] sin filtro" (the idea that everything could enter. In the nineties everything opens up without a filter [in the country]).[9] Living abroad during those years also gave Scherson the perspective to appreciate the accelerated pace through which modernization was taking place in post-transition Chile. The director sought to capture this process in the film by picturing a city as a construction site filling up with new modern-looking buildings.

The construction process, nonetheless, not only encompasses the material aspect but also includes the configurations of post-dictatorship identities, subjectivities, and models of citizenship impacted by the neoliberal modernity paradigm. In this sense, Scherson's debut film offers a visual account of the limited and partial access to modernization, along with the tensions in the construction of post-transition identity, by showing the extent to which Cristina is (un)able to experience the revamped neoliberal urban setting. Cristina begins her search around the city to find Tristán, the owner of the briefcase. With her finger she draws on a map of Santiago the distance that separates the place where she lives from the location of Tristán's house. An audience familiar with the racialized geography and class spatialization of the city would notice that she lives in a working-class area. Tristán, for his part, inhabits the whitened barrio *alto*: *alto* because the upper class (*clase alta*) dwells there and because it is higher in geographical terms, on the slopes of the Andean foothills. After a frustrating first attempt to trail Tristán across the upper-class neighborhood, Cristina comes back to the address and finds Irene (Aline Kuppenheim), Tristán's ex, in the house. Tristán and Irene had recently split up, which triggered an existential crisis for Tristán, who can afford to wander around the city purposelessly. Meanwhile, in the building site he supervises as an architect, the construction workers are on strike to demand better working conditions, a situation he does not relate to.

Consuming Modernity

Although Cristina uses the objects in the briefcase, she still does not know how to perform modernity. She is not in the arguably productive position of the architect (Tristán), building cities and transforming spaces. Instead, she is learning to navigate the segregated map of the capital. Her manner of smoking is clumsy, showing a lack of confidence in the performance of this modern identity. Intentionally, she starts following Irene as a way to decipher the codes of modernity from a female point of view. Using the condition of being unnoticeable that Cristina is given in the film as a "gift" (instead as an allegory of her invisibility as a *nana puertas adentro*), she can peek at Irene, sniff her scent (fig. 7.4), and mimic her behavior. By portraying Cristina as she uses haptic skills to learn the rituals of modernity, the film nonetheless seems to accentuate pristine qualities in her that are linked to a backward image of the Indigenous. Cristina scrutinizes what Tristán's ex does: how

FIGURE 7.4 Unnoticeable Cristina. *Play,* Alicia Scherson, 2005.

she applies makeup, how she dresses, what she buys in the shopping mall, what she eats at the restaurant. Nonetheless, the Mapuche character sees everything from afar, without being able to fully replicate Irene's acts of consumption. In this sense, while living in the capital brings Cristina closer to the modern lifestyle of the upper-middle class, her access to the status of modern female citizen like Irene is mainly symbolic, a process of learning yet not consuming through buying. Although it remains an exercise in fantasy for Cristina, consumption both symbolic and material is essential to belonging and to the exercise of citizenship in neoliberal modern Chile. On the other hand, if we approach consumption in the sense proposed by Néstor García Canclini (1995, 45)—that is, as a reflection of contemporary rationality, particularly neoliberal rationality—the act of consuming becomes part of Cristina's agency to navigate the city: even if consumption is not available to her, it serves her to grasp its meaning and central role in the production of identity, belonging, and distinction within neoliberal society.

In the context of Chilean neoliberalism, Tomás Moulián (1997, 100) has illuminated the central role of consumption in the "integration" of different sectors of society. Consumption, for Moulián (99–100), not only provides access to alleged modernity and its goods that were reserved only to well-off people but also encompasses a form of citizenship that is attached to the pleasure of consuming. Cristina's flaneur-like engagement with the city resembles this process; she walks around Santiago to grasp the modern identity of the city. In *Play* the space of the neoliberal modern city frames the representational paradigm of the Mapuche. The city is presented as the access point to a desirable modern lifestyle and a model of citizenship based on consumption, suggesting that the relationship with the urban milieu is predominantly marked by class distinction. The Mapuche woman accesses modernity through the city, by allegorically consuming it in her strolls like a flaneuse (Ramos 1989). For Julio Ramos (1989, 168), the original French expression to denote the idle and indolent street stroll acquires a particular meaning associated to modern commodification and consumption: "In the flânerie," says Ramos, "the privatized urban subject approaches the city with the eye of one who sees an object on display."[10] Other revisions of the act of flânerie have also addressed the invisibilization of women in the public space and, in consequence, as flaneuse (Elkin 2017). However, often the inclusion of women as flaneuse have been linked to consumption. This association prompted feminist critiques to note a sexist imagination of the flaneuse that associates her with the space of the shopping mall (Bowlby [1985] 2009). As *Play* shows, this connotation becomes even more problematic when it reproduces disempowering conceptions of women, mainly conceived as window-shoppers without purchasing power, as is the case of Cristina.

Since forms of belonging are intertwined with forms of consumption in Chilean neoliberal politics, Cristina's "consumption" through window-shopping provides her with an illusion of citizenship and of belonging to the modern city. As noted by Néstor García Canclini (1995, 19), "Being a citizen is not only about the rights recognized by the state apparatuses to those they were born in a territory, but also it has to do with the social and cultural practices that give a sense of belonging."[11] Forms of belonging to the modern nation are rendered through consumption, only possible as a chimera for Cristina. Despite the fact that Scherson presents Cristina as having the capacity to move around areas of the city reserved for light-skinned, upper-middle-class Chileans, barriers of race and class will prevent Cristina from actually belonging to those places. Cristina cannot cross the threshold of the theater where Irene goes; instead, she is scrutinized by the porter's gaze in a way that reinforces hegemonies of difference based on physical appearance. While there is no dialogue in the scene, the manner in which Cristina is looked at denotes the racialization of the gaze, the *way of seeing*.

What is at stake in that scene is the techniques of filmic representation in interaction with the nation's historic language of race. Racialized categories, despite mainly being anchored in the physical body, do not necessarily appeal to legible meanings of race. The cinematic production of racialized power relations depends on how the film form instates ways of seeing that attach "whiteness" and "Blackness" to certain characters. As Sara Ahmed reminds us, "Whiteness is not reducible to white skin, or even to 'something' we can have or be, even if we pass through whiteness" (2007, 159). Rather, as I suggest in my analysis, it is a *way of seeing*. My stance echoes Richard Dyer's understanding on the matter of whiteness where he states that "There is a specificity to white representation, but it does not reside in a set of stereotypes so much as in narrative structural positions, rhetorical tropes and habits of perception" (2017, 12). As a primarily visual technology, cinema is susceptible to the acknowledgment and perpetuation of visible difference.

By showing Cristina's adventures around the city as a mere act of impersonation, the film closes down the possibility of Cristina's real incorporation as a modern citizen with access to the allure of consumerism. Joanna Page (2017, 278), in her analysis of the representation of neoliberal ideology in *Play*, suggests that Scherson refuses to transgress solid class divisions. Scherson seems to confirm this vision by recognizing that in Chile the issue is that there is no social mobility: "In the case of *Play*, there is no social mobility. . . . There is no possibility of moving upwards in the social ladder, this girl no matter how hard she tries to dress up . . . it does not work" (Urrutia and Pinto 2005).[12] While Scherson frames the conflict as an issue of class barriers, her comment inadvertently supports a conflation of race and class. Cristina strives to learn the codes of modernity, but these will not be enough for her to be part of the modern project. Indeed, the scenes that show Cristina following Irene expose the workings of racial difference embedded into class difference. This system of embeddedness means that in this urban setting, where Cristina does not mention her own last name, she comes to be seen as a lower-class person instead of as a Mapuche woman, a nana when she wears the uniform. The Mapuche background is removed as a marker of difference and source of exclusion from the neoliberal modern nation. In this regard, the spaces of indigeneity in *Play* are equated to the spaces inhabited by *popular* lower classes, unwittingly resonating with the *politics of Indigenous erasure*, a term I use to define the fading of Indigenous identity into the modern language of the city. Through this process, some

Indigenous people have responded to the discrimination they face as indios by passing for members of racialized popular classes instead, even though both figures fall into the status of Other in Chile.

Appropriation of the modern urban lifestyle has been a process historically undertaken by Mapuche migrants to the city. The loss of a Mapuche surname and subscription to the ideological project of an urbanized life have contributed to erasing Indigenous visible identity. In this sense, Gissi (2004, 9) also remarks that it was common for some Mapuche to express their Mapuche-ness only in the private and safe space of the home. It is at home where Cristina speaks in Mapudungun when she phones her mother, who lives in the south. Although authors like Alejandro Lipschutz[13] recognized the power of Mapuche culture to adjust and modernize without necessarily neglecting the Mapuche-ness (in Crow 2007, 326), in the case of the film, phenotypic appearance seems to continue to have a role in the perpetuation of Otherness and the construction of difference around racialized bodies.[14] For Cristina, social status is attached to the color of her skin and her physical appearance. Despite the fact that Cristina modifies her aspect to look like Tristán's ex-girlfriend—she starts wearing makeup and gives herself a fringe similar to Irene's—when Cristina is in the hospital giving Tristán's details after his accident and she introduces herself as Tristán's friend, the nurse looks at her doubtfully. Rapidly, Cristina corrects herself by saying she is just an acquaintance. In this sense, I argue that in *Play* the racial burden of being indio is subsumed under discourses of class exclusion and lack of social mobility in post-transition Chile. This repeats the raceless racial narrative of neoliberalism accounted for by Goldberg (2008), while it exposes the impact of long-standing national narratives of exclusion around Indigenous people, intertwined with the production of belonging and access to citizenship in neoliberal Chile.

The historical and ongoing phenomenon of Indigenous erasure in the urban setting is also relevant to Paola Castillo's (2014) documentary feature film *Genoveva* that reflects on the conflation of race and class continued under the practice of raceless neoliberalism. The film explores the lost (and forgotten) Mapuche roots of the director's family settled in Santiago. As her family is confronted with the idea of having a Mapuche great-grandmother, Genoveva, a national history emerges, one of negation and discrimination against Indigenous people and Indigenous-looking Chileans with darker skin and hair color. Despite their Indigenous-looking phenotype and darker skin, Castillo's family *see* themselves as very distant from any Indigenous ancestry. The director's cousin claims that his closest connection to Mapuche people is his maid. This comment reproduces stereotypes of Mapuche women as nanas in the same way *Play* does. In the documentary, the great-grandmother Genoveva is included into the racial narrative of the family as "una mestiza más" (just another mestiza)—that is, as a Chilean resulting from the mix between Spaniard and Native people and not as an Indigenous person, exposing the legacy of the politics of Indigenous erasure today. This politics of erasure operates as the dissolution of the "stigma" of indigeneity by becoming a Chilean mestizo. Underlying this process is the historic negation of the Indigenous component of Chile in what José Bengoa (2007, 50) calls "un fuerte proceso de 'blanqueamiento imaginado'" (a strong process of "imagined whitening"). The contested meaning of *mestizaje* and the conflation of the image of popular classes and Indigenous people are also present in the production strategies of the film. In *Play* this conflation allows the character of Cristina to be performed by Viviana Herrera, an actress who is not actually Mapuche but whose physical appearance means that she could pass for Mapuche. This dynamic shows that skin color and appearance are not accurate indicators of race. Nonetheless, the fact that people continue to understand skin color as a key racial marker exposes the legacy of the racial formation of the nation and the effects of racialization on bodies. This legacy results in the fact that an actress like Viviana Herrera or Genoveva the great-grandmother can be seen both as mestizas and *sujetos populares* (urban poor), or as Indigenous peoples, indias. Although the film proposes that being a Mapuche is only one of the identities Cristina can play with, both Cristina's and Genoveva's bodies are Otherized—whether as *sujetos populares* or indias—according to the racial paradigm of the nation.

Just Playing Around

Following the logic of play advanced in the film, Cristina's Mapuche identity is plugged and unplugged to "connect" with the family in the south, expressing something of what García Canclini (1990) describes as strategies to enter and leave modernity. However, her Mapuche identity seems to be mainly accessorial and aesthetic in the film, an exotic touch without any engagement with the deeper meanings of being Mapuche, which includes being impoverished by the colonialist policies of the Chilean state without political recognition as people. In fact, Scherson has confessed that having Cristina speaking some lines in Mapudungun in the film was almost an arbitrary choice, since she liked the idea of having subtitles in the film (in Urrutia and Pinto 2005, 2). Cristina does not show any explicit identification with the historical territorial conflict in the south that has profoundly marked Mapuche identity and belonging up to the present day.[15] Her disconnection from Mapuche identity is also suggested by her position in support of her aunt's aims to sell some land, against her mother's criticism. It is understood that the aunt is trying to sell a field, which defies the traditional vision of Mapuche, in which identity is strongly linked to the symbolic value of the land corresponding to ancestral territories. For Cristina, her aunt "está en su derecho" (is in her right), supporting a vision of rights associated with the idea of individual property ownership and market consumption. By doing this, however, *Play* also supports a depoliticized and nonontologizing form of being Mapuche that does not make reference to attachment to land or take a political position in relation to the conflict disputing Mapuche territories. In this way, Scherson may be seen to question the extent to which Indigenous characters must necessarily be represented as taking up the fight against inequality, racism, and other forms of oppression in a way that effectively erases their individuality. Scherson mentioned that she requested Mapuche leaders to read the script to hear their opinion about Cristina's characterization.[16] Interestingly, in the view of the leaders from whom the director solicited comments, Cristina as a Mapuche character does not need to be identified with the ongoing territorial conflict taking place over Mapuche lands. Even though neoliberal politics have also sought to fragment Mapuche community, and the Mapuche are not a homogenous group and not all those who identify as Mapuche have the same political ideas in relation to neoliberalism, this response sounds contradictory in the context of the widespread recognition of the collective identity that supports Mapuche anticapitalist struggles for their territories. Nonetheless, this stance served to support Scherson's portrayal of Cristina as challenging an essentialized political identity, pointing instead to the possibility of representing the Mapuche in a broader range of options.

However, the way the film advocates for a deontologized Mapuche-ness becomes problematic since, in Cristina's act of appropriating and performing modernity, there is also a suggestion that the temporality of indigeneity needs to be updated and brought into the present tense in a way permitted by the nation. Indigenous Otherness is marked not only by the spatial segregation, belonging, and movement around the city, but also by the temporality assigned to being indio. The temporality of Indigenous Otherness seems to be attached to the premodern. The fact that Cristina has to acquire skills in order to move around the city and become part of the modern environment reinforces the sense that she belongs to the premodern. *Play* diverges from the previous film productions that engage with the Indigenous question wherein a romanticized image of traditional Indigenous ways of life is portrayed in contrast to the modernization and economic development sought by the Chilean nation-state. Nonetheless, premodern and backward ideas still underlie the representation and the current situation of Cristina in the city. Valentina Raurich and Juan Pablo Silva, in their study of the image of Indigenous people in Chilean documentary and fiction films, more particularly since the dictatorship and until the early 2000s, note that "the cinematic Indigenous is suspended between historical criteria, mythical stories and ecological struggles" (2011, 80).[17] According to their argument, "Representations of the Indigenous in Chilean cinema have modeled an exotic Indigenous, frozen in time and oblivious to their own historical processes" (80).[18] This imagery is brought about by an ideology they call an "exhumación de lo premoderno" (exhumation of the premodern), which materializes a cinematic image of the Indigenous trapped into residual and archaic features without the chance to update their identity and location in history. While Cristina's movement around the city and her condition of flaneuse also serve to challenge the temporal/spatial fixity imposed on Indigenous bodies, the only way she can "update her identity" and exercise citizenship is within the neoliberal framework of consumption and aspiration of social mobility.

This position regarding Cristina's Mapuche-ness suggests an *oblique engagement* with the politics of indigeneity and the representation of Mapuche people. I identify an *oblique engagement* in *Play* since it avoids addressing the status of Otherness that emerges from the interaction between the neoliberal modernization project and long-standing racism. The term *engagement* is used here to suggest an ideological intentionality in relation to the representation of the narratives of indigeneity. The notion of intentionality underlying the idea of *engagement* activates a hermeneutic of Otherness in the film that may refuse or subscribe to the hegemonic accounts of the nation. In this case, by deontologizing Cristina, the obliqueness challenges the paradigm of "exhumación de lo premoderno" that Raurich and Silva (2011) have identified as the dominant politics of Indigenous representation in Chilean cinema previous to the production of *Play*. However, the way in which Scherson attempts to deessentialize Cristina simultaneously prevents the film from addressing the power relations that sustain the location of Mapuche as an Other. Cristina's Otherness is confirmed after she attempts to experience the modernization project and her incorporation is denied.

The film also problematizes the image of Mapuche people connected to the land by noting that Cristina does not like the south, where she comes from, which is on the contrary idealized by the character of the gardener with whom she begins a romantic relationship. For the gardener, who has never been to the south, it is a green place, full of trees, which conjures a widespread misguided imagination that takes the growing of pine and eucalyptus of the timber industry for a nature sanctuary when it actually has caused the extinction of autochthonous forests and the collapse of the environment. Cristina prefers Santiago, the capital. She likes the Santiaguinos' smell of "desodorante, jabón, crema, auto, y plástico" (deodorant, soap, cream, cars, and plastic)—all the artificial scents that an urban modernity should smell like. The south for Cristina is synonymous with feeling cold and with poor people with a smoky odor. She cannot understand why the gardener wants to go to the south. She questions him: "A qué te vas a ir al sur tú si es lindo Santiago" (What are you gonna do in the south? Santiago's beautiful). Cristina also warns him, "Si te vai [al sur], vai a terminar más pobre . . . y con frío" (If you go there, you'll end up poor . . . and cold). Cristina makes a direct association of the south with poverty. Nonetheless, for Cristina it is a question of not fitting into the traditional Mapuche identity, and of what the south offers to her: "A mí me gusta Santiago, mamá. ¿Cuándo me va a entender? Yo no la puedo ayudar desde allá. No sé hacer nada" (I like Santiago, Mom. When are you going to understand? I wouldn't be of any help there. I do not know how to do anything).

The consequences of poverty are individualized in the film, as it does not fully explore the reasons why, for Cristina, the south is synonymous with poverty. According to the film, it is due to her incapacity to fit in there that Cristina must migrate. Nonetheless, as Gissi (2004, 6) explains,[19] "The need to emigrate to the capital is rather a consequence of state interests and decisions that have been detrimental to the Native peoples."[20] Cristina does not note the political and economic reasons of that condition. Her situation of migrant is disguised as an option and not as the consequences of the economic deprivation of Mapuche people in their territories. As an Indigenous migrant, her position in the film is as a domestic worker, whereas Milos, due to his Hungarian origin, is a foreigner to be taken care of. Considering Chile's nation building, Milos embodies the white European migrants promoted by the Chilean state to whiten, "civilize," and develop the incipient nation, while Cristina represents the Indigenous and Indigenous-looking subjects rejected from the racial paradigm.

(Im)possible Desires

Susana Domingo Amestoy (2020, 121) has argued that in *Play*, Scherson defamiliarizes Cristina as maid by removing her body from the usual spaces of domestic workers, the out-of-sight areas of the house. Notably, "*Play* transforms the city into the domestic worker's object of desire" (121). Nonetheless, despite this process of defamiliarization as a nana, I contend that Cristina remains attached to her social positioning as a racialized maid, which limits the pursuit of her desires. Building on Rabasa's (1997) notion of "the impossible," Gayatri Gopinath (2005, 5) develops the idea of "impossible desires" in order to frame the process of elision of queer female diasporic identities in mainstream transnational narratives of sexuality and subjectivity in South Asia. In the case of *Play*, Cristina's desire is undercut by the neoliberal regime, the same system that arguably grants her the "freedom" to migrate and inhabit the capital. Nonetheless, despite the impossibility of Cristina's belonging to the modern project of the neoliberal nation, which is available to Tristán and Irene, she does not renounce her desire to be part of the city. When Milos dies, Cristina refuses the gardener's proposal to go back to the south and decides to stay in Santiago by herself. Although as a racialized nana she cannot embody the modern citizen, Cristina imposes her presence on the city. In the last scene of the film, she goes up to the roof of a building from where she gazes at the urban landscape now at her feet (fig. 7.5). In Gopinath's (2005) analysis, desires themselves are not defined by their impossibility. They are deemed as impossible desires structurally speaking, but the filmic form provides an opportunity for agency. *Play* gives visual representation to Cristina's desires as a way of contesting the narrative of impossibility.

Nonetheless, in the interaction with other characters, Cristina is only seen as a nana. Similar to the case of *Lina de Lima* (González 2019)—a more recent Chilean film about an Indigenous maid of Peruvian origin working

FIGURE 7.5 Cristina gazing at the urban landscape. *Play*, Alicia Scherson, 2005.

in Santiago—*Play* also seeks to explore the domestic worker's desires beyond her location within the racialized division of labor in neoliberal Chile. However, Cristina's desires (as well as Lina's in María Paz González's film) become impossible to achieve within the framework of class and racial politics. In this regard, the fact that this chapter highlights that Cristina plays *Street Fighter II* as an arguably unusual interest for a Mapuche in a way also reproduces the regulatory projects over the Indigenous image. Certainly, like Domingo (2020) argues, Cristina resists her subjection to the space assigned to the maid.[21] Even more, for Cristina, the city represents a site of aspiration where everyday negotiations and resilience take place, offering opportunities for subaltern agency to play out. The defamiliarizing gesture of the film is relevant in relation to the inhabitation of space since it points to the disruption of the spatialized production of identities. Tim Cresswell and Deborah Dixon (2002, 6) note that the notion of identity has been mapped in some natural sense onto particular spaces such as women = home, workers = factory, Black people = ghetto. Here we could add Indigenous = countryside, and nana = private space. In the case of Mapuche migration and appropriation of the city space, their forms of mobility and inhabiting trigger anxieties as they challenge historically fixed identities of Indigenous as premodern or antimodernity and the spaces to where they "should" belong.

Play can be described as a fable of modern identities where the historical constructions of difference and Otherness are not addressed in Chilean neoliberal society. As Joanna Page points out, "Scherson shows no interest in radical political transformation; like Cristina, the film takes refuge in flights of fantasy that remove us from the realities of inequality in contemporary Chile" (2017, 278). Although the film introduces the context of a strike that makes a subtle allusion to the Chilean neoliberal scenario of precarious jobs, these sequences serve mostly to accentuate individualism as the backdrop of social relations in neoliberal Chile and the preeminence of the private world over collective identity.[22] More particularly, the film is silent about the ongoing policies of dispossession against the Mapuche and the racist politics that have legitimized their exclusion out of the borders of the nation. Despite this silence, the representation of indigeneity in the film encourages us to hesitate in equating Mapuche identity with the conflict, as is the case with Cristina in *Play*. However, Cristina is not able to embody a role model for possible Mapuche-ness since she cannot express Mapuche identity in the public space. Instead, Cristina belongs to the modern project of the nation only through learning to perform neoliberal modernity. The film shows the persistence of local beliefs about race and belonging of Indigenous people, rooted in the experience of coloniality and nation building. These beliefs entail epistemic consequences for the inclusion of racialized Chileans as modern citizens today. It is not only global neoliberal capitalism that affects Mapuche exclusion from the nation but also the legacy of the racial narrative of difference. Even as an illusion, Cristina's character challenges the idea of what it is to be a Mapuche woman in the city: poor, discriminated against, invisible, symbolic consumer, domestic worker, intended to marry a person of her social class. Cristina refuses to be that, believing in being part of the modernization project.

Notes

Unless otherwise noted, all translations are my own.

1. In the introduction of the book, Mignolo (2011, 1) explains how the essay "Coloniality and Modernity/Rationality" authored by Quijano (2007) provided intellectual stimulus for his examination of the notion of modernity.
2. Term coined to describe the rapid economic growth attributed to the neoliberal turn during the first decade of the dictatorship in Chile.
3. "La idea es que Chile se vea como un país moderno. Aquí no hay problemas étnicos, no tenemos gran tradición precolombina. Chile es básicamente un país

nuevo. . . . No nos interesa impactar al europeo con la imagen de un país exótico porque no lo somos. . . . Es simplemente la necesidad de que nos vean iguales a ellos y no como una curiosidad exótica."

4. Vidal Valenzuela has referred to the criticisms against the project, which indicated the ecological damage caused and also the uncritical validation of the neoliberal model installed during the dictatorship. According to Vidal Valenzuela (2017, 209), "El iceberg actuaba simbólicamente como un dispositivo de congelamiento de la memoria política en beneficio de relaciones comerciales a escala global" (The iceberg worked symbolically as a device for freezing the political memory for the benefit of commercial relations at a global scale).
5. The Concertación was the coalition of center-left political parties in Chile created to run for the "No" option in the plebiscite to decide the continuation of the military regime. After becoming the winners, this alliance was able to stay in power from the return to democracy in 1990 until 2010, when conservative candidate Sebastián Piñera won the Chilean presidential election. In 2013 the Concertación adopted the name of the Nueva Mayoría, the New Majority coalition, in an effort to update its image.
6. Patricio Aylwin, the first president after the transition (1990–1994), completed the sale of the LAN-Chile airline, while Eduardo Frei, his successor (1994–2000), privatized sanitation, port, and highway projects (Collier and Sater 2004, 394).
7. Larraín (2001, 162) describes the identity discourse of the post-dictatorship Chile as one embracing a "versión empresarial" (entrepreneurial version).
8. According to the 2017 census in Chile, 12.8 percent of the population consider themselves to be members of an Indigenous group, of which 9.9 percent identify themselves as Mapuche (Villalobos and Blanco 2018). The majority of the Mapuche population is concentrated in the capital city, followed by the region of La Araucanía (Navarro 2018).
9. Author's interview with director Alicia Scherson, held in person in Santiago de Chile, May 7, 2018.
10. "En la flanería el sujeto urbano, privatizado, se aproxima a la ciudad con la mirada de quien ve un objeto en exhibición."
11. "Ser ciudadano no tiene que ver sólo con los derechos reconocidos por los aparatos estatales a quienes nacieron en un territorio, sino también con las prácticas sociales y culturales que dan sentido de pertenencia."
12. "En el caso de *Play*, no hay movilidad social. . . . No hay posibilidad de moverse, esta mina por más que se vista . . . no."
13. Lipschutz was a prominent scientist from the 1960s and a nationalized Chilean. He was acknowledged by his challenging of biological theories of race, particularly to defend Indigenous people.
14. Despite the persistence of the image of the Indigenous as marginalized, it is worth noting that, as scholar Jo Crow (2013, 149) observed, a number of Mapuche people were part of the business entrepreneurial class in Santiago, although

this was mainly ignored by leftist discourses during the decades of the 1960s and early 1970s. Crow claims that this group proves that there were "Mapuche who were not part of the neglected and oppressed" (149). Nonetheless, the pervasiveness of racial politics in relation to the Indigenous body in Chile discussed in this thesis suggests that owning a business will not entirely protect from forms of racial discrimination.

15. The main antagonists of the conflict over Mapuche lands are the forestry and timber industries established in the area, the Chilean state that supports the entrepreneurial agenda of the private companies exploiting the land, and the Mapuche people reclaiming their territories.
16. Author's interview with director Alicia Scherson, held in person in Santiago de Chile, May 7, 2018.
17. "El indígena fílmico está suspendido entre criterios históricos, relatos míticos y luchas ecológicas."
18. "Las representaciones de lo indígena en el cine chileno han modelado un indígena exótico, congelado en el tiempo y ajeno a sus propios procesos histórico."
19. Gissi (2004, 6) also details the role of the ongoing colonial relationship between the Chilean state and Mapuche people on the economic deprivation of this Indigenous group. Changes in economic activities from wheat production to livestock and later to forestry have exacerbated the historic state-led impoverishment of Mapuche, pushing them to abandon their ancestral territories.
20. "La necesidad de emigrar hacia la capital es más bien consecuencia de intereses y decisiones estatales que han resultado perjudiciales para los pueblos originarios."
21. In the emblematic Peruvian film *La teta asustada* (*Milk of Sorrow*; Llosa 2009) about domestic work and indigeneity in contemporary Peru, the Indigenous nana is defined by the space. Upon arrival to the house where she is going to work, the order she receives is, "Quédate en tu cocina" (Stay in your kitchen), a phrase that makes emphasis on the possessive pronoun that denotes the place where she belongs. Additionally, the body is under scrutiny in order to meet the aseptic requirements to inhabit the "white space." The maid is thoroughly inspected to check whether her hands, nails, and ears look hygienic.
22. The construction manager tells Tristán about the strike they are planning, but Tristán replies he is external to the company. Lost in his thoughts and showing little interest in the strike or in the workers' situation, he mentions that his partner dumped him. "Hay cosas peores Don Tristán, mucho peores," replies the construction manager, noting Tristán's individualistic position and disconnection from social reality.

References

Ahmed, Sara. 2007. "A Phenomenology of Whiteness." *Feminist Theory* 8 (2): 149–68. https://doi.org/10.1177/1464700107078139.

Appelbaum, Nancy P., Anne S. Macpherson, and Karin Alejandra Rosemblatt. 2003. "Introduction." In *Race and Nation in Modern Latin America*, edited by Nancy P. Appelbaum, Anne S. Macpherson, and Karin Alejandra Rosemblatt, 1–31. Chapel Hill: University of North Carolina Press.

Bengoa, José. 2007. "Chile Mestizo." *Mensaje* 56 (564): 48–50. https://repositorio.uahurtado.cl/static/pages/docs/2007/n564_48.pdf.

Bowlby, Rachel. (1985) 2009. *Just Looking (Routledge Revivals): Consumer Culture in Dreiser, Gissing and Zola*. London: Taylor & Francis Group.

Castillo, Paola. 2014. *Genoveva*. Chile: Errante Producciones.

Collier, Simon, and William F. Sater. 2004. *A History of Chile, 1808–2002*. 2nd ed. New York: Cambridge University Press.

Cresswell, Tim, and Deborah Dixon. 2002. "Introduction: Engaging Film." In *Engaging Film: Geographies of Mobility and Identity*, edited by Tim Cresswell and Deborah Dixon, 1–10. Lanham: Rowman & Littlefield.

Crow, Jo. 2007. "Debates about Ethnicity, Class and Nation in Allende' s Chile (1970–1973)." *Bulletin of Latin American Research* 26 (3): 319–38. https://www.jstor.org/stable/27733940.

———. 2013. *The Mapuche in Modern Chile: A Cultural History*. Gainesville: University Press of Florida.

Domingo Amestoy, Susana. 2020. "Defamiliarizing the Maid: Alicia Scherson's *Play*." In *Domestic Labor in Twenty-First Century Latin American Cinema*, edited by Elizabeth Osborne and Sofía Ruiz-Alfaro, 121–42. Cham, Switzerland: Palgrave Macmillan.

Dyer, Richard. 2017. *White*. 20th anniversary ed. London: Routledge.

Elkin, Lauren. 2017. *Flâneuse: Women Walk the City in Paris, New York, Tokyo, Venice and London*. London: Vintage Books.

Escobar, Arturo. 2007. "Worlds and Knowledges Otherwise: The Latin American Modernity/Coloniality Research Program." *Cultural Studies* 21 (2–3): 179–210. https://doi.org/10.1080/09502380601162506.

———. 2010. "Latin America at the Cross-Road: Alternative Modernizations, Post-Neoliberalism or Post-Development?" *Cultural Studies* 24 (1): 1–65. https://doi.org/10.1080/09502380903424208.

Friedlander, Judith. 2006. *Being Indian in Hueyapán*. Basingstoke, U.K.: Palgrave Macmillan.

García Canclini, Néstor. 1990. *Culturas híbridas: estrategias para entrar y salir de la modernidad*. New ed. Mexico City: Grijalbo.

———. 1995. *Consumidores y ciudadanos: conflictos multiculturales de la globalización*. Mexico City: Grijalbo.

Gissi, Nicolás. 2004. "Los mapuche en el Santiago del siglo XXI: Desde la ciudadanía política a la demanda por el reconocimiento." *Cultura Urbana*, no. 1, 1–12.

Goldberg, David Theo. 2008. *The Threat of Race: Reflections on Racial Neoliberalism*. Malden, Mass.: Wiley-Blackwell.

González, María Paz. 2019. *Lina de Lima*. Chile: Quijote Films; Peru: Carapulkra Films; Argentina: Gema Films.

Gopinath, Gayatri. 2005. *Impossible Desires: Queer Diasporas and South Asian Public Cultures*. Durham, N.C.: Duke University Press.

Larraín, Jorge. 2001. *Identidad chilena*. Santiago, Chile: LOM Ediciones.

Llosa, Claudia. 2009. *La teta asustada*. Spain: Wanda Visión and Oberon Cinematográfica; Peru: Vela Producciones.

Mignolo, Walter. 2011. *The Darker Side of Western Modernity: Global Futures, Decolonial Options*. Durham, N.C.: Duke University Press.

Moulián, Tomás. 1997. *Chile actual: anatomía de un mito*. Santiago de Chile: LOM-ARCIS.

Navarro, Sofía. 2018. "Región Metropolitana concentra mayor población mapuche del país." *diarioUchile*, May 8, 2018. https://radio.uchile.cl/2018/05/08/region-metropolitana-concentra-mayor-poblacion-mapuche-a-nivel-nacional/.

Page, Joanna. 2017. "Neoliberalism and the Politics of Affect and Self-Authorship in Contemporary Chilean Cinema." In *A Companion to Latin American Cinema*, edited by Stephen M. Hart, Maria Delgado, and Randal Johnson, 269–84. Chichester, U.K. and Malden, Mass.: John Wiley & Sons.

Quijano, Anibal. 1989. "Paradoxes of Modernity in Latin America." *International Journal of Politics, Culture, and Society* 3 (2): 147–77. https://www.jstor.org/stable/20006945.

———. 1993. "Modernity, Identity, and Utopia in Latin America." *Boundary 2* 20 (3): 140–55. https://www.jstor.org/stable/303346.

———. 2007. "Coloniality and Modernity/Rationality." *Cultural Studies* 21 (2–3): 168–78. https://doi.org/10.1080/09502380601164353.

Rabasa, José. 1997. "Of Zapatismo: Reflections on the Folkloric and the Impossible in a Subaltern Insurrection." In *The Politics of Culture in the Shadow of Capital*, edited by Lowe Lisa and Lloyd David, 399–431. Durham, N.C.: Duke University Press.

Ramos, Julio. 1989. *Desecuentros de la modernidad en América Latina, Literatura y Política en el siglo XIX*. Mexico: Fondo de Cultura Económica.

Raurich, Valentina, and Juan Pablo Silva. 2011. "La exhumación de lo premoderno: la imagen de los pueblos originarios en el cine de ficción y documental chileno." *Estudios sobre las Culturas Contemporáneas*. 17 (34): 65–83. https://www.redalyc.org/articulo.oa?id=31620701004.

Richards, Patricia. 2013. *Race and the Chilean Miracle: Neoliberalism, Democracy, and Indigenous Rights*. Pittsburgh: University of Pittsburgh Press.

Rivera Cusicanqui, Silvia. 2010. *Oprimidos pero no vencidos: luchas del campesinado aymara y qhechwa de Bolivia, 1900–1980*. 4th ed. La Paz, Bolivia: La Mirada Salvaje.

Scherson, Alicia. 2005. *Play*. Argentina and Chile: Paraiso Production.

Subercaseaux, Bernardo. 1996. *Chile, ¿un país moderno?* Santiago de Chile: Ediciones B.

Urrutia, Carolina, and Iván Pinto. 2005. "Conversación/Entrevista a Alicia Scherson." *laFuga*, 1. http://lafuga.cl/conversacionentrevista-a-alicia-scherson/75.

Vidal Valenzuela, Sebastián. 2017. "El Pabellón de Chile en Sevilla '92 desde tres casos abortados de artes visuals." *Caiana*, no. 11, 209–16. http://caiana.caia.org.ar/resources/uploads/11-pdf/Vidal%20Valenzuela%20ESP.pdf.

Villalobos, Fernanda, and Benjamín Blanco. 2018. "Censo: Un 9,9% de la población se declara mapuche y persona por hogar se reduce de 4,4 a 3,1 miembros en 36 años." *Emol.com*, May 4, 2018. https://www.emol.com/noticias/Nacional/2018/05/04/904969/Censo-Un-99-de-la-poblacion-se-declara-mapuche-y-tamana-de-la-familia-se-reduce-de-44-a-31-miembros-en-36-anos.html.

Wade, Peter, Vivette García Deister, Michael Kent, María Fernanda Olarte Sierra, and Adriana Díaz del Castillo Hernández. 2014. "Nation and the Absent Presence of Race in Latin American Genomics." *Current Anthropology* 55 (5): 497–522. https://www.jstor.org/stable/10.1086/677945.

CHAPTER EIGHT

Indigenous Urbanization and Indigenous Urban Experiences in the Russian Arctic

The Cases of Yakutsk and Naryan-Mar

MARYA ROZANOVA-SMITH, STANISLAV SAAS KSENOFONTOV, AND ANDREY N. PETROV

Introduction

In a rapidly transforming world, urbanization is one of the defining signs of the ongoing demographic, social, cultural, and economic changes (Haase et al. 2018) facing the contemporary world. Urbanization (i.e., the growth of population, in absolute and relative terms, residing in urban settlements) has spread even to the remotest regions of the planet, although global peripheries tend to be less urbanized (United Nations 2019). The Arctic, however, is a significant exception, as it is a very remote region that stands out as one of the more heavily urbanized areas in the world (Heleniak and Bogoyavlensky 2015). The Arctic, covering northern parts of eight countries (Canada, Finland, Greenland [Kingdom of Denmark], Iceland, Norway, Russia, Sweden, and the United States), has approximately two-thirds of its population of four million living in cities and towns (Laruelle 2019; Zamyatina and Goncharov 2019), and this concentration is expected to increase (Rasmussen 2011). The proportion of urban dwellers is especially high in Arctic Russia (78.2 percent), Iceland (77.3 percent), and northern Sweden (70.8 percent; Zamyatina and Goncharov 2019). Nevertheless, other parts of the Arctic, such as the Faroe Islands and Nunavut, are less urbanized.

The Arctic is the homeland to Indigenous peoples who settled across a vast area of North America and northern Eurasia. Although the definitions and levels of recognition of the Indigenous status vary among the Arctic countries, the most inclusive estimates place the Indigenous population in the region at eight hundred thousand to one million (Jungsberg et al. 2019). The Arctic Indigenous peoples are highly diverse, with over forty major ethnic groups and hundreds of tribes that have, for millennia, called circumpolar lands and waters their home (Koivurova et al. 2020). Traditionally, most Indigenous groups in the Arctic were nomadic or seminomadic. However, the sedentarization and resettlement policies in the Arctic countries in the twentieth century, along with changing socioeconomic conditions that followed colonization, spurred a shift of the Indigenous population to larger settlements (Marcus 1992; Allemann 2020). The Indigenous peoples in the Arctic historically were under cultural, economic, social, and political pressure from strong and rich states, with extensive and well-funded urban development policies, developed infrastructure, and strong political will, leading to policies that were often conducted without considering the implications for Indigenous communities and that created urbanization on unequal and inequitable terms.

This urbanization trend[1] among Indigenous peoples is likely to accelerate in the future due to rapid climate and social changes in the Arctic (Stephens 2015). Given the speed and intensity with which Indigenous urbanization is taking place in the Arctic, a thorough examination of Indigenous urbanization in this region can make an important contribution to our understanding of the Indigenous urban experience globally. Unveiling, understanding, and valuing Indigenous urban livelihoods is an important task in respect to research and policy making, but also, most crucially, in terms of individual and collective self-determination of the Indigenous peoples. According to the UN Office for the High Commissioner for Human Rights (OHCHR), the reasons for Indigenous urbanization lie in the search for a new life in a framework of rural poverty, land grabbing, political conflicts, and other challenges. The Indigenous peoples "have moved from their traditional lands towards urban areas partly seeking opportunities for education and employment, partly because of human rights abuses and violations in particular to their land rights and partly for cultural survival" (OHCHR 2010).

In addition, there are significant underlying conditions related to a common historical trauma shared by all the Arctic Indigenous peoples, and Indigenous peoples around the world (Kirmayer, Gone, and Moses 2014; Joo-Castro and Emerson 2021; Smallwood et al. 2021). A long history of colonialism (Tomiak 2017) and oppression—accompanied by loss of land, forced sedentarization, westernization via boarding schools, the lack of recognition of Indigenous peoples' rights, and assimilation—were channeled through urbanization and aggravated by the mass migration of non-Indigenous populations to the Arctic. These historical events continue to affect the livelihoods and well-being of the Indigenous urban residents today.

Resettling to villages and, even more so, to cities and towns represents a striking departure from the traditional nomadic and seminomadic lifestyles and makes cultural and spiritual reconciliation with the urban environment extremely challenging. In addition, many Indigenous homelands are located thousands of miles away from cities in areas with low transportation accessibility and high travel costs. This limits physical access to ancestral lands and increases financial and logistical burdens for participating in subsistence practices for urban residents. The Arctic urban database includes fifty communities that range in size from approximately ten thousand (Anadyr) to over three hundred thousand (Yakutsk and Anchorage; Orttung 2020, 23–25). While definitions of the urban may vary, the common feature of these places—regardless of the size—is that the residents make their living primarily through employment in industry, services, and the public sector. Urban residents spend little or no time engaging in agriculture or traditional forms of subsistence. As people move to cities from rural areas, they experience existential challenges adjusting to a new urban reality. This transition is especially challenging for Indigenous people since, for them, fishing, hunting, gathering, and herding are more than simply economic activities but are integral to ways of life and imbued with spiritual significance, and, in many ways, the people are defined through these activities (Peters and Andersen 2013; UN HABITAT 2010).

Urbanization thus poses particular challenges for Indigenous peoples, and in this chapter we explore how Indigenous people of the Russian Arctic meet those challenges. We explore how they create new Indigenous identities that are meaningful in their new environments. As many of the other contributions to this volume show, just because being Indigenous has historically been associated with a rural existence does not mean that an urban Indigenous identity cannot be vibrant and meaningful as well.

Despite a number of important studies in North America,[2] and to a lesser degree in Greenland[3] and Fennoscandia,[4] the Russian case[5] is perhaps the least studied in the region because the proportion of Indigenous people in urban areas remains low, with the exception of Yakutsk, where more than 50 percent of the population identify as Indigenous. In this chapter we look at the Indigenous experience in two Russian cities: Naryan-Mar in European Russia and Yakutsk in the Asian (Siberian) part of the Russian Arctic.

The literature suggests that urban Indigenous identity is one of the most complex and challenging parts of the urban Indigenous experience (Stephens 2015). In cities, Indigenous identities are represented and manifested in a variety of forms and undergo transformations bound by generational, demographic, geographical, political, and cultural contexts and by characteristics of the identity bearers (Peters 2011), who, in addition, often face challenges in maintaining their ethnic identity (Weaver 2012). Similar to Indigenous peoples in other regions, Arctic Indigenous peoples have been excluded from the process of shaping and reimagining urban space and are seen as belonging to a rural milieu, as their traditional practices contrast with those of the urban environment. That is, Indigeneity has historically been defined as an explicitly rural identity, and so urban Indigenous peoples often appear as incongruous at best. In addition, urban environments provide few opportunities to pursue traditional practices, which are closely tied to identity, and it therefore becomes a challenge for Indigenous people to negotiate an ethnic identity that is both Indigenous and urban. In order to do so, however, Indigenous urbanites (and in some instances in cooperation with settlers' government institutions) re-create a cultural space in urban environments where some traditional practices, such as singing, dancing, crafting, and food sharing, can be pursued (Landry, Asselin, and Lévesque 2019) even as re-created spaces differ from the original one and traditional practices take place in different social contexts, often undergoing a substantial transformation. Urban Indigenous identities constructed through these practices may face accusations of inauthenticity, by non-Indigenous and other Indigenous people alike, an experience common to many other urban Indigenous people. Similarly, an urban Indigenous identity is seen as marginalized and not Indigenous enough, as moving to the city is seen as equivalent to assimilation (Nyseth and Pedersen 2014). This raises the question of the distinction between Indigenous lifestyles versus Indigenous heritage. Peters (2011), in her synthesis of the literature, demonstrates that today's Indigenous urbanites in Canada may not have a close connection to the land and may live completely different lives than their ancestors. In this case, Indigenous cultures, traditions, and identities (according to Peters 2011) may become heritage rather than lifestyle. This is not, however, to suggest that urban Indigenous identities are any less valid or authentic than rural ones but, rather, that they are not necessarily rooted in particular economic activities. An apparent exception here are the Canadian Mohawk, who have been closely associated with working on skyscrapers in U.S. cities such as New York from the early decades of the twentieth century (Simpson 2014).

Many scholars highlight the resilience and complexity of urban Indigenous livelihoods and argue that Indigeneity is not fading away in urban environments or becoming less meaningful but, rather, that it is evolving to face new realities (Peters and Andersen 2013). It is possible to (re)construct, retain, and revitalize urban Indigenous identities in the urban environment by creating space for cultural hybridity and innovation (Burke 2009; Balaram 2018; Smith and Leavy 2008). These may include the presence of Indigenous symbols in urban architecture as well as developed cultural infrastructure that encompasses Indigenous cultural centers, Indigenous peoples' organizations, Indigenous-owned businesses, Indigenous language courses, art studios, university/college/school programs, and museums, among many others (Chevalier 2017; Rozanova 2019; Korkina 2019).

We explore these issues through the following objectives: (1) to examine the recent history of Indigenous urbanization in Naryan-Mar and Yakutsk; (2) to identify how key elements of Indigenous identity—such as connection to land, traditional practices and customs, and Native languages—are manifested by the Indigenous urbanites; (3) to identify characteristics of urban Indigenous identities that emerge in the Russian Arctic and explore their connection with urban living and the cities' cultural landscapes.

Research Regions and Communities

This study was conducted in two Russian Arctic cities: Yakutsk (N 62.02°, E 129.40°), located in northeastern Siberia, and Naryan-Mar (N 67°38', E 53°03'), located in the western part of the Russian Arctic. Both cities function as regional administrative centers: the city of Yakutsk is the capital of the Republic of Sakha (Yakutia), the largest region in Russia by landmass, and Naryan-Mar, the administrative center and the only town in Nenets Autonomous Okrug.[6] Both cities are home to Arctic Indigenous peoples and are located on Indigenous ancestral lands, yet they represent two indicative/contrasting cases of history of Arctic colonization, Indigenous demographic, and urbanization patterns.

In this study we follow the international definitions of Indigenous peoples by the International Labour Organization Convention 169 (ILO C169) and the United Nations Declaration on the Rights of Indigenous Peoples (UNDRIP), which use self-identification, historical continuity, first occupation of the land, colonization in a nondominant condition in society, speakers of a Native language, and possessing their own social, political, and religious institutions as the key criteria. This definition includes both Sakha and Nenets. However, the Russian legislation recognizes and grants a special status only to the "small-numbered" Indigenous peoples (whose population does not exceed 50,000;[7] Federal Law-82 of April 30, 1999 "On Guarantees of the Rights of Indigenous Small-Numbered Peoples of the Russian Federation"), thus depriving larger ethnic groups of many Indigenous rights. In accordance with this classification, only the Nenets people, with a population of 44,000 (Russian Census 2010) are legally recognized as Indigenous and protected by a law that grants them special rights with regard to land and the preservation of their traditional way of life, while the Sakha people, with a population of 480,000 (Russian Census 2010), are not. Although this research does not address the question of how different legal statuses of Nenets and Sakha peoples affect the experiences of Indigenous urbanites, this might be an important direction for future research.

Methodology

In order to examine the urbanization process and its implications for different aspects of urban Indigenous residents' identities, we employed in-depth semistructured interviews with Indigenous young people aged eighteen to thirty-five who reside permanently in Yakutsk and Naryan-Mar. Interviews were conducted in 2020 and 2021. Young people are an important group to examine because they face the complex issues of identity and urbanity while representing the future of their Indigenous communities. In addition, we were particularly interested in Indigenous youth who were born in urban areas, or, at the very least, moved at a young age, to explore how they developed an Indigenous consciousness with little or no exposure to rural lifeways.

The interviewee pool was developed using the snowball sampling method. Initial participants—both male and female—were selected through personal contacts established over the years with these Indigenous communities. One of the authors, Stanislav Ksenofontov, identifies himself as Indigenous and comes from the case study area of Sakha Republic. He was born and raised in the rural area and moved to the urban setting and thus encountered similar experiences of ethno-cultural identity retention. Therefore, he expressed his deep interest and concern of studying Indigenous identity in the urban landscape. Marya Rozanova-Smith and Andrey Petrov are Western researchers who have long-term relationships with Arctic Indigenous communities in Russia. Working with Indigenous communities, Rozanova-Smith and Petrov are pursuing community-engaged and coproductive approaches that ensure the mutual benefit of research and the implementation of the principles of research conduct in the Arctic (IASSA 2020; Degai et al. 2022). All authors went through the ethics training and human subjects Institutional Review Board (IRB) process.

All the interview participants have been notified about the research and its objectives and have given consent for participation. Interviews involved Indigenous Sakha residents in Yakutsk and Nenets urbanites in Naryan-Mar. Interviews addressed the following topics: Indigenous language proficiency, traditional practices, familiarity with traditional art and sports, connections to rural areas, relations with relatives in rural areas, connections to nature and ancestral lands, diet preferences, and identity. Interviews were conducted in Russian, as it is the most commonly spoken and preferred language for the study participants. The interviews were recorded using an audio recorder, then transcribed online at oTranscribe website and analyzed in MAXQDA software, where transcript texts were coded into categories for data comparison.

Due to the global pandemic, which has significantly affected many Indigenous communities across the Arctic (Petrov et al. 2021), in-person interviewing was not feasible, and the authors conducted qualitative interviews online using Zoom and WhatsApp platforms. The online interview method was chosen due to its significant advantages during the pandemic, such as ensuring the health and safety of research participants, convenience and flexibility, and the opportunity for interview participants to remain in the comfort of their homes, as well as providing the opportunity to develop meaningful communication and discuss personal matters if necessary (Gray et al. 2020).

Results and Discussion

Arctic Indigenous Urbanization: A Tale of Two Cities

THE CASE OF YAKUTSK

Yakutsk, one of the oldest urban settlements in Siberia, was founded in 1632 by Russian Cossacks and, until recently, ethnic Russians mainly populated the city. Indigenous peoples, predominantly the Sakha, a Turkic-speaking people, historically inhabited rural areas with large pastures as they actively practiced seminomadic horse and cattle breeding at that time, as well as hunting, fishing, and gathering. By the end of the seventeenth century, rural residents began migrating to the city and its vicinity for trade, and this pattern was amplified in Soviet times. Currently, the population of Yakutsk is 330,615 (Sakhastat 2021). According to the last available census (Russian Census 2010), Indigenous residents constituted 50.7 percent of the city's population, comprising the Sakha (48 percent), Evenki (1 percent), Eveny (0.7 percent), and other Indigenous groups such as Dolgans, Chukchee, and the Yukaghirs, among others. The non-Indigenous population is predominantly ethnic Russian (Russian Census 2010).

In 1989, toward the end of the USSR, 74 percent of Sahka lived in rural areas, and only 13 percent lived in cities and towns (Vsesoiuznaia Perepis' Naseleniia 1996). In the 1990s many ethnic Russian workers returned to western Russia due to the deep economic crisis and the closure of mining industries. At the same time, migration of Sakha from rural areas to Yakutsk and other cities has increased as a result of the reorganization of *kolkhoz* (collective farms existed in Sakha under the rule of communism since the 1920s), reorganized in *sovkhoz* in the 1960s (Vinokurova 2016) after the collapse of the Soviet Union (Ferguson and Sidorova, 2018). Rural-urban migration has increased in recent decades: for example, in 2017 it constituted 66.7 percent of the total migration flow to cities in the Republic of Sakha (Tomaska et al. 2018).

It is worth noting that Yakutsk is a rapidly growing city: its population has grown by about 100,000 since 2005.[8] In 2019 alone, 14,252 people migrated to Yakutsk, mainly from rural areas of the Republic of Sakha (Sakhastat 2021). This massive migration inflow was predominantly generated by Indigenous Sakha people as part of the rural-to-urban education and labor-related migration caused by unemployment and lack of higher educational opportunities in the villages. In the context of an urban setting, however, traditional activities tend to be practiced less compared to rural areas, where these activities are the primary economic activity, whereas in the city they are largely recreational.

THE CASE OF NARYAN-MAR

In Nenets Autonomous Okrug (NAO), urbanization began in the twentieth century, when the settlement of Naryan-Mar (in Nenets, "Red City") was established in 1931 as a symbol of the Soviet "conquest" of the Arctic and the exploration of its natural resources (Rozanova 2019). Before the 1930s, the Indigenous population, predominantly Nenets eople, pursued a traditional nomadic lifestyle on these lands and engaged in a subsistence economy based on reindeer herding, fishing, hunting, and gathering. For the local Indigenous Nenets population, urbanization was not the result of internal development but rather was an external forcing accompanied by an "abrupt reformatting of the very principles of the existence of a socio-historical and geographical space" (Martianov 2016, 118). Urbanization dramatically changed the ethnic composition of the region as a result of the rapid increase of the non-Indigenous settler population and the influx of temporary workers from different regions of the Soviet Union.

As described below, in the rapidly growing urbanized industrial center of Naryan-Mar, urbanization was not accompanied by the Indigenous population's grassroots support. Initial Nenets' resistance to urbanization can be explained by the fact that, until relatively recently, their livelihoods were deeply rooted in a traditional subsistence economy and thus inseparable from the Arctic ecosystems. Also, Nenets maintain traditionally strong kinship ties and often follow principles of commonality and traditions of sharing as opposed to the urban sociocultural norms often characterized by a greater degree of isolation and individualism (Föllmer 2020; Klinenberg 2001; Emerson and Smiley 2018; etc.).

In NAO, the total population reached 44,389 people in 2021, of whom 32,948 were urbanites, and 11,441 were rural dwellers. The regional administrative center, the city of Naryan-Mar, is home to more than half the population of NAO (25,536 people in 2021).[9] Urbanization in NAO has affected different ethnic groups to varying degrees. As the most recent Russian census, conducted in 2010, revealed, in urban settings, the share of ethnic Russians at 80 percent makes them a dominant group. Nenets are also progressively urbanizing but at a much slower pace. The share of Nenets urbanites in the total Nenets population is nearly 23.6 percent in 2010, which demonstrates a minor increase from 20.4 percent in 2002 (Russian Census 2002).

In the city of Naryan-Mar, the two major ethnic groups that represent Indigenous peoples are Nenets, comprising 6.7 percent of the total city dwellers, and Komi, 7.3 percent (Russian Census 2010). The ethnic imbalance and the overwhelming dominance of the Russian culture and Russian language in NAO, among other factors, largely contribute to significant language shifts among Nenets urbanites. The most recent census data with a focus on urban dwellers showed that only 25.3 percent of the city's Nenets population speaks the mother tongue (Russian Census 2002).

For decades, among key drivers of rural-urban migration of Nenets people, predominantly youth, were educational and professional opportunities in the city (Rozanova 2019). However, ongoing unprecedented climate-induced environmental change in the Arctic will likely affect the traditional lifestyle of Indigenous Nenets people and bring further social, economic, and institutional transformations and accelerate urbanization processes.

Arctic Urbanity and Emerging Indigenous Identities

We now move to a consideration of Indigenous youth (aged eighteen to thirty-five) for whom urban life is a basic part of their existence but who yet maintain an Indigenous identity.

CONNECTION TO LAND

As mentioned earlier, in rural areas Arctic Indigenous communities maintain a close connection to their lands through traditional practices such as fishing, hunting, gathering, and herding, as well as spiritual practices. For urban residents, practicing cattle/horse breeding or (semi)nomadic reindeer herding is nearly impossible on a regular basis, whereas this is often the single economic activity for rural Indigenous peoples, around which much of their culture evolves. Nevertheless, for Indigenous urbanites, other land- and water-based activities, such as fishing, hunting, and gathering, are much more accessible. As our research revealed, most of the male interview participants, and some women, go fishing in their free time, and many people, predominantly women, also engage in foraging.

> I love fishing. This love has been with me since childhood. My father and grandfather are ardent fishers and hunters. When I was a kid, I used to spend the whole summer in the village at my grandparents'. Grandfather used to take us to hay harvesting and fishing, we used to pick berries and mushrooms with grandmother. (Yakutsk, Sakha female, twenty-three)

> I love fishing. . . . Last year I did my best to fish every week, but due to some circumstances and time shortage, it wasn't always possible. (Yakutsk, Sakha male, thirty)

> We try to have more fish in our diet, and it is desirable that we catch it ourselves. Every year we try to go fishing, especially for smelt, and we also collect goose and partridge eggs, and pick cloudberries. (Naryan-Mar, Nenets female, thirty-three)

Hunting, traditionally perceived as a male domain, depends on the season and availability or acquisition of licenses for hunting, so few people practice it regularly. "Well, it depends on the season. If I have a license, then I do my best to go hunting every season, but it is not always possible to acquire a license" (Yakutsk, Sakha male, thirty-two).

Although hunting rules and regulations in Russia are applied differently to various groups of hunters and the rural Nenets pursuing a traditional way of life are given some special rights, there are no exceptions for Indigenous urbanites. Thus, the lack of legal recognition becomes an obstacle for pursuing their traditional activities and maintaining cultural practices: "I grew up in the village, and I have relatives who are reindeer herders, so I went fishing and hunting all my childhood. My parents taught me. You can say that I was perfectly proficient in this. Now it is difficult because you need to get a hunting permit and a hunting rifle. These days, there is only fishing with friends. But it is happening more and more rarely" (Naryan-Mar, Nenets male, twenty-eight).

Subsistence gathering is an important traditional activity among Indigenous youth. They pick up various berries and mushrooms every summer, but most of the time while in a village or tundra. Furthermore, gathering tends to be practiced more among women. As our female interview participants reported:

> In summer when I have time and when I am in a village, I go to pick mushrooms three-four times per week if the weather is fine, and to pick berries once a year. (Yakutsk, Sakha female, eighteen)

> We pick the berries ourselves every year, then freeze them, make jam. (Naryan-Mar, Nenets female, twenty-seven)

Almost none of the interview participants mentioned cattle breeding or reindeer herding as a regular practice, as they are rather rural activities. In Yakutsk, only one male interview participant aged twenty-three stated to have a horse breeding farm, although not his own but father's:

Author (A): Do you practice cattle breeding or reindeer herding?
Interview Participant (IP): My father has a horse breeding farm.
A: Does it mean you are involved in this activity?
IP: Yes.
A: How often do you help?
IP: Once, twice a year.

In Naryan-Mar, the urban sedentary lifestyle is viewed by many older Nenets as less desirable and even risky, and some Nenets parents see their children's future in the tundra pursuing (semi)nomadic lifestyle: "Every summer, I go to the chum[10] in the Bolshezemelskaya tundra for about ten days, where relatives have reindeer herding. And my parents also go to the chum and help with the reindeer. There, I also go fishing, picking berries. . . . It happens to get out there only once a year. My parents want to send me to work in the tundra. And for me, ten days a year in the tundra is enough, and most preferably, not in winter" (Naryan-Mar, Nenets male, twenty-one).

Young Indigenous urbanites also connect to ancestors' lands through their relatives in rural areas. All of the interview participants have relatives in villages, and many pay their grandparents a visit on weekends or holidays. Even though their lifestyle is urban, they continue to maintain strong links to rural lifestyles, and this is an important element in their Indigenous identity and practice (Solovyeva and Kuklina 2020). A young woman (Yakutsk, Sakha female, twenty-three) stated, "Most of the time we go to a village—to my grandfather and grandmother—to Amga, this is one of my favorite places because all my life I've gone there for the whole summer."

However, not all of them visit their relatives in a village, or they visit them rarely. A young man (Yakutsk, Sakha male, twenty-nine) said, "I was in Nyurba only once, in Maya two, three times in my whole life. I have never been to hay making, I have never spent summer in a village. I don't know what it's like."

The loss of ties to rural areas is often associated with the death or resettlement of relatives. As our participants reported:

> I used to go there when my great grandmother was alive. She died, and no one goes now. (Yakutsk, Sakha male, twenty-nine)

> I used to visit a village when I was a kid. I don't go now since many relatives moved to the city. (Yakutsk, Sakha female, twenty-three)

Economic factors and the remoteness of some communities also create barriers for the city dwellers to keep ties with their Arctic homelands, sometimes creating an emotional distance. Despite a strong desire to visit their relatives and their ancestor's lands, many young Indigenous urbanites cannot afford to travel to remote Arctic areas:

> I rarely pay a visit these days; I have not been there [in my village] in the last year. Only a one-way ticket costs 6,200 rubles [US$85]. We have our own hut in the tundra on Kolguev Island, that is where we used to go for two weeks in the summer with our relatives. And at this time, almost all the relatives live in Naryan-Mar, and on the whole, young people are leaving [the village] due to lack of jobs there. (Naryan-Mar, Nenets female, thirty-three)

> It is difficult to reach my mother's village, the return ticket costs 50 thousand rubles [US$670]. And there's nothing there, food is very expensive. (Yakutsk, Sakha female, nineteen)

Even if the interview participants may not be visiting their relatives in villages often, they keep an important tradition of exchanging goods associated with subsistence activities. Access to traditional food is another important component shaping Indigenous identity. For Indigenous urbanites, it is directly linked to the spiritual tradition of sharing, which is central for Arctic Indigenous cultures. Sharing helps maintain connections between rural and urban relatives and keeps ties with Indigenous home communities. Sharing food is a traditional practice that helps establish close relations with individuals, nature, and spirits. Sharing is meant not only to support livelihoods and potentially extend the family through marriage to other community members, but also to construct and maintain ethnic identity (Ksenofontov, Backhaus, and Schaepman-Strub 2017). At the same time, a tradition of food/goods sharing provides means for strengthening the resilience of Indigenous urbanites who receive culturally and nutritionally important foods and other items (Solovyeva and Kuklina 2020). Most of the time rural relatives share meat and fish with their urban family members:

> My grandmother lives in a village, and she shares meat with us. They also produce butter. (Yakutsk, Sakha female, twenty-three)

> Relatives bring over horse meat from ulus [a rural district]. Relatives and friends from the northern districts send along fish. (Yakutsk, Sakha male, thirty)

> Relatives bring us meat from the tundra. It is important [to keep this tradition]. In our childhood, we did not get sick as we consumed our traditional food. (Naryan-Mar, Nenets female, twenty-seven)

> At present, it is getting more problematic to eat our traditional food regularly. Venison is very expensive in our stores, and you cannot afford it. That is when my relatives had their own reindeer herd on Kolguev Island,[11] they always used to send us venison. (Naryan-Mar, Nenets female, thirty-three)

Naryan-Mar Indigenous residents also mentioned that, over time, preferences in food consumption are changing in correlation with urban lifestyle and access to science-based information about food-related risks: "*In my childhood, we ate raw fish, but now I prefer only cooked fish. Fish can catch parasites, after all. I just did not know that before. However, when it comes to venison, I eat it raw when relatives pay a visit*" (Naryan-Mar, Nenets male, twenty-eight).

Through this tradition of sharing, city residents maintain linkages at a distance and also participate in reciprocal sharing by sending city-bought items (e.g., electronics) to rural communities. This way, sharing also helps villagers to receive additional produced goods from the city and thus support rural community resilience (Solovyova and Kuklina 2020).

Language Use

The ability to speak an Indigenous language is another key component for the (re)construction of urban Indigenous identity. In many of Russia's "ethnic" republics (such as the Republic of Sakha) or ethnic autonomous regions (such as the NAO), two or more languages are spoken: Native and Russian. Some people may speak both languages equally well, or only one of the languages. In our case study areas of Yakutsk and Naryan-Mar, we identified different patterns: the majority of the Sakha interview participants spoke both Sakha and Russian, and the majority of Nenets spoke only Russian, most likely due to a different history of assimilation and Indigenous population size.

In Yakutsk, while Sakha is largely spoken within Indigenous families, Russian is used mostly for work and is considered to be spoken more often than Sakha: "*It depends on the setting. For example, it is easier to communicate in Sakha at home with my husband or parents; at work, we predominantly speak Russian*" (Yakutsk, Sakha female, twenty-three). Surrounding settings are one of the major factors that impact language proficiency. Some of the interview participants spoke Native Sakha when they traveled to a rural area or went to a specialized Sakha school: "*I stopped learning Sakha after the third grade when I transferred to another school and at that point my Sakha had significantly vanished. . . . My spoken Sakha got revived in the seventh grade when I started traveling to a village where I began to speak Sakha from* scratch" (Yakutsk, Sakha male, thirty-two).

In Yakutsk many young people ceased speaking their Native Sakha when they moved to an urban area or went to a regular public school with classes taught in Russian only: "*I speak very poor Sakha, but I do understand it. I used to speak Sakha until I* was four or maybe even five years old. When I moved to Neryungri [another city in Sakha Republic], let's *say to a Russian-speaking environment, I completely stopped speaking* Sakha" (Yakutsk, Sakha male, thirty). Furthermore, changing from a specialized Sakha school to a standard public school often led to the loss of ability to read in Native Sakha, and many interview participants experienced difficulties in reading Sakha texts: "*I used to read in Sakha only in elementary school when subjects were taught in Sakha. Then I transferred to a Russian school and now it's difficult to read in* Sakha" (Yakutsk, Sakha female, eighteen).

Speaking Native Sakha for some interview participants constitutes belonging to a local society and sense of Indigeneity. However, for some young people, or for their parents, proficiency in Native Sakha does not make much sense.

> I don't feel I am Indigenous here in Yakutsk because of a language barrier. (Yakutsk, Sakha male, thirty)

> I don't think speaking Sakha is a must, it doesn't make any sense. Russian is enough for me. (Yakutsk, Sakha male, twenty-nine)

In Naryan-Mar, some of our participants mentioned that in their Nenets families, parents/grandparents were not practicing their Native Nenets language with children and grandchildren: "*No, I do not speak Nenets, just a few phrases. My mother and grandmother speak fluently. In my childhood, in my family, the parents communicated with us [children] in Russian and among themselves in Nenets*" (Naryan-Mar, Nenets male, twenty-eight). This appears to be a reflection of a common strategy when parents prefer promoting an assimilation/integration in the larger community for their children over the cultivation of their ethnic identity, often thinking that it is an advantage to speak the national language to ensure greater education and employment opportunities (e.g., Mander 2015).

Interview participants also identified serious issues coming from "refined" forms of their Native language. As some of them pointed out, the literary, or standard, Nenets language that was developed by Western linguists in cooperation with Indigenous folklorists and writers[12] deviated significantly from local dialects[13] used in everyday life in different rural settings: "*There is a big difference between literary and spoken Nenets language. Original Nenets language mainly used simple formulations. While at school and in language courses, they teach a rather literary language, which is more difficult to learn and is little spoken on an everyday basis. For communication in everyday life, we need a more tundra-type conversational* Nenets" (Naryan-Mar, Nenets female, thirty-three).

However, in both Yakutsk and Naryan-Mar, some interview participants revealed the path of "how Indigenous identities might be constructed and sustained in adulthood" (Quigley 2019). These young urbanites indicated that in their late twenties and thirties they realized the importance of speaking Native Sakha and Nenets and started learning them: "*After school [graduation] I realized the importance of [my] native language, and at that time I tried to start speaking Sakha* well" (Yakutsk, Sakha female, twenty-four).

In Naryan-Mar, some Indigenous young adults started actively partaking in their Native language through language courses[14] only after relocating to the city: "*I speak a little Nenets. We did not have many Nenets lessons in primary school [in the village], and back then, it seemed that the Nenets language was unnecessary and unimportant. However, I started learning Nenets deliberately when the language courses were introduced in the city [of Naryan-Mar]. I will proceed to do so when the courses are held again*" (Naryan-Mar, Nenets female, twenty-eight).

Although more research is necessary to better understand our study participants' perspectives on the Indigenous language learning, as well as mechanisms of Indigenous language revitalization in urban milieus connected to reconstruction and empowerment of Indigenous identities, the phenomenon of Indigenous languages resurgence can be observed among Indigenous urban populations across continents (e. g., Sánchez et al. 2018; Donna 2014).

The constitution of the Russian Federation and federal and regional laws guarantee that the Native languages be taught at schools in regions with Indigenous populations. Yet the effective implementation of these norms in practice is often challenging, and the situation with Indigenous language education and education in Indigenous languages differs from region to region (for Nenets Okrug, see Zmyvalova 2015; for Sakha, see Sokolova, Panikar, and Beloshitskaya 2019). Both Sakha and Nenets languages are recognized as official languages along with the Russian language in our two study regions, but the language policies vary significantly. For instance, in Sakha, the regional government makes efforts to facilitate indigenization of the education system by supporting nomadic schools and kindergartens, in addition to school education delivered in non-Russian languages, particularly in Sakha (Arefiev 2014; Zamyatin 2017). At the same time, Nenets Okrug is experiencing a severe shortage of Nenets language teachers, and the Nenets language is taught at schools only as one of the subjects in the educational program.[15]

Native languages may be well-preserved if they are widely spoken and traditional subsistence activities (e.g., cattle breeding, reindeer herding, hunting, fishing, gathering) are well maintained (Petrov and Chernyshova 2019). Our research results demonstrate this pattern well. Sakha is spoken by the majority of the study participants in Yakutsk, although mostly at a colloquial conversational level predominantly with their family members. Language is a significant marker of ethnic identity for the Sakha people, especially compared to other ethnic groups of Siberia (cf. Buddhism as a key factor of identity among Buryat rather than the Buryat language; Ferguson and Sidorova 2018). However, while the population of Yakutsk in 2020 increased by 65 percent compared to 1989, mostly due to the influx of Sakha from rural areas (Boldyrev 1990; Sakhastat 2021), the proportion of Sakha speakers in the city has not risen accordingly (Maximova 2019). This points to an increasing share of Sakha urban residents who do not speak their mother tongue. This pattern can be explained by several factors, including interethnic marriages, globalization, the dominant status of the Russian language in media and social networks, and the lack of software in Sakha (Maximova 2019). Ivanova (2014) reported that the increase of bilingualism in everyday use of both Sakha and Russian languages in Yakutsk enabled the formation of a persistent bilingualism. However, the assertive nature of bilingualism and the dominance of Russian in communication practice may over time oust an ethnic Sakha language, as has happened to some other Native languages (Nenets, Buryat, Tyvan) in Russia (Ivanova 2014; Rozanova 2019).

Spiritual Ties: Traditional Ceremonies, Customs, and Spiritual Practices in the City

Indigenous communities maintain their ethnic identity in part through traditional cultural and spiritual practices such as religious rituals, customs, dances, songs, ceremonies, including festivals. For Sakha people, traditional cultural practices of Sakha include circle dance (*ohuokhai*), throat singing (*toyuk*), playing mouth harp (*khomus*), embroidery, and wood and mammoth tusk carving. In the city of Yakutsk, only a few interview participants reported practicing traditional art. An interesting conversation took place with a young man who performs wood and mammoth tusk carving as a hobby. He stated, "I carve products from wood and mammoth tusks. Back in the days I studied Sakha symbols, which symbols mean what, and based on that I attempted to draw symbols. First, I used to make a list, then draw symbols, and finally sell drawings to jewelers to create jewelries. Later, I started to create my own products with my own sketches" (Yakutsk, Sakha male, thirty).

Sakha and Nenets peoples, like many other Indigenous peoples across the Arctic, have their own system of religious beliefs, customs, and spiritual practices and ceremonies. This traditional heritage brings a strong connection to ancestors and the spiritual world, predominantly practiced by elders, spiritual knowledge holders, in rural areas (Petrov and Chernysheva 2019). In urban settings, the level of engagement with traditional heritage and spirituality varies.

In Yakutsk, all the interview participants are familiar with some main Sakha customs and beliefs. However, not all of them perform these customs on their own; usually they are carried out by parents or other elders. One young man reported: "Yes, I follow the customs, but I don't perform the rituals myself" (Yakutsk, Sakha male, thirty). Another interview participant voiced that she knows about the existence of spirits and gods but not their names and what beliefs or customs should be carried out and when: "I know main *sier-tuom* [customs] that it is necessary to feed a river and fire while in nature. I know there are spirits and gods, but I don't know their exact names and what exactly one should do" (Yakutsk, Sakha female, twenty-three).

In Naryan-Mar, most interview participants admitted that they have neither a profound knowledge of Nenets customs and rituals nor many opportunities to practice them:

> I do not practice rituals in everyday life. There are no sacred sites in the city. All sites of power [sacred sites] are in the tundra. (Naryan-Mar, Nenets female, twenty-seven)

> The Nenets have become modern. . . . I know some customs, but they are not followed. Sacred places remain [in rural areas], but few rituals are held even in the Kanin tundra. (Naryan-Mar, Nenets male, twenty-eight)

In traditional (precolonial) societies in the Arctic, the elders ensured the transfer of Indigenous knowledge and skills necessary to perform the rituals, while shamans were deemed to possess extraordinary skills and abilities to perform sacred actions. Nowadays, the system of the Indigenous knowledge transfer and continuity of Indigenous traditions might have been disrupted: "*Some of our elders know the rituals, but they keep them secret. And there is not a single shaman in the NAO*" (Naryan-Mar, Nenets female, thirty-three).

In Yakutsk, the majority of young people responded that they attend traditional ceremonies, such as Sakha summer solstice day festival Yhyakh: "When there is an opportunity and time, we go to Yhyakh with friends and family" (Yakutsk, Sakha female, twenty-three). However, some interview participants expressed reluctance to participate in Yhyakh for various reasons. One young man explained his unwillingness to attend the public celebration of Yhyakh by the presence of drunken people during the festival: "There are always many drunken crazy people" (Yakutsk, Sakha male, twenty-nine). Another reason why the interview participants do not join Yhyakh is the reluctance of their family members or friends to participate. One young woman responded, "We used to attend Yhyakh often when I was a kid and when my grandmother was alive. But we stopped going there because my parents as well as my friends don't like it" (Yakutsk, Sakha female, twenty-four).

Similarly, some Indigenous urbanites in Naryan-Mar prefer to celebrate Nenets cultural festivals in the village or in the tundra. As a Nenets young man stated: "*I participate in traditional celebrations only outside Naryan-Mar. For example, we fly off to celebrate the Reindeer Day in the chum. It is the collective farm Ya Erv that organizes [the trip]. I also participate in the winter races on a snowmobile in Nelmin Nos—our shops sponsor this event. It is not interesting to participate in Naryan-Mar; they [festivals] are always the same and more tourist-oriented*" (Naryan-Mar, Nenets male, twenty-one).

In Naryan-Mar, all participants recognized the symbolic importance of the Nenets cultural institutions operating in the city. They also supported the idea to have more Nenets-oriented public events as a sign of the presence (empowerment) of Nenets culture in the urban landscape:

> The [Nenets] culture in the city is modernized. Real preservation of culture is possible through familiarizing with the original way of life—outside the urban environment. On the other hand, regarding the city sections and studios of the Nenets culture, and the Nenets theatre: young people have started getting involved; through performances, they become familiar with the language and customs; and there is a good atmosphere. The same in the Ethnocultural Center.[16] It turns out that these places of Nenets culture in the city are places of communication and memory. (Naryan-Mar, Nenets female, thirty-three)

> In the city, it is still necessary to support [Nenets] cultural organizations; otherwise, everything will be forgotten. (Naryan-Mar, Nenets male, twenty-eight)

Interviews also revealed a phenomenon of cultural hybridity and the devaluation of cultural authenticity in performance of "traditional" ceremonies (Burke 2009; Balaram 2018; Smith and Leavy 2008; Graham and Dadd 2021). For instance, our participants in Naryan-Mar described some of the rituals as explicitly designed for the settlers or tourists and yet were presented as Indigenous Nenets customs and traditions. Highly popular among the non-Indigenous population, both transformed Indigenous rituals and newly invented ceremonies lack profound (sacred) meaning in the urban environment. For instance, among them is "the rite of initiation into the Northerners" designed for the tourists and often performed by Nenets using stylized eclectic elements of Nenets rituals (Naryan-Mar, Nenets female, thirty-three); and "Buran Day" (Naryan-Mar, Nenets male, twenty-one), a snowmobile race organized with a concert, an outdoor theater, reindeer sled rides, contests, and a funfair.[17] Similar hybrid cultural events take place in Yakutsk.

This cultural appropriation and co-optation of activities are not unique to Naryan-Mar and Yakutsk and are well-documented elsewhere in the Arctic (Viken and Müller 2017; Mankova 2017) and the world (Hinch and Butler 2007). In Russia they have taken different forms—from government political instrumentalism to Indigenous revivalism and ethnocultural tourism (Viken and Müller 2017). The events typically attract tourists and non-Indigenous residents but have variable buy-in from the local Indigenous communities (Pashkevich 2017). Similar to other countries with Indigenous populations, there is also a growing engagement of Indigenous urbanites in ethnocultural tourism in the Arctic. This newly developing economic sector is heavily promoted by Russian Arctic regional governments. Despite its great potential for future growth and employment opportunities, some of our interview participants perceive it as somewhat controversial due to risks of devaluation of Indigenous cultural specificity, commodification of culture, and possible emotional hardships and "authenticity gaps," feelings also articulated in the literature (e.g., Graham and Dadd 2021; Butler and Hinch 2007).

Self-Identification of Indigenous Urbanites

In the two Arctic cities, our research revealed the presence of different types of Indigenous urban identities. Among them are various ethnic identities, including positive (an identity where a person feels joy, pride, confidence, kinship and belonging to a particular ethnic group), hybrid (an identity where the global interacts with the local to create a new identity), and negative (an identity where a person feels anxiety, uncertainty, or discomfort with his/her own ethnic group and identity; Efimov, Lapteva, and Borisova 2014; Smith and Leavy 2008), as well as an emerging nonethnic territorial identity (an identity restricted to a specific place; Paasi 2000; Anisimova and Echevskaya 2018).

Some of the interview participants, especially those proficient in their Indigenous language and closely connected to rural communities, exhibited a strong claim to their ethnic identity. These Indigenous positive identities are prevalent among recent migrants and the first-generation migrants to the city. Remarkably, the young urban Indigenous participants with a positive identity stressed significant changes in self-identification they have experienced throughout their lives. A surprising number of them, especially in their late twenties and thirties, demonstrated a "self-(re)constructed" positive Indigenous identity, which surfaced later in their lives when they rediscovered their belonging through cultural learning available in the city (such as Indigenous language classes and ethnic studios):

> I am Nenets! And this is a conscious choice I made. In my childhood, in the "village" school, I had a different attitude toward my ethnicity, as special attention was paid to the Slavic culture only, and there was a feeling of unequal treatment. . . . We did not have Nenets classes in our school, and only later, when I started attending various Nenets cultural centers in college [in the city], I started to get into it. (Naryan-Mar, Nenets female, twenty-seven)

> I feel myself more Sakha. I didn't really think about that before. I started thinking about that after school and at university because I started identifying myself as Sakha and realized the importance of the native language. (Yakutsk, Sakha female, twenty-four)

In certain cases, self-identification is based more on ethnicity rather than cultural identity, or is linked to geographical territory as a dominant marker: *"Definitely not Russian. Probably depends on the environment, because when I'm in western Russia or abroad, I feel myself Asian, because of the attitude toward non-Russians. Here in Yakutsk I feel myself as non-Indigenous, probably it is what it is. Language barrier is a force, but anyway I consider myself Sakha" (Yakutsk,* Sakha male, thirty).

In our study, we identified the presence of *hybrid identity* based on ethnicity among Indigenous youth. The nature of city experience contributes to the hybridity of urban Indigenous identities. As a result of external influences, many elements of Indigenous traditional culture (e.g., dancing, singing, carving, embroidering, etc.) in the cities have ceased to be sacred and meaningful and have become secular and aesthetic. In the urban environment, Indigenous sacred symbols and unique artifacts are outside of their semantic field and are often replaced by inauthentic substitutes. They are also modernized or refined, often without the participation of the Indigenous knowledge holders, under the influence of new technologies, societal demands, and expectations. Some interview participants expressed hesitancy or difficulties in ethnic self-identification. This may be associated with their dual ethnicity.

> Nobody. Well, mom is Evenk, dad is Sakha. (Yakutsk, Sakha female, nineteen)

> It's a difficult question. I think in any case I am more Sakha. (Yakutsk, Sakha female, twenty-three)

There is also a growing trend of bilingualism among young urbanites. As a result, young people may hold dual identification, considering themselves as both Indigenous and Russian. One of our participants revealed an emerging trend of creating highly inclusive Arctic/Northern identity, a territorial identity based on wide geographical area that gathers and mixes diverse elements from various Indigenous and non-Indigenous cultures and traditions of the Northern region (cf. Siberian identity; Anisimova and Echevskaya 2018): *"Don't even know [who I am]. Probably I feel more like a Northerner"* (Naryan-Mar, Nenets female, twenty).

The interviews indicate the generational effect on formation of negative identity, with the second and third generation urban residents identifying less as Indigenous and even finding themselves in denial about their Indigeneity and cultural background: *"Honestly? I don't consider myself Sakha. Because I hate the majority of Sakha people, the majority of Sakha people are so mean, and it freaks me out to be next to Sakha people. I try to isolate myself from them"* (Yakutsk, Sakha male, twenty-nine).

Similarly, Efimov, Lapteva, and Mikhailova, in their analysis of the impacts of urbanization on Sakha identity, revealed that urbanization may significantly affect second and further generations of Sakha people, "threatening both demographic reproduction of the [Sakha–*A.*] ethnic group, and its transmission as a cultural and linguistic community" (2015, 134). We also observed that the second generation of Sakha urbanites are less connected to their rural relatives and less interested in traditional culture. Their ethnic identity is combined with Sakha and Russian, while Russian is a dominant language of communication in their daily life (Efimov, Lapteva, and Mikhailova 2015).

Conclusions

Our study shows that an urban Indigenous identity exists, but the city transforms it into a complex, fluid, fractured, or overarching identity. In fact, we see many types of Indigenous identities in our case cities. While in traditional cultures ethnic identities are more constant and resistant to changes from the outside, modern urban identities are complex, inclusive, fluid, and hybrid, epitomizing different paths of self-identification. Jacobs (2019) points out that Indigenous identities are in constant transition as they attempt to reconcile the dominant and Indigenous cultures. Indigenous youth is a particular case of this hybridity that in turn delineates their interests, literacies, and identity (63–64). Arctic urban youth has been described as trying to negotiate traditional values and teachings with the dominant societies by relying on newly developed abilities to generate a hybrid cultural space (Korkina 2019).

The literature points out (e.g., Stephens 2015) that Indigenous urban experiences often diverge between larger cities with a substantial presence of Indigenous populations (like Yakutsk) and smaller places with just a few Indigenous residents (such as Naryan-Mar). We observe the same pattern in our case studies, with Yakutsk providing more opportunities and infrastructure to stay culturally connected to Sakha society. The Nenets living in Naryan-Mar find themselves in a minority with comparatively fewer resources to support their Indigenous livelihoods and retain their Native language.

The study identified a number of key factors to support resilience of an Indigenous identity in cities, mostly relevant to urban Indigenous youth. Among them are connection to land, spiritual ties, and Indigenous language use. First is the access to nature and nature-based traditional activities, such as hunting, fishing, and gathering, as well as retaining strong ties to relatives living on the ancestral lands and in rural communities. However, in the Arctic, many urban Indigenous residents live thousands of miles away from their ancestral lands and do not have the physical and financial means to visit their Native lands. In addition, Indigenous urbanites often face the lack of legal recognition or additional procedural hurdles that may become an obstacle for pursuing traditional lifestyle and maintaining cultural practices such as hunting and fishing. It leads to further alienation from their Indigenous heritage and ancestors' lands and losses of Indigenous knowledge linked to traditional skills, and ultimately widens the gap between rural and urban Indigenous communities.

As seen from the above discussion, the Indigenous urban experiences of young people in Yakutsk and Naryan-Mar are unique yet indicative of Indigenous city livelihoods in other parts of the Russian Arctic and across the circumpolar region and, indeed, the world. A struggle to retain Indigenous culture and heritage and emerging hybrid identities, and search for new forms, meanings, and spaces of Indigeneity in the city, underline the contemporary modernities of Arctic urban Indigenous youth.

Understanding Arctic Indigenous urbanization and urban experience is an important exercise to ensure not only that these experiences become a part of multigenerational heritage and cultural being, but also that urban Indigenous livelihoods are articulated and valued. Arctic cities shed light on unique urbanization processes and outcomes while providing valuable lessons for other remote urban regions around the globe as more Indigenous peoples settle in cities and towns.

We find that urban Indigenous identity in Naryan-Mar and Yakutsk is shaped by several leading factors, namely the relationship to the land and their rural relatives/communities, shared spiritual ties, and language use. It is evident that having these components in place may create settings in which Indigenous identity is most resilient. Staying connected to nature and being regularly involved in traditional land- and water-based activities (hunting, gathering, fishing, reindeer herding, etc.) is one of the leading conditions of thriving urban Indigeneity. This is complemented by the consumption and sharing of traditional food. Notably, a rural-urban food-sharing tradition appears to persist in both cities, strengthening the links of urban communities to ancestral lands. The ability to speak an Indigenous language is another indicator of resilient urban Indigenous identity. Erosion or loss of proficiency of the mother tongue is associated with emerging dual or non-Indigenous identities among study participants.

This research indicates that Indigenous experiences in cities can be less problematic if there are conditions and capacities to maintain stronger ties to rural communities, culture, and tradition while fully participating in an urban society. Under such circumstances, Indigenous identities remain resilient, although they also become flexible and complex. As our participants pointed out, a crucial condition for maintaining Indigenous identities is a developed cultural infrastructure in the cities. Both community and government institutions appear to play a major role in creating such an enabling environment. Thus, policies that strengthen these institutions and practices may yield positive results, particularly if co-designed with and led by the Indigenous peoples.

From the policy perspective, it is also important to recognize that Indigenous urbanites, particularly youth, may feel unwilling to articulate their Indigenous identity in order to fit in an urban setting. This may lead to official invisibility and nonrecognition of the Indigenous peoples by authorities, which often leads to less attention paid to the Indigenous peoples' needs in cities in favor of rural communities (Stephens 2015). Consequently, further policy-focused research needs to be conducted to improve our understanding of Indigenous urban livelihoods, especially of urban Indigenous youth.

This study relied on a limited number of interviews in two case cities. More work is required to refocus urban research and policy making on understanding and recognizing urban Indigenous communities. The Indigenous peoples' livelihoods in cities are diverse and complex. Although very much localized, they are also a part of broader processes of urbanization and globalization, and thus should be examined in a variety of contexts and at various scales. Better connecting case studies around the world could be one of promising directions. A critical task for future research is to place Indigenous youth at the center of attention and explore multigenerational experiences of Indigenous urban residents. Finally, engaging with coproductive methodologies, where the leadership in research and policy making is given to the Indigenous peoples, would substantially advance our collective knowledge and policy practice of sustainable development in Indigenizing cities.

Acknowledgments

We would like to express our deep gratitude to all interview participants in Naryan-Mar and Yakutsk, who shared their perspectives on living in a city, visions of their cultures, hopes, and concerns. We would also like to thank Dr. Tuyara Permyakova and Ms. Irina Kim for their help in recruiting interview participants in Yakutsk, Varvara Korkina Williams for valuable discussions, and Dr. Valery Mikheev for his invaluable support in the course of undertaking the study in Naryan-Mar. Our deep appreciation goes to the editors of the volume, Dr. Dana Brablec and Prof. Andrew Canessa, and the two anonymous reviewers for their highly valuable comments and great ideas for future research directions. This research was supported by the U.S. National Science Foundation (award number 1545913).

Notes

1. Today, by some estimates, cities and towns concentrate nearly 85 percent of the Indigenous Greenlanders, 60 percent of Indigenous Alaskans, 50 percent of Arctic Indigenous Canadians, and 45 percent and 36 percent of Indigenous people in Arctic Russia and Scandinavia, respectively (Laruelle 2019).
2. E.g., Tomiak 2017; Norris and Clatworthy 2011; Nejad et al. 2019; Patrick and Budach 2014; Huskey, Berman, and Hill 2004.
3. E.g., Pedersen 2008; Hamilton and Rasmussen 2010.
4. E.g., Nyseth and Pedersen 2014; Berg-Nordlie 2018; Vuolab 2016.
5. E.g., Efimov, Lapteva, and Mikhailova 2015; Rozanova 2019; Kuklina and Krasnoshtanova 2016.
6. The Russian Federation presents a complex federal system, combining both models of territorial federalism (based on a strictly spatial division of power) and a national-territorial model (granting non-Russian peoples the right to some kind of statehood within the federation; see Lynn and Novikov 1997). The constituent units of the federation are divided into multiple types of regions: oblasts, republics, krais, autonomous okrugs, federal cities, and autonomous oblasts. Republics and autonomous okrugs are homes to specific Indigenous peoples (often minorities) with their own culture, language, and traditions.
7. The Explanatory Note to the Federal Law "On Guarantees of the Rights of Indigenous Small-Numbered Peoples of the Russian Federation" (September 11, 1997) states that "the specified quantitative criterion for classifying ethnic groups as small-numbered peoples, according to ethnographers, reflects the fact that self-reproduction of peoples numbering less than 50 thousand people is impossible without additional socio-economic assistance from the state and society."
8. Goroda Rossii, https://города-россия.рф/sity_id.php?id=65.
9. Russian Federal State Statistics Service, www.gks.ru.
10. A *chum* (tent) is a temporary dwelling used by the nomadic Indigenous peoples specializing in reindeer herding in Russia.
11. Kolguev Island, located in the southeastern Barents Sea, witnessed one of the greatest tragedies in reindeer herding. Weather extremes with ice rains combined with oil-influenced grazing land grabs, the abandonment of traditional livestock husbandry practices, and over-exploited pasture lands led to reindeer mass death. Within three years, with the culmination in 2014, reindeer livestock dropped from approximately 12,000 to less than 100 (data varies) (Pristupa et al., 2019).
12. Nenets writing appeared only in the 1930s as a result of the joint efforts of Nenets scholars and Western linguists of the Institute of the Peoples of the North in Leningrad (now St. Petersburg). Among those who stood at the origins of Nenets literature were the Nenets poet Nikolai Vylka and the Nenets folklorist Anton Pyrerka. They contributed to creating the Nenets literature and the first textbooks for Nenets schoolchildren (Vorob'yova, 2014).

A literary, or modern standard, Nenets language (Nenets-Yurak) is based on the Bolshezemelskaya tundra dialect. In the process of codification of Indigenous language, linguists had to overcome the challenge of the existing regional and local dialects (nowadays, linguistic differences between local Nenets dialects are considerable; Laakso 2020) and make the Nenets language suitable for describing various political, economic, social, and cultural developments of the modern world.

13. The process of the Nenets language codification was particularly damaging to the Forest Nenets by excluding and marginalizing these small communities and putting them at a disadvantage (Toulouze 2003).
14. In Naryan-Mar, the Nenets language courses for adults (eighteen and older) are organized with the financial support of the regional government in the form of grants to the local Nenets Indigenous association, Yasavey (https://narianmar.bezformata.com/listnews/kursi-po-izucheniyu-nenetckogo-yazika/101966590/).
15. https://nazaccent.ru/content/28873-neneckij-yazyk-v-shkolah-nao-prepodayut.html.
16. Ethnocultural Center (www.etnonao.ru) in Naryan-Mar is one of the government-sponsored institutions that serves as the manifestation of the official recognition and support of Indigenous cultures of Nenets and Komi peoples in Nenets Autonomous Okrug (for more details, see Rozanova 2019).
17. Arctic Russia Tourism, https://tourism.arctic-russia.ru/en/.

References

Allemann, Lukas. 2020. "Soviet-Time Indigenous Displacement on the Kola Peninsula: An Extreme Case of a Common Practice." In Koivurova et al. 2020, 92–105.

Anisimova, Alla, and Olga Echevskaya. 2018. "Siberian Regional Identity: Self-Perception, Solidarity, or Political Claim?" In *Russia's Regional Identities*, edited by Edith W. Clowes, Gisela Erbslöh, and Ani Kokobobo, 189–205. London: Routledge.

Arefiev, A. L. 2014. *Yazyki korennykh malochislennykh narodov Severa, Sibiri i Dal'nego Vostoka v sisteme obrazovaniya: istoriya i sovremennost'*. Moscow: Tsentr sotsial'nogo prognozirovaniya i marketinga.

Balaram, Arita. 2018. "(Re)theorizing Hybridity for the Study of Identity and Difference." *Social and Personality Psychology Compass* 12 (10): e12413–n/a.

Berg-Nordlie, Mikkel. 2018. "The Governance of Urban Indigenous Spaces: Norwegian Sámi Examples." *Acta Borealia* 35 (1): 49–72.

Boldyrev, V. A. 1990. *Itogi perepisi naseleniya SSSR / Goskomstat*. Moscow: Finansy i statistika.

Burke, Peter. 2009. *Cultural Hybridity*. Cambridge, U.K.: Polity Press.

Butler, Richard, and Tom Hinch, eds. 2007. *Tourism and Indigenous Peoples: Issues and Implications*. Amsterdam: Butterworth-Heinemann.

Chevalier, Joan F. 2017. "School-Based Linguistic and Cultural Revitalization as a Local Practice: Sakha Language Education in the City of Yakutsk, Russian Federation." *NationalitiesPpapers* 45 (4): 613–31.

Degai, Tatiana, Andrey N. Petrov, Renuka Badhe, Parnuna P. Egede Dahl, Nina Döring, Stephan Dudeck, and Thora M Hermann. 2022. "Shaping Arctic's Tomorrow through Indigenous Knowledge Engagement and Knowledge Co-Production." *Sustainability* 14 (3): 1331.

Efimov, V. S., A. V. Lapteva, and E. I. Mikhailova. 2015. "The Impact of Urbanization on the Transmission of Culture and Language of the Sakha People: A Sociological Analysis." *Arheologiâ, ètnografiâ i antropologiâ Evrazii* 43 (4): 127–34.

Efimov, Valeriy, Alla Lapteva, and Ul'yana Borisova. 2014. "Problemy vosproizvodstva etnicheskoy prinadlezhnosti naroda sakha (po materialam etno-sotsiologicheskikh issledovaniy v respublike Sakha-Yakutiya)." *Problemy istorii, filologii, kul'tury* 2 (44): 333–49.

Emerson, Michael Oluf, and Kevin T. Smiley. 2018. *Market Cities, People Cities: The Shape of Our Urban Future*. New York: New York University Press.

Ferguson, J., and L. Sidorova. 2018. "What Language Advertises: Ethnographic Branding in the Linguistic Landscape of Yakutsk." *Language Policy* 17 (1): 23–54.

Föllmer, M. 2020. "The Sociology of Individuality and the History of Urban Society." *Urban History* 47 (2): 311–26.

Graham, Marnie, and Uncle Lexodious Dadd. 2021. "Deep-Colonising Narratives and Emotional Labour: Indigenous Tourism in a Deeply-Colonised Place." *Tourist Studies* 21 (3): 444–63.

Gray, Lisa M., Gina Wong-Wylie, Gwen R. Rempel, and Karen Cook. 2020. "Expanding Qualitative Research Interviewing Strategies: Zoom Video Communications." *Qualitative Report* 25 (5): 1292–301.

Haase, Dagmar, Burak Güneralp, Bharat Dahiya, Xuemei Bai, and Thomas Elmqvist. 2018. "Global Urbanization." In *Urban Planet: Knowledge Towards Sustainable Cities*, edited by T. Elmqvist, X. Bai, N. Frantzeskaki, C. Griffith, D. Maddox, T. McPhearson, et al., 19–44. Cambridge: Cambridge University Press.

Hamilton, Lawrence, and Rasmus Ole Rasmussen. 2010. "Population, Sex Ratios and Development in Greenland." *Arctic* 63 (1): 43–52.

Heleniak, T., and D. Bogoyavlensky. 2015. "Arctic Populations and Migration." In *Arctic Human Development Report: Regional Processes and Global Linkages*, edited by J. N. Larsen and G. Fondahl, 53–104. Copenhagen: Nordic Council of Ministers.

Hinch, Tom, and Richard Butler. 2007. "Introduction: Revisiting Common Ground." In Butler and Hinch 2007, 19–30.

Huskey, Lee, Matthew Berman, and Alexandra Hill. 2004. "Leaving Home, Returning Home: Migration as a Labor Market Choice for Alaska Natives." *Annals of Regional Science* 38 (1): 75–92.

IASSA (International Arctic Social Sciences Association). 2020. "IASSA Principles and Guidelines for Conducting Ethical Research in the Arctic." IASSA. https://iassa.org/about-iassa/research-principles.

Ivanova, N. I. 2014. "Osobennosti Yakutsko-Russkogo dvuyazychiya: leksiko-semanticheskaya interferenciya pri nesootvetstvii obyema znacheniy slov" [Patterns of Sakha-Russian Bilingualism: Lexical-Semantic Interference in Discrepancies of Meanings]. *Sibirskiy Philologicheskiy Journal*, no. 3, 225–32.

Jacobs, Curran Katsi'Sorókwas. 2019. "Two-Row Wampum Reimagined: Understanding the Hybrid Digital Lives of Contemporary Kanien'kehá:ka Youth." *Studies in Social Justice* 13 (1): 59–72.

Joo-Castro, Lucy, and Amanda Emerson. 2021. "Understanding Historical Trauma for the Holistic Care of Indigenous Populations: A Scoping Review." *Journal of Holistic Nursing* 39 (3): 285–305.

Jungsberg, L., E. Turunen, T. Heleniak, S. Wang, J. Ramage, and J. Roto. 2019. *Atlas of Population, Society and Economy in the Arctic*. Stockholm: Nordregio.

Kirmayer, Laurence J., Joseph P. Gone, and Joshua Moses. 2014. "Rethinking Historical Trauma." *Transcultural Psychiatry* 51 (3): 299–319.

Klinenberg, Eric. 2001. "Dying Alone: The Social Production of Urban Isolation." *Ethnography* 2 (4): 501–31.

Koivurova, Timo, Else Grete Broderstad, Dorothée Cambou, Dalee Dorough, and Florian Stammler. 2020. *Routledge Handbook of Indigenous Peoples in the Arctic*. London: Routledge.

Korkina, Varvara. 2019. "Indigenous Youth in Russia: Challenges and Opportunities." In *Global Indigenous Youth: Through Their Eyes*, edited by Dali Angel, Victor A. Lopez-Carmen, and Elsa Stamatopoulou, 142–57. New York: Institute for the Study of Human Rights, Columbia University.

Ksenofontov, Stanislav, Norman Backhaus, and Gabriela Schaepman-Strub. 2017. "'To Fish or Not to Fish?' Fishing Communities of Arctic Yakutia in the Face of Environmental Change and Political Transformations." *Polar Record* 53 (3): 289–303.

Kuklina, Vera and Natalia Krasnoshtanova. 2016. "The Urbanization of Indigenous Peoples of Northeastern Siberia." In *New Mobilities and Social Changes in Russia's Arctic Regions*, edited by Marlene Laruelle, 133–57. London and New York: Routledge.

Laakso, Johanna. 2020. "Contact and the Finno-Ugric Languages." In *The Handbook of Language Contact*, edited by Raymond Hickey, 519–35. Hoboken, N.J.: John Wiley & Sons.

Landry, Véronique, Hugo Asselin, and Carole Lévesque. 2019. "Link to the Land and Mino-Pimatisiwin (Comprehensive Health) of Indigenous People Living in Urban Areas in Eastern Canada." *International Journal of Environmental Research and Public Health* 16 (23): 4782.

Laruelle, Marlene. 2019. "Postcolonial Polar Cities? New Indigenous and Cosmopolitan Urbanness in the Arctic." *Acta Borealia* 36 (2): 149–65.

Lynn, Nicholas, and Aleksei Novikov. 1997. "Refederalizing Russia: Debates on the Idea of Federalism in Russia." *Publius* 27 (2):187–203.

Mander, David J. 2015. "Enabling Voice: Aboriginal Parents, Experiences and Perceptions of Sending a Child to Boarding School in Western Australia." *Australian Journal of Indigenous Education* 44 (2): 173–83.

Mankova, Petia. 2017. "Heterogeneity and Spontaneity: Reindeer Races, Bureaucratic Designs and Indigenous Transformations at the Festival of the North in Murmansk." *Acta Borealia* 34 (2): 159–77.

Marcus, Alan R. 1992. *Out in the Cold: The Legacy of Canada's Inuit Relocation Experiment in the High Arctic*. Copenhagen: IWGIA.

Martianov, Viktor. 2016. "Urbanizatsiia rossiiskoi Arktiki: severnaia gorodskaia identichnost' kak faktor razvitiia." In *Rossiiskaia Arktika v poiskakh integral'noi identichnosti: Kollektivnaia monografiia*, edited by O. B. Podvintsev, 112–39. Moscow: Novyi khronograf.

Maximova, M. I. 2019. "Problemy sokhraneniya Yakutskogo yazyka" [On Preservation of Sakha Language]. *Vestnik sovremennykh issledovaniy* 5.1 (32):12–16.

Nejad, Sarem, Ryan Walker, Brenda Macdougall, Yale Belanger, and David Newhouse. 2019. "'This Is an Indigenous City; Why Don't We See It?' Indigenous Urbanism and Spatial Production in Winnipeg." *Canadian Geographer* 63 (3): 413–24.

Norris, M. and S. Clatworthy. 2011. "Urbanization and Migration Patterns of Aboriginal Populations in Canada: A Half Century in Review (1951–2006)." *Aboriginal Policy Studies* 1 (1):13–77.

Nyseth, Torill. and Paul Pedersen. 2014. "Urban Sámi identities in Scandinavia: Hybridities, Ambivalences and Cultural Innovation." *Acta Borealia* 31 (2): 131–51.

OHCHR. 2010. *OHCHR Report 2010*. https://www.refworld.org/pdfid/4ee9ec902.pdf.

Orttung, R., ed. 2020. *Urban Sustainability in the Arctic: Measuring Progress in Circumpolar Cities*. New York and Oxford: Berghan Books.

Paasi, Anssi. 2000. "Territorial Identities as Social Constructs." *Hagar: International Social Science Review* 1 (2): 91–113.

Pashkevich, Albina. 2017. "Empowering Whom? Politics and Realities of Indigenous Tourism Development in the Russian Arctic." In Viken and Müller 2017, 105–21.

Patrick, Donna, and Gabriele Budach. 2014. "'Urban-Rural' Dynamics and Indigenous Urbanization: The Case of Inuit Language Use in Ottawa." *Journal of Language, Identity, and Education* 13 (4): 236–53.

Peters, Evelyn J. 2011. "Emerging Themes in Academic Research in Urban Aboriginal Identities in Canada, 1996–2010." *Aboriginal Policy Studies (Edmonton, Alberta, Canada)* 1 (1). 78–105.

Pedersen, Birgit Kleist. 2008. "Young Greenlanders in the Urban Space of Nuuk." *Études Inuit Studies* 32 (1): 91–105.

Peters, Evelyn, and Chris Andersen, eds. 2013. *Indigenous in the City: Contemporary Identities and Cultural Innovation*. Vancouver: University of British Columbia Press.

Petrov, A. A., and S. L. Chernyshova. 2019. "Cultural Heritage of the Indigenous Arctic Peoples of the Sakha Republic (Yakutia)." *IOP Conference Series: Earth and Environmental Science* 302 (1): 12035.

Petrov, Andrey N., Mark Welford, Nikolay Golosov, John DeGroote, Michele Devlin, Tatiana Degai, and Alexander Savelyev. 2021. "Lessons on COVID-19 from Indigenous and Remote Communities of the Arctic." *Nature Medicine* 27 (9): 1491–92.

Pristupa, Alexey O., Machiel Lamers, Maria Tysiachniouk, and Bas Amelung. 2019. "Reindeer Herders Without Reindeer: The Challenges of Joint Knowledge Production on Kolguev Island in the Russian Arctic." *Society & Natural Resources* 32 (3): 338–56.

Quigley, Dawn. 2019. "Indigenous Identity Construction: Enacted Upon Us, or Within Us." *Social Identities* 25 (5): 694–703.

Rasmussen, Rasmus Ole, ed. 2011. *Megatrends*. Copenhagen: Nordic Council of Ministers.

Rozanova, Marya. 2019. "Indigenous Urbanization in Russia's Arctic." *Sibirica* 18 (3): 54–91.

Russian Census. 2002. "2002 All-Russian Population Census." Russian Federal State Statistics Service data. https://rosstat.gov.ru/vpn_popul.

Russian Census. 2010. "2010 All-Russian Population Census." Russian Federal State Statistics Service. https://rosstat.gov.ru/vpn_popul.

Sakhastat. 2021. State Statistics Service of the Republic of Sakha (Yakutia). https://rosstat.gov.ru/territorial

Sánchez, L., E. Mayer, J. Camacho, and C. R. Alzza. 2018. "Linguistic Attitudes toward Shipibo in Cantagallo: Reshaping Indigenous Language and Identity in an Urban Setting." *International Journal of Bilingualism* 22 (4): 466–87.

Simpson, Audrey. 2014. *Mohawk Interruptus: Political Life across the Borders of Settler States*. Durham, N.C.: Duke University Press.

Smallwood, Reakeeta, Cindy Woods, Tamara Power, and Kim Usher. 2021. "Understanding the Impact of Historical Trauma Due to Colonization on the Health and Well-Being of Indigenous Young Peoples: A Systematic Scoping Review." *Journal of Transcultural Nursing* 32 (1): 59–68.

Smith, Keri E. Iyall, and Patricia Leavy. 2008. *Hybrid Identities: Theoretical and Empirical Examinations*. Leiden: Brill.

Sokolova, Flyora Kh, Marina M. Panikar, and Nataliya N. Beloshitskaya. 2019. "Legislation on Language Policy in Komi and Sakha (Yakutia) Republics of the Russian Federation." *Polar Journal* 9 (1): 64–74.

Solovyeva, Vera, and Vera Kuklina. 2020. "Resilience in a Changing World: Indigenous Sharing Networks in the Republic of Sakha (Yakutia)." *Polar Record*, no. 56, E39.

Stephens, Carolyn. 2015. "The Indigenous Experience of Urbanization." In *State of the World's Minorities and Indigenous Peoples*, 55–61. London: Minority Rights Group International.

Tomaska, A. G., N. D. Fedotova, Y. M. Sannikova, and D. M. Vinokurova. 2018. *Respublika Sakha (Yakutia): osobennosti territorialnoy i socialnoy mobilnosti*. Yakutsk: IHRISN SB RAS.

Tomiak, Julie. 2017. "Contesting the Settler City: Indigenous Self-Determination, New Urban Reserves, and the Neoliberalization of Colonialism." *Antipode* 49 (4): 928–45.

Toulouze, Eva. 2003. "The Forest Nenets as a Double Language Minority." *Pro Ethnologia: Multiethnic Communities in the Past and Present*, no. 15, 95–108.

UN HABITAT. 2010. *Urban Indigenous Peoples and Migration: A Review of Policies, Programmes and Practices*. United Nations Housing Rights Programme, Report No. 8.

United Nations, Department of Economic and Social Affairs, Population Division. 2019. *World Urbanization Prospects: The 2018 Revision*. New York: United Nations.

Viken, Avrid. and Dieter Müller, eds. 2017. *Tourism and Indigeneity in the Arctic*. Blue Ridge Summit, Pa.: Channel View Publications.

Vinokurova, Liliya. 2016. "Transformatsiya kolkhozov v sovkhozy v Yakutii v 1960-kh gg.: sotsial'nyye i ekonomicheskiye posledstviya." *Nauchnyy dialog* 11 (59): 193–202.

Vorob'yova, O. I. 2014. "Sozdatel' bukvarya i nenetskoy pis'mennosti pervyy nenetskiy lingvist-perevodchik Anton Petrovich pyrerka." *Vestnik Severnogo (Arkticheskogo) federal'nogo universiteta*, no. 2, 56–60.

Vsesoiuznaia Perepis' Naseleniia. 1996. *Itogi Vsesoiuznoy perepisi naseleniia 1989 goda*. Minneapolis: East View Publications.

Vuolab, Siv Eli. 2016. "Negotiating an Urban Indigenous Identity: Expectations, Prejudices and Claims Faced by Urban Sámi in Two Contemporary Norwegian Cities." Master's thesis, UiT Arctic University of Norway.

Weaver, H. N. 2012. "Urban and Indigenous: The Challenges of Being a Native American in the City." *Journal of Community Practice* 20 (4): 470–88.

Zamyatin, Konstantin. 2017. "Indigenous Peoples and Education in the Russian Federation," In *State of the World's Indigenous Peoples: Education*, 187–206. New York: United Nations.

Zamyatina, Nadezhda, and Ruslan Goncharov. 2019. "Arctic Urbanization: Resilience in a Condition of Permanent Instability. The Case of Russian Arctic Cities." In Resilience and Urban Disasters: Surviving Cities, edited by Kamila Borsekova and Peter Nijka, 136–53. Cheltenham, UK: Edward Elgar.

Zmyvalova, E. A. 2015. "Indigenous Children's Right to Learn Their Mother Tongue at School: Implementation and Realization in Russia." *Arctic Review on Law and Politics* 6 (2): 151–74.

AFTERWORD

Indigenous Cities as Fields and as Nodes

CHRIS ANDERSEN

When the editors of *Urban Indigeneities: Being Indigenous in the Twenty-First Century* invited me to write an afterword for their edited volume, I hesitated. Though I have published fairly extensively on issues and dynamics pertaining to urban indigeneity, I know comparatively little about the geographical and empirical foci emphasized in this volume, which is predominantly South American. In chatting with the editors, however, it became clear that my lack of direct scholarly experience in these geographical regions potentially constituted an interesting vector of analytical departure. After all, even though these cities and regions are otherwise rarely researched or written about in a field of urban Indigenous studies that continues to cement a longstanding bias toward English-based and global north–focused scholarship, Indigenous urbanization and urban indigeneity nonetheless constitute phenomena that span the entirety of the globe (indeed, from a purely numerical perspective, far more urban Indigenous people live in the global south than in the north). As such, I was fairly confident that the locales studied in the volume's chapters would bear affinities with those I had studied (mainly Canadian, American, Australian, and New Zealand); that turned out to be the case.

A little less than a decade ago, I wrote a chapter in an edited collection (Peters and Andersen 2014) on what I thought made urban Indigenous communities in Canada distinctive—and what made the character of urban indigeneity so city specific—arguing that (at least) a dozen elements were shaped by the force of the cities that Indigenous communities resided in / were part of (see Andersen 2014). Among these, I highlighted the continuing presence of economic marginalization, even in the midst of a growing Indigenous middle class; the continued presence of racism/exclusion; the sheer diversity of Indigenous tribes and nations in any particular city; given Canada's particular approach to dealing with Indigenous peoples legally, the wide array of legal statuses that urban Indigenous community members possessed; the complexities of social service delivery in the midst of legal and other complexities; the distinctiveness of urban Indigenous institutions/organizations; the specific ethos that shaped urban Indigenous policies; the creation and maintenance of more "informal" networks (including immediate and extended family networks, as well as those of friends and "friends of friends"); continued connections to nonurban communities; and the distinctive place of Indigenous women in urban milieus, both socially and politically (see Andersen 2014). Each of these meso-level characteristics combined in ways specific to individual cities, producing distinctive, local—and even vernacular—urban Indigenous communities within them.

As I write this afterword, I am surprised, given the specificity to the Canadian context of my original discussion, by the extent to which these components laid out nearly a decade ago resonate with this volume's contributor essays. I probably should not be so surprised: globally, much of the force that drives Indigenous urbanization profoundly shapes urban Indigenous residents' access to basic human rights that most urban residents in most cities in the world otherwise take for granted but that many—and in some nation-states, most—urban Indigenous residents cannot: housing, employment, education, and the recognition that our distinct humanity not only constitutes an important component of the broader urban milieu but co-constitutes it.

This volume's contributions clearly demonstrate the convergences and commonalities that exist regarding urban indigeneity across regional, national, and even global contexts: the complexities of migration to and from urban centers that often continue to include nurtured links to rural communities that take the forms of circulating bodies, objects, information, and cultural meanings; the context-specific reimagining of the very (and varied) meaning(s) of indigeneity—politically, socially, economically, and spiritually—in urban spaces; the dynamic entanglements of authenticity and identity that contour urban Indigenous experiences; the racism and discrimination—including entrenched primitivist discourses and practices and the ongoing attempts at erasure—faced by urban Indigenous residents and communities; the multiple and often complicated forms that urban Indigenous organized/

organizational resistance and collective action take as exemplars of social movements over a broad range of rights and desires; and the continued intrusion of the cultural projects of nation-states. And yet, as we will see, a good deal of context- and locality-specific institutions, discourses, and practices shape urban indigeneity.

In the introductory chapter to their enormous edited volume on global urbanization, Peake and Bain (2017, 2) suggest that despite its own internal diversity, the long span of urban scholarship can be divided in two major camps, between which they suggest a longstanding tension exists: the first focuses on "understanding the city as an empirical container (an inert, preexisting product or thing)" and the second on "perceiving it as a socio-spatial process (an ongoing production of spatialized relations of power)." In the former context, the city is understood—and thus, positioned—as a knowable and, as such, measurable object (2017, 5), the kinds of measurement that we normally associate with demographic and policy-oriented expertise. The latter context has tended to position their discussions around the character of urban life. Less an object to be subjected to, say, statistical analysis, cities in a socio-spatial conception serve instead as a distinctive basis for studying the cultural meanings and social life it generates (2017, 10).

Clearly, the contributions to this volume fall squarely into the second category. In what may be regarded as a departure from the ways that afterwords are normally structured (which normally accord a preponderance of space to summarizing volume chapters; in this case, Brablec and Canessa's excellent introduction ably covers that ground), I wish instead to invite readers to *re*-read this excellent volume through one or both of two distinctive lenses I will share, both of which may be used to position "the city" according to isomorphic properties that I will lay out shortly.

This afterword turned out to be a good deal more theoretical than I had originally intended, based on my attempt to contextualize the city's real and powerful gravitational pull on the social lives of Indigenous residents, identities, families, settlements, and nations, as well as the ways in which the agentic presences of urban Indigenous residents have not only pushed back against that pull (as it typically gets positioned in ontologies of resistance), but actually played a role in constituting the city anew. In the context of my own grateful engagement with these excellent contributions, I thus offer two lenses for reading them in the context of urban spaces: (1) understanding the city as an example of a *social field*; and (2) positioning the city as a *node*, rather than a locale, in a broader conceptual and geospatial tapestry of relations of social power. Though the majority of this afterword has been given to discussing these conceptual lenses, as I unpack the elements of each, I will nonetheless endeavor to connect both to moments in the various chapters where they resonated most strongly with me.

Toward these ends, I will begin with a brief discussion of what it means to position the city as a social field, following it with a discussion of the elements of the volume that stood out to me as best evidencing that analytical tack. Before I do so, however, I want to briefly relay a key Bourdieusian concept—*homology*—to help make sense of how and why the same patterns of urban indigeneity seem to repeat themselves globally across urban contexts, despite their intense vernacularity in any given urban context. *Homology* is a term that Bourdieu borrows from biology—defined there as "similarities in structure and anatomy between different organisms" (Wang 2016, 354)—to account for the structural similarities across different social fields. Defining homology as a "resemblance within a difference" (Bourdieu and Wacquant 1992, 106), Bourdieu uses it as part of his explanation for why we repeatedly find analogous inequalities across otherwise disparate social arenas (i.e., hospitals, the education system, the criminal justice system, etc.).[1] Bourdieu's concept of *homology* allows for the balancing of local particularities in any given social field on the same analytical footing as others and, in so doing, derives a sense of their structural similarities, even as we mark their differences. First, however, I will turn to a conceptual discussion of what social fields are, why they are important, and what we can learn about (in this case) urban indigeneity through the analytical lens they provide.

Cities as Social Fields

Like the term *homology* just discussed, my use of the term *social field* is indebted to French sociologist Pierre Bourdieu's decades-long attempts to come to grips with the complexities of everyday life as they connect to broader structural contexts (and vice versa). In the words of Loïc Wacquant (2018, 92)—perhaps the most well-known of Bourdieu's pupils and, later, collaborators—the enduring analytical power of the social field in particular, part of a more complex/complicated conceptual toolbox, stems from its heuristic ability to range along levels of abstraction and to travel smoothly across analytic scales to link large structures of power (a country, state, or metropolis) and the meso-level of institutions (such as fields of cultural production, science, journalism, and politics) to the minutiae of everyday interaction and the phenomenological texture of subjectivity encapsulated by the term of practice.

Bourdieu understood the social world as being divided into a number of distinct, hierarchically structured and (only) semipermeable spheres of professional practice that possessed within them specific rules, forms of knowledge, interrelations, and forms of socialization (i.e., habitus) through which field members struggle and within which a field's relations are governed and reproduced.[2] Meanwhile, the field itself analytically *mediates* the operation of power at the levels of the global and the everyday local while simultaneously providing us with a heuristic device to better envision the entanglement of these levels of abstraction (see Bourdieu and Wacquant 1992, chap. 7, for a useful explication of the social field methodology).

In his valuable discussion of social field methodology, David Swartz (1997, 122–26) highlights four major elements of social fields, being attentive to the fundamental social fact of power that exists within all fields: (1) fields are foundationally locales of *struggle*; (2) these struggles occur in fundamentally *hierarchical* circumstances; (3) struggles unfold according to specific *practical logics*; and (4) as such, social fields are *semiautonomous* to the outside world.[3] These structural elements of social fields may seem abstract, but nonetheless they have much to teach us about how to understand the operation of power in urban contexts and the local specificity of its operation within any given city and in that analytical context, and they offer a valuable lens for thinking about the unfolding operations of social power with respect to urban indigeneity more specifically. They likewise provide us with analytical contacts for thinking through the touch points of homology discussed earlier.

If cities operate in the nexus of a number of different kinds of power and resources that define and concentrate unequally (and inequitably) in their geopolitical space—that is, if they operate as distinctive instances of social fields—what does their operation look like in practice, particularly with respect to Indigenous presence(s) within them? As it turns out, much of the immediate answer to this question depends on both local and more global contexts, and while each play out in specific ways according to the social field of any given city (including their long histories of bio- and necro-engagement with urban indigeneity), they continue to exhibit startling similarities in their structural forms. I will now turn to the volume chapters to offer some examples of structural similarities that I found illuminating. In her chapter on the role played by Indigenous art in making a place for Shipibo people living in Lima, Peru, Borea notes the specific kinds of struggle faced by many Shipibo as they have attempted to fashion their community of Cantagallo. The lack of adequate housing for Indigenous migrants necessitated the creation of an entirely new neighborhood, a hard-fought space that, though still lacking basic utilities service, had at least offered a locale of belonging and comfort. This community has nonetheless been under constant threat since its construction. Indeed, its members were recently relocated as part of Lima's urban renewal strategy, but without a new space (in a context where the original was burned to the ground). Similarly, several authors note the extent to which urban employment opportunities get curtailed by housing dynamics: in chapter four, Brablec, for example, explains why so many urban Indigenous women migrants end up working as nannies as a result of this work including housing. Such examples—the volume possesses others—demonstrate both the distinctiveness of urban indigeneity specific to its social context and a structural convergence across different national contexts.

A second major aspect of inequitable struggle that resonates with a social field lens is the force that cities exert on the *employment* contexts of urban Indigenous residents, particularly women. Certainly a trope of urban Indigenous scholarship worldwide is that, though Indigenous people migrate to cities for myriad reasons, chief among them is the potential for expanded employment opportunities. And indeed, volume authors writing in geographical contexts as diverse as the Arctic, Japan, and South America have emphasized this element of the urban migration experience in those national contexts. But these authors also make clear just how constrained such opportunities can be and the kinds of tolls they can take on women, especially, who undertake migration in search of these opportunities.

In this context, I already noted Brablec's observation about the relationship between certain forms of employment and housing opportunities, but labor itself has constituted a stake in the very creation of urban Indigenous communities. In her chapter on Indigenous urbanization in Fiji, for example, Stevens discusses the ways that colonial administrators controlled geographies of labor to effectively shape the racial composition of Fiji's population (involving the importation of laborers from India), policies that in turn exerted an enormous impact on the makeup of Fiji's urban communities today; Ikemura Amaral smartly explores the gendered, classed, and racialized vectors of gendered labor in Bolivian markets (particularly in its ontological relationship to "nonwork") and their potential impact on individuals' relationships to indigeneity; and Brablec notes the gendered exploitation of Indigenous women's labor in Chile (and their agency in counteracting it through their engagement in "ethnic" organizations).

Given the imperial/colonial backdrop that shapes modernity globally, the economic marginalization of urban Indigenous individuals and communities is but one instance of broader and deeply racialized inequities that shape much—and, given the neoliberal policies that are increasingly impacting nation-states around the world, very much by the beginning of the twenty-first century—of the life opportunities of urban Indigenous residents, and women in particular. Moreover, the racism and discrimination so apparent in the Canadian context is, in their own empirical contexts, equally apparent in this edited collection's chapters, in a wide array of forms and manifestations.

Borea, for example, documents the various forms of discrimination the Shipibo in Lima faced, from the policing of their presence in urban spaces to garden variety face-to-face prejudice; Brablec demonstrates how discrimination was baked into the cake of labor opportunities such that "working as live-in nanas often implied [Indigenous women] immersing themselves in spaces where indigeneity was defined by its exploitability"; Uzawa relayed an instance of discrimination against her Indigenous people, the Ainu, so engrained in Japanese society that they could, on national television, be compared to dogs as a humorous trope (though perhaps a more shocking example, this is nonetheless part of a broader array of discrimination forms practiced by the Japanese state against the Ainu people); and del Valle Casals's discursive analysis of a mainstream film demonstrates how many Mapuche people might attempt to protect themselves from discrimination in urban Chilean society.

My point in offering a "city as a social field" as an analytical lens is not to declare the "total power" of cities to shape (read: burden) the lives of Indigenous residents. The volume's chapters demonstrate the potential, to one degree or another, for this to be the case, but the agentic tone of the authors makes it equally clear that Indigenous residents shape just as they are shaped, and they do so in ways distinctive to their local contexts. Usually not equally (centuries of colonialism make it difficult to imagine fully equitable relations in colonial nation-states) but like all urban residents, Indigenous residents act with agency, even while being constrained by structure.

As such, my inviting us to think about cities in terms of social fields and their associated gravitational pull is to make the point that such framings are useful for imagining (and analyzing!) the boundaries around and mostly within which those involved in any given urban context struggle and for taking seriously the lived density of any given city: its "tempo" as Simmel (1950) termed it or its "texture" as urban studies doyen Henri Lefebvre (1991) phrased it. It is in this sense that social fields operate as a "relational configuration endowed with a specific gravity which it imposes on all the objects and agents which enter into it" (Bourdieu and Wacquant 1992, 17). In this context, the volume's contributors have ably demonstrated how incredibly complicated and intensely local the pull of any particular city can be. As scholars we seek to draw comparisons between the goings-on of different locales. This is a necessary part of undertaking scholarly analysis, given the extent to which we understand the enduring power of imperial/colonial/capitalist projects to make such comparative positioning bear analytical fruit so regularly. And yet, though different national and even regional contexts certainly play a role in shaping how institutions, discourses, and practices play out in any given urban context, cities possess their own histories that deserve to be respected and analyzed in their vernacularity.

Indeed, one is struck repeatedly, in reading these chapters, by how carefully the authors have respected and thus emphasized this deep sense of place. However, even as we note the analytical value of positioning the city as a social field, urban indigeneity needs to be understood not simply in terms of the force of individualized or localized places but rather (or additionally) for the power of cities within a broader chain or network within which they act as *nodes* (an element that the volume contributors also emphasized). Though the social field methodology lends itself well to understanding locality or vernacularity, it turns out that it is also useful for understanding how cities operate in the context of larger / more abstract and smaller / more local configurations of power (see Savage 2021, 2011; Wacquant 2018). I turn now to that discussion.

Cities as Nodes

In his discussion of power in the ancient world, sociologist Anthony Giddens (1985) positioned city-states as *power containers*, a term he used to denote circumscribed areas for the generation of administrative power. "A locale is a power container insofar as it permits a concentration of allocative and authoritative resources. In . . . class-divided societies, castles, manorial estates—but above all cities—are containers for the generation of power" (Giddens 1985, 13). Though Giddens argued that the modern nation-state has eclipsed the city to become the preeminent example of a power container, as the previous section on understanding cities as social fields makes clear, I contend that cities continue to produce their own anchorages (or, to use a slightly more dynamic nautical term, *vortices*) of power, and the larger the city, often the larger the allocatively and authoritatively generative capacity.

If cities are to be understood as fields, it is important to emphasize that they operate not just as locales but as powerful *nodes* within broader flows and networks of power—that is, in spite of the power of their local pull, cities are not self-contained. Good historical reasons exist for thinking of and analyzing cities in nodal terms. In the introductory discussion to their edited volume on mobile communications in urban spaces, for example, Sheller and Urry (2006b, 1) argue that as a result of their general tendency to be built in historically strategic locations (waterways or overland routes, to provide but two examples of many), many cities grew into hubs for various kinds of infrastructural systems (railways, highways, air, etc.) that drew people, goods, information, and meanings in and out of their ambit. As such, "All places are tied into at least thin networks of connections that stretch beyond each such place and mean that nowhere can be an 'island'" (Sheller and Urry 2006a, 209).

Sheller and Urry (2006a, 2006b) were part of a cadre of scholars who drew together and built on previously existing scholarship on mobility to create a new set of lenses for understanding and analyzing the character of social institutions and social action, part of a "new mobilities paradigm" (see Sheller 2021, chap. 2, for a discussion of the genealogy and evolution of this paradigm). Critiquing what they regarded as the "sedentarist" tendencies of several academic disciplines that (of particular relevance here) tended to understand places as self-contained containers or "buckets," so-called new mobilities scholars instead appealed for a scholarly disposition focused on positioning *movement* as being of elemental importance to understanding the operations of social institutions and practices (see Hannam, Sheller, and Urry 2006; Sheller and Urry 2006a, 2006b; also see Urry 2000).

Calling for no less than a "fundamental recasting of social science," Sheller (2021, 10) has more recently suggested that the new mobilities paradigm has aspired over its genealogical unfolding to three fundamental characteristics: (1) It began in a "metaphysics of mobility" such that studying the constitutive power of *movement* in the formulation and sustainability of social institutions and practices becomes its major orienting lens.[4] Sheller and Urry (2006a, 208) argue, for example, that the social sciences have otherwise minimalized "the importance of the systemic movements of people for work and family life, for leisure and pleasure, and for politics and protest" *or* have overemphasized the relationship between movement and freedom, as though all bodies had the same opportunities (or desires) for movement. (2) The paradigm emphasized the *different modes and modalities* of movement, singularly and in combination, including (but not limited to) corporeal travel, physical movement of objects, virtual travel (a mode made especially pressing in the last several years of a pandemic), and imaginative travel (more on this below). And (3) the paradigm was rooted in the idea that movement and mobility is always *co-constituted by immobilities and moorings*, such that "new places and technologies . . . enhance the mobility of some peoples and places *and* heighten the immobility of others" (Sheller and Urry 2006b, 207). In sum, "The new mobilities paradigm involves analyzing networks, relations, and flows and circulation, not fixed places. Yet it also analyzes the processes of mooring, grounding, dwelling, waiting, and homing. It challenges the idea of space as a container for social processes" (Sheller 2021, 10).

Importantly, the new mobilities paradigm's concern with movements prioritized both their different spheres (physical movement, movement of information, objects and meanings, etc.) and—arguably more importantly—their interdependence: How do various movements act in congruence or friction, what consequences ensue (locally and globally), and what kinds of meanings and, indeed, what new forms of social life are co-constituted in and with such movements (Sheller and Urry 2006a, 213)? Perhaps equally importantly, Sheller and Urry (2006a, 2006b) push back against an ontological separation of people from places, arguing instead that "a complex relationality of places and persons [is] connected through performances" and further, that "the places travelled to depend in part upon what is being practiced within them" and as such, "places are . . . not so much fixed as implicated within complex networks" (2006a, 214).

Understanding places like cities as nodes rather than (just) locales or containers places into conversation the everyday lived complex realities of urban Indigenous residents with their immediate surroundings while concomitantly respecting the ways that people, goods, meanings, and even identities flow (and/or are restricted) in part based on any given city's gravitational (push and) pull.[5] As such, it merits close attention. And indeed, the volume authors emphasize the central importance of a mobility lens to properly understanding Indigenous presence in cities and urban indigeneity. Thinking in terms of Sheller's (2021) three major characteristics—an ontology of movement, different forms and modalities of movement, and the co-constituted relationship between mobility and immobility—we can better understand the power of cities to shape (or warp) these conditions.

Each of the volume's authors are concerned with mobility in various forms and modalities. Certainly, a major focus of the edited collection includes the migration of Indigenous individuals and families from rural areas to cities. In her valuable discussion of "colonial mobility," Toomey (2021) articulates three overlapping types of mobility produced in a colonial context: hyper mobility (those encouraged to travel for work and leisure), compelled mobility (the result of global/neoliberal forces), and forced mobility (whereby those who travel are punished for doing so). The contributors to this volume demonstrate the value of understanding mobility/migration in the context of an overlapping framework like Toomey's (that is to say, Indigenous urban migration is rarely wholly forced but likewise is never wholly free, either).

In chapter one, for example, Borea uses works of art to explore the movement of the Shipibo people from more rural Amazonian rural communities to building their own community within the capital city of Lima, Peru (and how the migratory experiences of Andes and Amazonian-based communities differed); Stevens likewise documents the long histories of migration within Pacific society (and Pacific cultures) as a backdrop for understanding the specific contexts of migration to Suva, Fiji—including both diverse, cosmopolitan forms of Indigenous migration from across the Pacific and that of indentured laborers from India—that come to shape its urban indigeneity and the struggles that these migrations produced; and, emphasizing the impact of neoliberal reforms of migration dynamics in Bolivia, Ikemura Amaral's chapter emphasizes the social mobility that accompanied geospatial mobility, and the forms of cultural miscegenation it precipitated, as well as individual relationships *to* indigeneity (which, as she sophisticatedly demonstrates, is deeply gendered in its own right).

Brablec's chapter explores the role that rural-to-urban Chilean migration has played—also deeply gendered and racialized—in shaping leadership opportunities for Indigenous women in their efforts to produce new forms of Indigenous cultural (re)generation in urban spaces, while also documenting the tremendous emotional toll of migration. In her chapter on the importance of imagery to "broadcasting" Indigenous authenticity in Bolivia and Peru, Peluso's chapter makes the case for forms of mobility that include circulatory, contingent, and bilateral migrations, pointing to a broader range of reasons than we often see connected to migration explanations (while also emphasizing how previous generations of migration shape urban perceptions of more recent ones). In her discursive analysis of a popular film, del Valle Casals's chapter notes the role of the nation-state in encouraging "white" movement to Chile while noting the extent to which Mapuche migration to urban spaces "triggered anxieties" and unsettled otherwise historically congealed understandings of indigeneity as primitive or premodern and, as such, less deserving of urban than rural spaces. And in their chapter on Arctic urbanization, Rozanova-Smith et al. note that rapid non-Indigenous migration into otherwise Indigenous spaces impacted the well-being of urban Indigenous residents.

Part of the new mobilities paradigm is additionally founded on the idea that mobility always includes more than bodies; objects, images, information, and cultural meanings are also/always on the move, as well. Adey, for example, explains that "mobilities means societies are interlinked by the mobilities of peoples *and* things" (2017, 10; emphasis added). Further, in their discussion of the relationship between migrant worlds and material culture, Basu and Coleman (2008, 317) argue that in migratory contexts, people and things not only interact but, in fact, are mutually constitutive. More specifically with respect to communication of information, Adey et al. (2014, 4) note that "mobilities of data, media and information . . . can come to replace, mediate and compliment physical mobilities," and in his founding treatise on recasting society into "the social" through consideration of a mobile ontology, sociologist John Urry (2000, 2) argued for the importance of respecting the movement of *images* and *information* in its reconfiguration.

This volume's contributing authors complexly explore the importance to analyzing urban indigeneity not only of the movement, migration, circulation, and *friction* (see Cresswell 2014) of brown bodies but also of the movement of objects and perhaps more specifically, images, information, and communication. In the first sentence of their volume introduction, for example, Brablec and Canessa note the continued circulation in whitestream society—and thus the enduring power of the images—of the "noble savage," living in harmony with rural nature (a primitivist discourse the dynamics of which most of the volume contributors engage). Such mental geographies (Said 1993) about where Indigenous people(s) *really* belong are both rooted in and reproduce the deep colonial binary through which urban Indigenous residents are mentally—and in some cases, as this volume demonstrates, physically—removed and erased from urban locales. Brablec and Canessa later remark on the power of goods and images to connect otherwise geographically distance locales, noting this as an example of the power of the urban (and I would contend more specifically, the power of the urban Indigenous) to penetrate more rural and often traditional locales.

The circulation of Indigenous images and objects plays a role in exploring the dynamics of urban indigeneity and Indigenous urban communities in a number of the chapters. Borea documents the creation of Shipibo art as a form of collective urban Indigenous self-building and agency; Peluso intriguingly explores the power of stereotypical imagery to shape the kinds of public discourses (in popular culture but also in policy) regarding "authentic" indigeneity, and the dynamics this poses for Indigenous leaders who engage with constituents in urban and rural Indigenous communities; and del Valle Casals also explores the relationship between Indigenous presence and urban modernity through the image(s) of the movie *Play*.

Though the new mobilities paradigm has nodded to the importance of social mobility, it has mainly been interested in the relationship between mobility and space, and in particular the power of technological advances to produce new forms of social life in and between spaces. As Urry (2000, 33) put it, in describing the globalization literature at the turn of the millennium, there exists a "wide variety of new objects, of new machines and technologies, which dramatically compress or shrink time-space. . . . Such technologies include fiber-optic cables, jet planes, audiovisual transmissions, digital television, computer networks including the Internet, satellites, credit cards, faxes, electronic point-of-sale terminals, portable phones, electronic stock exchanges, high speed trains and virtual reality." The volume authors offer several examples of this compression of time-space between rural and urban nodes. Several authors highlighted, for example, the increased communications infrastructure that connected urban and rural locales, as well as the power of cell phones (in Peluso's chapter), social media (Facebook in Borea's chapter, WhatsApp in Peluso's, and Spotify in del Valle Casals's), and television (Peluso, Uzawa) to communicate across space and time.

Third and finally, the new mobilities paradigm was careful from its inception to understand and position mobility in terms of power and, as such, to locate it in its relationship to *im*mobility (Adey et al. 2014, 4). Initially positioned in the context of the kinds of immobile infrastructure necessary to support the mobilities that came to shape the contemporary (read: modern) world (see Urry 2000), new mobilities scholars came to position mobility, first, as not always uniformly positive and, second, as attached to various forms of racialized and heteropatriarchal exclusions (Sheller 2014, 57). As Sheller (60) argues, "The very processes that produce movement and global linkages also promote immobility, exclusions and disconnection" (also see Toomey's [2021] valuable discussion on mobility in colonial contexts).

Certainly the volume's contributing authors have pointed out the forms of spatial immobility in the form of physical segregation that accompanies their discussions of urban indigeneity in their various local contexts. Here, however, I want to stretch the metaphor of im/mobility slightly to account for the kinds of racial mobility often present in Indigenous experiences in urban locales. And indeed, the volume contributors are very much aware of and delve into the nuances of this social/racial mobility. Brablec and Canessa note in the introduction that part of the complexity of urban indigeneity lies in the manners in which any given urban locale powerfully shapes the contexts for identifying as Indigenous (arguing that urban indigeneity is not different than that of more rural areas, just different). In her chapter, Uzawa powerfully engages in an autoethnographic account of her identifying as Ainu based on her relationship to locales and institutions in Tokyo, and the forms of Ainu community therein.

As urban Indigenous scholarship has long noted, urban spaces were often seen and treated by state, regional, and municipal officials—virtually all of whom were not Indigenous—as though they represented spaces where Indigenous people came to live and Indigenous culture came to die (Andersen 2012, 151). Contributors to this volume have ably proven the lie of such an assertion, but they have done so in productively complicated ways, demonstrating both the mobilities and the immobilities that shape urban Indigenous experiences and identities. While Borea's chapter focuses on Shipibo attempts to reproduce urban Shipibo identities anew by community building in Lima, Peru (thus tacitly demonstrating the mobility of Shipibo culture and identity from rural to urban spaces), other contributors (Stevens, Peluso) focus more on the racial politics of their respective urban contexts that complicate narratives about the innate mobility of Indigenous identities into newer, urban spaces (though Brablec also noted the power of mestizo/whiteness to produce immobility in urban Indigenous place making in Santiago).

Authors also explored the forms of immobility that adhere to colonial/racial regimes, in which various elements of racial comportment (skin color, clothing, general mannerisms, etc.) command forms of long-standing immobility that stand in the face of situated self-understandings regarding indigeneity. In her chapter, for example, del Valle Casals's discursive analysis of the movie *Play* demonstrates that "the fact that people continue to understand skin color as a key racial marker exposes the legacy of the racial formation of the nation and the effects of racialization on bodies." To the extent that this remains the case, such racial fixity can and does serve as a form of immobility with respect to social and geographical mobility.

Conclusion

In his discussion of the power of Bourdieu's concepts to the field of urban studies, Savage (2020, 150) suggests that their value lies in their "capacity to synthesize across sites, to link micro and macro, to engage pragmatist concerns with daily life to a wider political economy, and to foreground the role of accumulation." As I think about the chapters in this volume, I am struck not by the extent to which the lenses I offer in this afterword encourage such a tack, but rather by the extent to which the chapters themselves demonstrate a richness of both theoretical-conceptual sophistication and empirical granularity that lend themselves to such approaches. Indeed, it was only after having read the collection several times that my plan for writing the afterword revealed itself, and it is highly unlikely that I would have taken this approach with a different set of chapters.

This volume represents an important addition to the global field of urban Indigenous scholarship. I make this claim for two main reasons. First, because the authors are writing in geographical areas that have not otherwise been sufficiently explored (or cited!) by conventional urban Indigenous scholarship, mine included. As such, it offers empirical diversity that enriches the field as a whole. Second, this edited collection includes a wide range of methodological approaches that depart from the usual discourse analysis–based discussions. My emphasizing this point should not be construed as a knock on previously existing urban Indigenous scholarship: nearly all of us deal with urban indigeneity in ways that push back against constant attempts at our erasure, historically and today, and discourse analysis is a ready-made tool for undertaking such labor. Yet it is gratifying to read such a wide range of methodological approaches to analyzing urban indigeneity, and I thank the volume's authors for their contributions.

Notes

1. In his discussion of the principles of homologies, Wang (2016, 355) identifies four: (1) the opposition between the dominant and the dominated in any given field; (2) an opposition between the orthodoxy and heterodoxy; (3) the opposition between economic and cultural capital; and (4) the distinction between the autonomous and heteronomous poles of a field. Since fields are heuristic devices (cognitive—and in this case, analytical—shortcuts), they are not directly interchangeable, and Wang's discussion provides valuable context for understanding the level of convergence between any given fields.
2. Bourdieu studied numerous social fields, among them law, medicine, religion, art, literature, and the criminal justice system.
3. A given field's internal logics, rules, and mechanisms of development (Swartz 1997, 126) mean that their shape is the result of the intergenerational, rulebound struggle of those within it rather than the result of a broad structural principle such as racism, sexism, heteropatriarchy, etc.; each and all of these must be translated or refracted into the field.
4. Adey (2017, 7) defines mobile ontologies as "a set of apprehensions about the world characterized by movement, flow and vortices of matter, even if things appear fixed."
5. At the risk of didacticism, gravity does not actually push *or* pull; from a general theory of relativity perspective, it "bends" space/time in ways that accelerate objects toward larger objects. I use the phrasing here in a rhetorical context.

References

Adey, Peter. 2017. *Mobilities*. 2nd edition. London and New York: Routledge.

Adey, Peter, David Bissell, Kevin Hannam, Peter Merriman, and Mimi Sheller. 2014. "Introduction." In *The Routledge Handbook of Mobilities*, edited by Peter Adey, David Bissell, Kevin Hannam, Peter Merriman, and Mimi Sheller, 1–20. London: Routledge.

Andersen, Chris. 2012. "Urban Landscapes of North America." In *The World of Indigenous North America*, edited by Robert Warrior Robert. 149–70. London: Routledge.

———. 2014. "Urban Aboriginality as a Distinctive Identity, in Twelve Parts." In Peters and Andersen 2014, 46–68.

Basu, Paul, and Simon Coleman. 2008. "Introduction: Migrant Worlds, Material Cultures." *Mobilities* 3 (3): 313–30.

Bourdieu, Pierre, and Loïc Wacquant. 1992. *Invitation to a Reflexive Sociology*. Chicago: University of Chicago Press.

Cresswell, Tim. 2014. "Friction." In *The Routledge Handbook of Mobilities*, edited by Peter Adey, David Bissell, Kevin Hannam, Peter Merriman, and Mimi Sheller, 107–15. London: Routledge.

Giddens, Anthony. 1985. *The Nation-State and Violence*. A Contemporary Critique of Historical Materialism 2. Cambridge, UK: Polity Press.

Hannam, Kevin, Mimi Sheller, and John Urry. 2006. "Mobilities, Immobilities, and Moorings." *Mobilities* 1 (1): 1–22.

Lefebvre, Henri. 1991. *The Production of Space*. Translated by Donald Nicholson-Smith. Oxford: Blackwell.

Peake, Linda, and Alison Bain. 2017. "Introduction: Urbanization and Urban Geographers." In *Urbanization in a Global Context*, edited by Alison Bain and Linda Peake, 1–15. Oxford: Oxford University Press.

Peters, Evelyn, and Chris Andersen, eds. 2014. *Indigenous in the City: Contemporary Identities and Cultural Innovation*. Vancouver: University of British Columbia Press.

Said, Edward. 1993. *Culture and Imperialism*. New York: Alfred A. Knopf.

Savage, Mike. 2011. "The Lost Urban Sociology of Pierre Bourdieu." In *The New Blackwell Companion to the City*, edited by Gary Bridge and Sophie Wilson, 511–20. Chichester: Blackwell Publishing.

———. 2021. "Interventions—Bourdieu Comes to Town: Part II." *International Journal of Urban and Regional Research* 45 (1): 150–53.

Sheller, Mimi. 2014. "The Mobilities Turn." In *The Routledge Handbook of Mobilities*, edited by Peter Adey, David Bissell, Kevin Hannam, Peter Merriman, and Mimi Sheller, 45–54. London: Routledge.

———. 2021. *Advanced Introduction to Mobilities*. Cheltenham, U.K.: Edward Elgar Publishing.

Sheller, Mimi, and John Urry. 2006a. "Mobile Cities, Urban Mobilities." In *Mobile Technologies and the City*, edited by Mimi Sheller and John Urry, 1–17. London: Routledge.

———. 2006b. "The New Mobilities Paradigm." *Environment and Planning A* 38 (2): 207–26.

Simmel, Georg. (1950). "The Metropolis and Mental Life." In *The Sociology of Georg Simmel*, edited by K. Wolff, 409–24. New York: Free Press.

Swartz, David. 1997. *Culture and Power: The Sociology of Pierre Bourdieu*. Chicago: University of Chicago Press.

Toomey, Nisha. 2021. "The Nexus of (Im)mobilities: Hyper, Compelled, and Forced Mobile Subjects." *Mobilities* 17 (2): 269–84.

Urry, John. 2000. *Sociology Beyond Societies: Mobilities for the Twenty-First Century*. London and New York: Routledge.

Wacquant, Loïc. 2018. "Bourdieu Comes to Town, Part I: Pertinence, Principles, Applications." *International Journal of Urban and Regional Research* 42 (1): 90–105.

Wang, Yingyao. 2016. "Homology and Isomorphism: Bourdieu in Conversation with New Institutionalism." *British Journal of Sociology* 67 (2): 348–70.

CONTRIBUTORS

Dr. Aiko Ikemura Amaral is a lecturer in International Development at King's College London, and her work takes on an interdisciplinary approach to address intersectional identities and inequalities in Latin America. The chapter in this book is based on her PhD research (Sociology, University of Essex/UK), which explored processes of racialization and urbanization of indigeneity and their intersections with gender and class. This research started from Bolivian urban street markets in São Paulo (Brazil) and El Alto (Bolivia), where she met the women (and some men) whose personal narratives underpin her work. Aiko is a mixed-race, middle-class Brazilian, a Latin American woman who works from the Global North, and her experiences of labor, migration, and racialization are certainly different from those of the women she met at the street markets. She hopes that the privileges she holds from her position can be employed to advance the anticolonial commitment that motivates her research. She is also a non-Indigenous academic. By underscoring her interlocutors' emphasis on the ambivalent character of their personal experiences of navigating these colonial, patriarchal, and neoliberal contexts, she hopes this work can eschew essentialist representations of what it means to be Indigenous and highlight the intersectional forms of exclusion and the spaces for inclusion that characterize the dynamicity of urban Indigeneity today.

Dr. Chris Andersen is a professor and the dean of the Faculty of Native Studies at the University of Alberta. He is the author of two books, including, with Maggie Walter, *Indigenous Statistics: A Quantitative Indigenous Methodology* (Walnut Creek, Calif.: Left Coast Press, 2013) and *"Métis": Race, Recognition and the Struggle for Indigenous Peoplehood* (Vancouver: UBC Press, 2014), which won the Native American and Indigenous Studies Association's Best Subsequent Book Award for 2015. With Evelyn Peters, he also coedited *Indigenous in the City: Contemporary Identities and Cultural Innovation* (Vancouver: UBC Press, 2013). Andersen was a founding member of the Native American and Indigenous Studies Association Executive Council, is a member of Statistics Canada's Advisory Committee on Social Conditions, and is editor of the *Journal of Aboriginal Policy Studies*. He was recently named to the Royal Society of Canada's College of New Scholars, Artists and Scientists.

Dr. Giuliana Borea is a lecturer in Latin American Studies in the School of Modern Languages at Newcastle University. Before joining Newcastle in 2021, she was a Marie Curie Research Fellow at the University of Essex and a Stipendiary Fellow at the Institute of Latin American Studies, SAS, University of London. She is also an affiliated lecturer of Anthropology at the Pontificia Universidad Católica del Perú. She is a social anthropologist informed by an interdisciplinary perspective of the arts and culture. Her research and teaching explore the political economy of contemporary art worlds and their transnational networks: museum theories, politics, and practices; place making; and sensory knowledge, with a focus on Latin America, particularly on Peru. She is the author of the book *Configuring the New Lima Art Scene: An Anthropological Analysis of Contemporary Art in Latin America* (Abingdon: Routledge, 2021); and editor of the volume *Arte y Antropología: Estudios, Encuentros y Nuevos Horizontes* (Lima: PUCP, 2017). Borea has served as Perú's director of Museums and Cultural Heritage at the National Institute of Culture (Ministry of Culture) and coordinator of the Chavín National Museum, the Qhapaq Ñan Museum Network, and the Lima Contemporary Art Museum. She was cofounder of Tandem: Cultural Management for Development association, which promoted grassroots organizations fostering cultural policies from below. The chapter for this book is based on research for the AmazonArt Project. The participatory and interdisciplinary approach of this research seeks to contribute to dialogues between anthropology, art history, and curatorial studies, and to benefit Indigenous artists and museum practices and policies. AmazonArt focuses on Peru's Amazonian contemporary art, with particular attention to Uitoto and Shipibo artists, who are playing an important role in the growing visibility of Amazonian art at national and international levels. The artists played a primary, public, and participatory role in the development and dissemination of this project. This research understands the practices of Amazonian contemporary artists and their contributions to the art world and the society at large by addressing the condition of mobility of these practices and their aesthetic influences and negotiations across the community, urban centers, and international art circuits. It not only focuses on shamanic aspects but also explores the large spectrum of agendas that these works mobilize and the challenges they posit to the narratives and protocols of art. Finally, it goes beyond semantic and discursive practices to engage with the artists themselves—their projects, their voices and dreams—as it contributes to open channels for self-representation.

Dr. Dana Brablec is an Assistant Professor in Race, Decoloniality and Intersectionality at the Centre for Latin American Research and Documentation (CEDLA), University of Amsterdam. She holds a PhD in sociology from the University of Cambridge (2020), where she explored Indigenous urbanization in Santiago de Chile and the state's role in this process. Her research has been published by the *Bulletin of Latin American Research*, *Sociology*, and the *Journal of Ethnic and Migration Studies*, exploring issues such as Indigenous civil society organizations, identity re-creation, language revitalization, place making, authenticity/hybridity, and identity politics while also engaging with urban, intersectional, and decolonial studies. Previously, she worked as a postdoctoral researcher at the Wales Institute of Social and Economic Research and Data (WISERD)—Bangor University, and as an affiliated lecturer in the Department of Politics and International Studies and bye-fellow in sociology at the University of Cambridge. Dana has worked with Indigenous Mapuche organizations for over seven years, pursuing a participatory-based methodological approach. The emphasis of her research has been placed on empowering Mapuche people, especially women, through the development of horizontal, fluid, and dialogical links, making them an active part of her research as well as long-term collaborators.

Professor Andrew Canessa is a social anthropologist who has been working with Indigenous people in highland Bolivia since 1989. A fluent speaker of Aymara, Andrew has published widely on issues of identity, gender, sexuality, history, and politics. Among his key publications are: *Natives Making Nation: Gender, Indigeneity and the State in the Andes* (Tucson: University of Arizona Press, 2006); *Intimate Indigeneities: Exploring Race, Sex, and History in the Small Spaces of Andean Life* (Durham, N.C.: Duke University Press, 2012); and *Género, complementariedades y exclusiones en Mesoamérica y los Andes* (Quito: International Work Group for Indigenous Affairs [IWGIA] and Abya Yala, 2012). The latter brought scholars (including Indigenous scholars) from Mesoamerica and South America to construct a comparative framework for understanding gender relations in Indigenous communities in these regions. At the core of his work is to see the world through Indigenous people's eyes, to understand their lived realities, and to render these for wider audiences without exoticizing Indigenous people. He draws on over thirty years of not only collaboration but also lifelong friendships with Indigenous people in Bolivia. Although he is unable to share his written work with the people he works closest to, he has long discussed the contents of his writing and engages in regular dialogue with friends and community leaders.

Dr. Sandra del Valle Casals, with more than fifteen years of experience in the film industry and cultural sector working in various positions (film producer, director of partnerships, event manager, and consultant), has sought to develop a multifaceted career led by her passion for social impact-driven endeavors with global outreach. Being the only Cuban to receive a PhD from Cambridge University in a long time and being also woman, biracial, and migrant, Sandra has sought to promote cultural events and scholar debates that help push boundaries and visibilize underrepresented identities. In particular, Sandra's doctoral research on racial politics, citizenship, and migration in contemporary Chilean cinema shows the convoluted way in which race and nation have historically been interwoven, determining the exercise of citizenship for marginalized groups such as Mapuche people. Her essays have been published in a number of books, such as *Afrocubanas: History, Thought, and Cultural Practices* (Lanham, Md.: Rowman & Littlefield, 2020), *Conquistando la utopía: el ICAIC y la revolución 50 años después* (Havana: Ediciones ICAIC, 2010), and *Desafíos feministas en América Latina: la mirada de las jóvenes* (Montevideo: Cotidiano Mujer, 2009).

Dr. Stanislav Saas Ksenofontov is an Indigenous Sakha social scientist from the Republic of Sakha, NE Siberia, Russia. He earned his PhD from the University of Zurich (Switzerland), where he conducted his research on the vulnerability of social-ecological systems of Arctic Sakha to global change drivers, namely climate change, land use change, and sociopolitical transformations. Saas is a postdoctoral scholar at the ARCTICenter, University of Northern Iowa (U.S.), where he continues his research on the impacts of global change on Arctic social-ecological systems, particularly urbanization effects on Indigenous identities, Russian energy megaproject impacts on ecosystems and traditional practices, and climate change effects to urban infrastructures. In addition, Dr. Ksenofontov's research interests include Asian interests in the Arctic, sustainability of Indigenous communities, and Indigenous knowledge. Dr. Ksenofontov is an Indigenous collaborations project group leader of the Association of Polar Early Career Scientists (APECS) and fellowship program coordinator of the International Arctic Science Committee (IASC).

Dr. Daniela Peluso is a cultural anthropologist who has worked over the last three and a half decades in Lowland South America with Indigenous communities in mostly Peru and Bolivia. She has been actively involved in various local grassroots efforts on issues relating to health, gender, Indigenous urbanization, and human and land rights. She works in close collaboration with Indigenous federations and organizations, always ensuring that her research is aligned with Indigenous pursuits, facilitates relevant concerns, and is impactful in meaningful ways. Her publications focus mostly on Indigenous ontologies, urbanization, empathy, violence, corruption, relatedness, and the anthropology of finance. She received her PhD in 2003 from Columbia University and is an emeritus fellow in social anthropology at the University of Kent. She is the recipient of numerous research grants.

Dr. Andrey Petrov is ARCTICenter director and associate professor of geography at the University of Northern Iowa (U.S.). Dr. Petrov is an economic and social geographer who specializes in Arctic economy, regional development, and post-Soviet society, with an emphasis on the Indigenous peoples and local communities in Russia and other circumpolar countries. His current research is focused on regions of the Arctic and concerns regional development, spatial organization, and restructuring of peripheral economies, human well-being, dynamics of social-ecological systems, and sustainable development. He has published on issues pertaining to socio-economic change, development, and demographic dynamics of Indigenous and non-Indigenous populations, relationships between communities and extractive industries, and sustainability science and sustainable development in the Arctic. Dr. Petrov is the president of the International Arctic Social Sciences Association (IASSA) and chair of the International Arctic Science Committee (IASC) Social and Human Working Group.

Dr. Marya Rozanova-Smith is a research professor at George Washington University. In addition to her work in academia, she participated in a wide range of social projects. She was the founder and chairperson of the Center for Civil, Social, Scientific, and Cultural Initiatives (STRATEGIA) and served as a Galina Starovoitova Fellow for Human Rights and Conflict Resolution at the Kennan Institute, the Woodrow Wilson International Center for Scholars. Dr. Rozanova-Smith has been (co)organizing international academic projects on a wide range of Arctic issues and engaging with Indigenous communities and their leaders in the Arctic regions to ensure their voices are heard. Dr. Rozanova-Smith has been teaching the Arctic Affairs course at the George Washington University's Elliott School of International Affairs since 2018. Her current research interests include Arctic governance, Indigenous urbanization, and gender empowerment in the Arctic. Dr. Rozanova-Smith is a principal investigator of the project Understanding the Gendered Impacts of COVID-19 in the Arctic (COVID-GEA), supported by NSF. She has also initiated educational programs and informal surveys conducted in close collaboration with Indigenous communities and their leaders in Russian Arctic regions. Dr. Rozanova-Smith's research interests include Arctic governance, Indigenous empowerment, diversity, and women's participation in politics and government in the Arctic.

Dr. Kate Stevens (Pākehā/settler) is a senior lecturer in history at the University of Waikato in Aotearoa, New Zealand. Her research and teaching focus on histories of cultural, environmental, and economic exchange in the colonial and postcolonial Pacific. She has previously published on interracial whaling communities in New Zealand (with Prof. Angela Wanhalla); sexual violence and colonial criminal justice in Fiji, Vanuatu, and New Caledonia;

and coconut commodities across the Pacific. Stevens is currently working on a new project on the environmental and social history of Suva, supported by the Marsden Fund Council from government funding, managed by Royal Society Te Apārangi (grant number UOW2012). It builds on a 2019 workshop hosted at the National Archives of Fiji on Suva's pasts and the forthcoming volume *Suva Stories*, edited by Nic Halter (Canberra: Australian National University Press). The project is a collaboration with scholars and cultural advisors at the University of the South Pacific and the University of Waikato and will support new student research in 2022–2024, further develop the website and app fijianhistory.com, and fund community symposium and workshops on Suva's history. The project has ethics approval from the University of Waikato FASS Human Ethics Committee (approval number FS2021–63). At the time of writing, COVID-19 outbreaks and the resultant closures of the Fiji and New Zealand borders delayed the planned community engagement and the research itself. This chapter was consequently developed based on a published literature and newspaper review. Once the research resumes in 2023, the team will conduct *sevusevu* and meet with Suvavou leaders and the iTaukei Trust Board in Suva to ensure the research follows culturally appropriate protocols (originally planned for late 2020) and focuses on areas of relevance for community members. During this research, the team will support iTaukei, Pasifika, and Māori students to develop their own research projects and publications on Indigenous urban histories in Suva or the wider Pacific region as relevant to their own interests and communities through funded summer scholarships and mentorship. One Waikato-funded student already produced an award-winning poster (on Pacific women's poetry on urban life) and continued into postgraduate study. As a settler/non-Indigenous academic, helping to facilitate the development of Indigenous Pacific research and researchers is an important way to contribute to the field, and we hope that this project will help nurture new scholars and thinkers into postgraduate historical research and/or related careers. Team members, including students wherever possible, will share their findings in person as part of community workshops on Suva's past toward the end of the project.

Dr. Kanako Uzawa is a Norwegian-based Ainu scholar, advocate, and artist. She is a multilingual and multifaceted cultural scholar who speaks Japanese, English, and Norwegian. She is an affiliated researcher at the Research Faculty of Media and Communication at Hokkaido University. She contributes to collaborative research and Ainu performing art on the multidimensional articulations of Indigenous knowledge. She also engages with the ArCSII (Arctic Challenge for Sustainability) as a research collaborator, where she contributes her expertise on both the Sámi and Ainu issues. She is an editorial board member of *AlterNative: An International Journal of Indigenous Peoples* in New Zealand, Aotearoa. Dr. Uzawa obtained her doctorate in Community Planning and Cultural Understanding from the UiT Arctic University of Norway, Tromsø, in 2020. Her PhD focused on urban Ainu livelihood and its contemporary expressions based on autoethnography as one of the research methods. Dr. Uzawa works and engages with a number of academic and international forums, lectures, and artistic work on Indigenous identity making. She is particularly active in working on promoting contemporary aspects of Indigenous livelihoods (the Ainu) using her website as a means of communication with an international audience (see more in AinuToday.com). Her current work engages with a curational project on the Ainu exhibition in collaboration with the University of Michigan Museum of Art in the United States. One of her museum works in the past can be seen at the Ainu exhibition *A Soul in Everything: Encounters with Ainu from the North of Japan* at the Rautenstrauch-Joest Museum in Cologne, Germany: https://rautenstrauch-joest-museum.de/A-Soul-in-Everything.

INDEX